Job
Analysis

Job Analysis

AN EFFECTIVE MANAGEMENT TOOL

Stephen E. Bemis
Ann Holt Belenky
Dee Ann Soder

The Bureau of National Affairs, Inc., Washington, D.C.

The Bureau of National Affairs, Inc.
Washington, D.C. 20037

LIBRARY OF CONGRESS CATALOGING IN PUBLICATION DATA

Bemis, Stephen E.
  Job analysis.

  Bibliography: p.
  Includes index.
  1. Job analysis. I. Belenky, Ann Holt. II. Soder, Dee Ann. III. Title.
HF5549.5.J6B42   1983   658.3'06   83-18923
ISBN 0-87179-412-8

Printed in the United States of America
International Standard Book Number: 0-87179-412-8

Dedication

This book is dedicated to the late Harry E. Bose. At the time of his death in 1979, Dr. Bose was working as a psychologist with the Boston regional office of the United States Civil Service Commission, and serving as an instructor at universities in the Boston area. Throughout the public personnel community, he was known as a true professional; he combined high standards with practicality.

Harry was a colleague and friend of two of the authors of this book. We share a tremendous sense of loss with his many other friends and colleagues over his untimely death.

Contents

List of Exhibits

Preface

Numerous books currently exist that deal with issues surrounding the law and equal employment opportunity (EEO). Some, like Miner and Miner (1978), treat the subject of job analysis as *one* of those issues which must be considered in building an effective and defensible selection system. Other books, such as *Job Analysis: Methods and Applications* (McCormick, 1979), concentrate on job analysis as a personnel research mechanism. *Job Analysis: An Effective Management Tool*, however, deals directly with the challenge of constructing an empirical and legally defensible job analysis system with specific procedures and forms. This book was written to fill that void—to provide a system to balance judicial dictates and EEO needs with the limited personnel resources of the typical employer. The system recognizes the dictates of law, regulation, court action, and everyday organizational practices.

This book is written for the people who need accurate information about jobs to carry out their human resource management responsibilities. These include the line supervisor or manager and the personnel professional. Labor and civil rights attorneys, and personnel and industrial psychologists are currently showing an increased interest in job analysis procedures. This interest parallels the interest that judges are showing in the nuances of job analysis. Nevertheless, the prime user of job facts is the prime source of job facts—the manager who designs jobs, selects people to perform the jobs, and evaluates the employee's performance on those jobs. The human resource professionals who support the manager are also important users of job facts as they evaluate jobs, or recruit, select, and train individuals. While lawyers, psychologists, and others may find this book useful, our primary goal is to be of assistance to the manager and the human resource professional.

Numerous people contributed ideas and suggestions to this book, especially Gerald P. Fisher, who had the initial inspiration for it and the initiative to suggest the idea to The Bureau of National Affairs, Inc. We thank him for his dream of a book on the roles of job analysis, equal employment opportunity, and the law, as well as for his input in the book's early stages. We regret that personal and business commitments prevented him from continuing active participation in its preparation.

Donald J. Schwartz of the Equal Employment Opportunity Commission offered many valuable suggestions for chapters in addition to chapter 6 that shows his name. Although his ideas were considered in revising those other chapters, none of the views presented in them should be interpreted as a reflection of his views or those of the EEOC. We also wish to thank Elizabeth Aberant who edited and typed the final manuscript. Her conscientiousness and professionalism were an inspiration to the authors during the final weeks of preparing the manuscript for the publisher. Finally, we wish to express our appreciation to Barbara J. Smith, who formatted and typed the VERJAS forms and many of the other exhibits. Her patience and ingenuity were critical to the successful completion of the book.

1. Overview

In the years ahead, employers face an unprecedented set of challenges. To remain viable or to grow and prosper, they must be efficient. At the same time they must be seen by the users of their goods or services, and by the public who keeps them in business, as productive and responsive to consumer or public needs. Moreover, they must meet legal and social demands to employ a diverse and representative work force, which often means employing members of minority groups or women in jobs traditionally held by whites or men, and vice versa. In short, organizations must be more productive while meeting complex, often contradictory, legal, social, administrative, and economic demands.

There is no single or simple solution to these interacting pressures on employers, but a focal point for addressing them is at the level of the jobs that people perform in the organization. An understanding of how a job is designed, how people are sought and selected for a position, and how they are evaluated and rewarded by an organization is crucial for efficient human resource management. The first step in looking at jobs for human resource management purposes is job analysis.

What Is Job Analysis?

Job analysis is a systematic procedure for gathering, documenting, and analyzing information about three basic aspects of a job: *job content*, *job requirements*, and *the context* in which the job is performed.

Job content identifies and describes the activities of the job. Depending upon the particular job analysis method used, descriptions of job content may range from general statements of job activities through detailed descriptions of duties and tasks, or from more detailed statements of the steps or elements involved in a particular process, to descriptions of motions needed to perform an activity.

In the past, *job requirements* have included factors such as years of education and experience, degrees, licenses, and so forth—credentials assumed to be evidence that an individual possesses the qualifications for

1

successful job performance. A more modern view of job requirements identifies the skills, abilities, areas of knowledge, and physical and other characteristics which are required to perform the content of the job in a particular situation or context.

The *context* in which a job is performed generally includes factors such as its purpose, the degree of accountability or responsibility of the employee, the availability of guidelines, the extent of supervision received and/or exercised, the potential consequences of error, and the physical demands and working conditions of the job.

The purpose of job analysis is to provide an objective description of the job, not of the person performing it.

Sources of Data

The prime source of job facts is the manager. It may therefore seem surprising that managers should have to engage in a formal process to gather data that will be primarily used by them. Nevertheless, there are sound practical and legal reasons why this process is necessary:

1. Other people have to use the information as well. Poorly documented information is seldom useful to others who need job data, whether for purposes of human resource management or for purposes of litigation.

2. Others may have to supply missing data. For instance, nuances of the job must sometimes come from the employee.

3. Managers may often be unaware of how much they know or don't know about a job until they think it through and write it down. Information in their mental data banks is useless if it cannot be retrieved in a way that makes it relevant to other information.

4. If an employment decision is challenged through a grievance or a legal action, a post-hoc memory search as to why a decision was made will not suffice. The same holds true if a personnel research study is needed that requires an analyst or a reviewer to look at job facts for similar positions.

Although the manager is usually the prime source of job analysis data, job analysts frequently consult other sources. These include job incumbents, engineers, technical manuals, organization studies, professional associations, external experts, and clients or customers. A comprehensive job survey will include as many of these sources as needed to understand the job in question and to carry out the purpose of the job analysis. Numerous techniques are used to tap these various sources; a brief description of these follows:

Background research. This involves a review of existing job descriptions, training materials, technical manuals, and previous job studies. This technique should be part of any job analysis process.

Observation. When an analyst (or a supervisor who works in a different location) is doing a job study, he or she should spend a period of time observing the employee at work. This is the best way to get an understanding of the job context or environment. If the job involves both physical and mental tasks, for example, observation is the best means of determining just how the tasks are performed and interrelated. In the authors' opinion, this data-gathering technique is so important that it should be common practice for all job analysts from outside the work unit. If a personnel action needs to be defended in court, analysts are in a much better position to establish credibility if they have actually observed the job. (The reasons for the observation should be explained to the employee to minimize suspicion.)

Individual interview. The individual interview is frequently conducted concurrently with observation, but it may take place away from the job site, particularly where interviewing is precluded by safety considerations or noise. A supervisor may interview an employee to determine exactly what tasks must be performed to accomplish an agreed-upon duty. A job analyst may interview a manager about a job the manager supervises.

The group meeting. There are two kinds of job analysis group meetings. One is a *technical conference* where, typically, design engineers and outside experts get together to identify what tasks will be necessary to perform a job created as a result of technological change. At this point there are no incumbents to observe or to interview. The other kind of group meeting is known as a *structured interview.* In this situation a number of job experts (supervisors or incumbents or both) discuss a job under the direction of, and according to a structure determined by, a job analyst.

The worker log. An infrequently used but effective job analysis technique is to have workers keep a diary on what they are doing at certain predetermined times. For some jobs, it might be every 15 minutes for a week. For other jobs, workers may be asked to keep a complete diary for ten randomly selected days over a period of six months. The specific procedure is dictated by the nature of the job and the organization. The U.S. Postal Service uses an innovative variation on the worker log to gather information needed for a unique purpose, the establishment of rates for various classes of mail. A "snapshot" is taken by designated supervisors throughout the country at predetermined times, using a rather imposing looking form to show what a large sample of workers are doing at the indicated time. A copy of the form is included in Appendix 3.

The questionnaire. Questionnaires may be administered to employees and/or supervisors on a one-to-one basis, in a group setting, or even by mail. Normally they are administered to all job incumbents (or supervisors), or to a randomly selected sample. The technique is particularly useful when a large number of employees do similar jobs. The questionnaire may be of two types. An *unstructured questionnaire* basically asks employees what it is they do. Such a questionnaire is easy to put together but difficult to analyze or summarize. A *structured questionnaire* can be developed only after certain other techniques have been applied (e.g., background research, observation, interview). This questionnaire, inventory, or checklist normally requests information on whether a specific thing is part of the respondents' job, and the importance they attach to it. A structured questionnaire compares with an unstructured one in much the same way that an "objective" test compares with an "essay" test. A structured questionnaire with limited open-ended questions is among the most frequently used. (Some sample job analysis questionnaires are shown in Appendix 1.)

Participation. If the supervisor is the job analyst and has performed the job, he or she has, in effect, employed the participation technique. Even though it is effective, time and safety factors frequently preclude outside job analysts from "walking in the incumbent's moccasins." Job analysts obviously should not be piloting commercial airliners, but there are ways of simulating jobs that can be quite realistic. Where these simulators have been developed for training or assessment purposes (e.g., pilot simulators), job analysts should consider using them. The "simulator participation" technique has been used in analyzing the job of nuclear power plant operator.

Uses of Data

Job analysis data are needed to design a job and evaluate it in relation to other jobs in the organization. Once a position has been established and classified, the manager must make sure that appropriate job information is used in the recruitment of qualified candidates. Then, with the assistance of the personnel office, the manager must determine which candidates are best qualified for the job. Once an employee has been hired or promoted, the manager has the responsibility of training the employee. This includes initial training, upgrading of skills, retraining, and development. Managers must also make sure that employees know what is expected of them, appraise employees to see if these expectations are being met, and take necessary actions to improve performance. How often do managers or human resource management staff have the necessary data in the format needed to assure that actions taken in carrying out these functions are job related? Court decisions and professional experience provide the same answer: "Not often enough." Thus, the time spent by a manager in gathering and documenting job data can be easily justified.

Exhibit 1 summarizes how job analysis data can be used in each stage of the human resource management cycle. It includes job design, job classification or evaluation, recruitment, selection, training, performance appraisal, and performance management. These applications are discussed more fully in Chapter 4. Although the personnel office can furnish information in many of these areas and may actually assume primary responsibility for performing some of these functions, the manager or supervisor has the most complete understanding of the job and the biggest stake in the results.

Exhibit 1.   The Human Resource Management Cycle: Application of Job Analysis Data

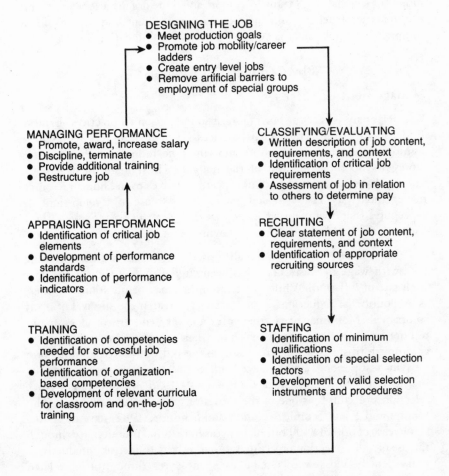

DESIGNING THE JOB
- Meet production goals
- Promote job mobility/career ladders
- Create entry level jobs
- Remove artificial barriers to employment of special groups

MANAGING PERFORMANCE
- Promote, award, increase salary
- Discipline, terminate
- Provide additional training
- Restructure job

CLASSIFYING/EVALUATING
- Written description of job content, requirements, and context
- Identification of critical job requirements
- Assessment of job in relation to others to determine pay

APPRAISING PERFORMANCE
- Identification of critical job elements
- Development of performance standards
- Identification of performance indicators

RECRUITING
- Clear statement of job content, requirements, and context
- Identification of appropriate recruiting sources

TRAINING
- Identification of competencies needed for successful job performance
- Identification of organization-based competencies
- Development of relevant curricula for classroom and on-the-job training

STAFFING
- Identification of minimum qualifications
- Identification of special selection factors
- Development of valid selection instruments and procedures

The State of the Art

No one job analysis system is generally accepted as best suited for all purposes. Numerous systems have been developed to meet particular needs (ten are discussed in Chapter 2) and many variations on these systems are used daily in the field. Sometimes the variations are dictated by organizational needs or constraints but typically they reflect the preferences of the users. Both professional and legal guidelines avoid dictating a particular methodology. They leave it to the users to apply the job-analysis techniques that are appropriate for their purposes.

Although the state of the art in job analysis is best described as fluid, personnel experts are responding to management concerns and to the legal/regulatory climate by devoting considerable attention to the subject of job analysis. Meanwhile, more and more organizations are taking a systems approach to human resource management and looking for a comprehensive job-analysis system to provide a foundation.

Why Conduct Job Analysis?

Management Concerns

Job analysis is at the heart of most sound personnel practices. Exhibit 1 identified a number of such practices. Human resources represent a significant cost to all employers and, in some industries, this resource represents 80 to 90 percent of the budget. Thus, many managers are finding that their most important concerns revolve around human resource management, and that it makes good business sense to develop rigorous procedures that document what they are doing in this area. Some of these concerns are highlighted in the following paragraphs.

Employee productivity. Nationally, productivity has not been keeping pace with wage increases. This has been cited as one of the reasons for a high rate of inflation. While this relationship may be questionable, there is no doubt that reductions in productivity threaten the survival of many companies. Most managers, therefore, are very concerned about maintaining or increasing productivity in their organizations. One way to accomplish this is to select workers with the skills or potential to perform jobs in a superior way. A New York Stock Exchange publication on productivity (New York Stock Exchange, 1979) identifies poor employee selection procedures as one of the causes of productivity problems. John Hunter and Frank Schmidt (Hunter and Schmidt, 1982) have estimated an increase of $80 to $100 billion per year in material productivity through the use of valid selection procedures. Another way to increase productivity is to identify and reward outstanding employees through a job-related performance appraisal system. Improved selection and appraisal procedures can increase the productivity of blue collar workers, white collar workers, and managers. Both procedures depend on a comprehensive system for capturing and documenting job facts.

Social responsibility. Most managers feel a responsibility to hire individuals from the community they serve. Such individuals may not have the academic credentials or work experience normally expected in job applicants. Job-related selection procedures, based upon a sound job analysis, can help the employer identify the skills needed for effective performance of the jobs. Further, if the employer cannot find applicants with the needed skills and chooses to develop a training program to help meet this social responsibility, job analysis data are needed both to design an efficient training program and to develop procedures for selecting applicants who can benefit from the training.

Managers also feel a responsibility to hire individuals with physical or mental handicaps. In hiring such individuals, a manager wants to be sure that they can contribute to the organization's productivity without creating a safety hazard to themselves or to others. Job analysis is needed to identify (a) jobs where a particular handicap will not limit performance, (b) jobs which may be redesigned to accommodate the individual, and (c) possibilities for the reassignment of tasks within a work group (see Chapter 4).

Informed decision making. Managers are decision makers. Many of the decisions they make involve people—what applicant gets hired, what employee gets trained, who gets promoted, who gets fired. Managers are concerned that they have all relevant information before making such decisions. Information on the skills needed on a job and the skills possessed by applicants helps to assure that the hiring or promotion decision is sound; it also helps the manager to resist pressures from executives or union officials for priority treatment of their relatives or friends.

Efficient human resource management. Because people are frequently a manager's most valuable—and most expensive—resource, managers know that they must handle this resource efficiently. For instance, they will take a critical look at expensive training programs during "belt-tightening" times. If applicants with needed skills are available in the labor market, the training may be an unnecessary expense. On the other hand, if people with the skills are either unavailable or too expensive, training may be a wise course of action.

Other aspects of human resource management can be helped by job analysis information. It may not be cost effective or good for employee morale to hire engineers to spend most of their time drafting, when drafting technicians are available for less money. On the other hand, it may not be wise to pay "stenographer wages" for a clerk who will type and may transcribe from a dictating machine but who will never take shorthand.

The Legal/Regulatory Climate

An additional reason for increased interest in job analysis is the Civil Rights Act. Section 703(h) of Title VII of the Civil Rights Act of 1964, as amended (42 U.S.C. Sec. 2000e-2(h)), states, in part, ". . . nor shall it be an unlawful employment practice for an employer to give and to act upon the results of any professionally developed ability test provided that such test, its administration or action upon the results is not designed, intended, or used to discriminate because of race, color, religion, sex, or national origin." In a series of cases and regulatory issuances that followed the Act, it has become clear that "test" has been interpreted very broadly to include all significant personnel decisions. Thus all such decisions should be based on professionally developed selection methods. Each of the methods accepted by the profession and by the courts relies in whole or in part on some form of job analysis. Although forms of job analysis have existed since the early part of this century, the legal/regulatory climate makes a professionally acceptable form more important than ever.

The primary federal regulatory issuance in the area of job-relatedness is a document entitled "Uniform Guidelines on Employee Selection Procedures" (Uniform Guidelines, 1978). These Uniform Guidelines were issued on August 25, 1978, under authority of Title VII of the Civil Rights Act as well as other federal authorities in the area of equal employment opportunity. They apply to almost all employers. The history, content, and interpretation of the Uniform Guidelines are summarized in other places and will not be repeated here. Their impact on the employment practices of employers cannot be overstated.

The procedures covered by the Uniform Guidelines include any personnel action which enhances one employee or class of employees compared to another class. These actions include not only paper and pencil tests, but also oral interviews, minimum qualification standards, selection for training when there is potential career enhancement, granting of bonuses and other awards, performance appraisal, and classification/pay decisions.

The key to the successful defense of an employment practice under the Uniform Guidelines is job-relatedness. The primary vehicle for demonstrating the job-relatedness of most decisions about employees or applicants for employment is job analysis. For instance, in 1980, Professors Herbert S. Feild and William H. Holley, Jr., of Auburn University studied 66 employment discrimination court cases involving performance appraisal. As reported by The Bureau of National Affairs, Inc. (*Daily Labor Report*, No. 249, 1980), the performance appraisal systems which employers defended successfully possessed four characteristics, one of which was the use of job analysis to develop the content of the appraisal system. The employer successfully defended practices in all three cases where job analysis was used to develop the appraisal system; it lost 11 of the 14 cases which did not use job analysis.

Adverse impact and the relevant labor market. Once a contested employee selection procedure is identified, it is the responsibility of the complaining party (employee, unsuccessful applicant, Equal Employment Opportunity Commission, or other complainant) to establish the adverse impact of the procedure. This may be done by comparing selectees to applicants, selectees to the relevant labor market, or employees to the relevant labor market. (The term "relevant labor market" refers to those persons in the geographical recruitment area where a job exists who have the basic experience or education needed to perform adequately in the job.) Job analysis must be used to establish the skills and abilities necessary for adequate job performance before determining who, among the numerous persons in the labor market, will fall into the specific category of "relevant."

Correcting or defending the selection procedure. If adverse impact is demonstrated by showing that there are meaningful differences between groups, employers have two choices: (1) to modify or eliminate the selection procedure that is creating the adverse impact or (2) to defend it by showing that it is valid and that there is no other equally valid procedure with less adverse impact. Job analysis plays a prominent role in each of these alternatives.

If the first alternative is chosen, employers may use job analysis procedures to restructure or to redesign the job or they may modify the selection process or that aspect of the process (e.g., a height requirement, a requirement for a master's degree, a specific number of years of experience) that is causing the adverse impact. Interestingly, restructuring the job may facilitate the modification of the selection procedure. Further, a new job may be created for which it is easier to find a more diverse applicant pool; an upward mobility training program may be created; or an aggressive, targeted recruitment program may be established to reduce the adverse impact in the specific job category.

If the second alternative—validating the procedure—is chosen, employers need to be aware that job analysis (and the quality of that analysis) plays a prominent role in enforcement agency and judicial decisions on the acceptability of selection procedures.

Employers are cautioned that failure to comply with various civil rights laws and regulations cannot be justified by pointing to "excessive" administrative costs. Indeed, such expenditures may be a false economy, as when State of Illinois officials discovered that the state was spending $200,000 per year for its EEO program and $4,000,000 per year defending itself against EEO law suits. Probably if these figures had been reversed the state "could have avoided a lot of disruption to its regular work and could have built the foundation for a better personnel system in the process" (Seberhagen, 1978). This appears to be particularly true for selection and promotion practices with job analyses providing the needed undergirding.

The new legal perspectives, including the five major legal concerns in cases involving job-relatedness, are discussed in Chapter 5. Although job analysis is important, it must be recognized that whether a court will find an employment practice to be legal depends on many more variables than the existence of a careful and rigorous job analysis. The four-factor framework presented at the end of Chapter 5 is the product of a long-term analysis of major court decisions. The framework can help the manager to "put it all together" and assess an organization's situation in order to take appropriate action to improve it.

The Need for an Integrated Approach: A Versatile Job Analysis System

As described above, many types of personnel management activities require accurate job information. Managers or supervisors (referred to collectively as "managers" in this book) of salaried, nonexempt or exempt employees take actions with an awareness of job information, but frequently without focusing on what is really important to the job. In many organizations, upper level managers and those in charge of the personnel function frequently act without getting accurate job information from first-level managers. In other organizations, requests for job information impose on the manager's time repeatedly over the course of a year. Both these scenarios reflect inefficiencies which can have a substantial negative impact on organizational productivity.

For a number of years, personnel managers and human resource experts have said that there must be a better way—a systematic way to record basic job data and then access it as needed for different human resource management purposes. It is inefficient and unproductive to gather job facts independently for each of the purposes shown in Exhibit 1, or even for three or four of them. Economics and common sense necessitate a coordinated, integrated approach to the gathering and documenting of job facts because:

- Each use of job analysis may put slightly different emphasis on what the worker does (tasks), on the knowledges, skills, or abilities (competencies) required to do the work effectively, and on the

structure or environment (context) in which the work is performed.
- Each use of job analysis has some reliance on all three kinds of information.
- While job analysis is necessary, carrying out any job-analysis process may be time consuming.
- Various people in the organization have a role to play in the job analysis process.

An integrated job analysis approach is called for in responding to these diverse needs.

The documentation and use of such data is increasing in proportion to the amount of litigation and regulation in human resource management areas. Organizations which try to refute a charge of discrimination by gathering job data when the case is brought or "on the eve of trial" are looked at negatively by the courts; nevertheless, considerable time and dollar resources must be expended to gather the data.

Current federal regulations and court decisions make it clear that when personnel actions are challenged as discriminatory, an employer's defense must be based on job relatedness. Thus, many of today's employers are documenting personnel actions. The VERJAS system was developed to help managers document and use job information in decision making.

The procedures presented in Chapters 3 and 4 represent a comprehensive system for developing, documenting, evaluating, and updating job and worker information so that it is accessible for making informed and objective personnel management decisions about recruiting, hiring, training, disciplining, and rewarding employees. The procedures have been written with a concern for both legal requirements (discussed in Chapter 5) and the practical realities of organizational life.

VERJAS is composed of procedures utilized in other job analysis methods integrated into a single system to meet management's total job analysis needs. The system is a job analysis melting pot in both origin and use.

Chapter 3 shows the manager or job analyst how to gather and document job facts. It is a "how to" manual, complete with step-by-step instructions. Because it is instructional in nature, the tone of Chapter 3 differs from that used in the rest of the book. Chapter 3 is also supplemented by Appendices 1, 2, and 3. Appendix 1, Planning and Conducting A Job Analysis Study, focuses on the broader issue to be considered. Appendix 2 offers specific suggestions for conducting interviews. Appendix 3, A Job Analysis Case Study, discusses an actual job analysis project. It provides an example of how the concepts and techniques discussed in this book can be applied to situations much broader than the main thrust of this book.

Chapter 4 describes how to use the data generated by VERJAS to carry out a variety of human resource management functions. A key concept of the system is that data from a single base can be the focal point for multiple uses. For instance, this chapter outlines the use of competency data for initial applicant screening and selection, for performance appraisal, and for the determination of training needs. It also shows the use of content, competency, and context information to design, evaluate, or classify a job. The chapter also shows how task and competency information can be critical in developing useful training programs for an employee or an entire organization.

Future Perspectives

Chapter 6, a commentary on the likely job analysis agenda for the next decade, is contributed by Donald J. Schwartz. Currently Dr. Schwartz is staff psychologist for the Equal Employment Opportunity Commission; formerly he held the same position with the U.S. Department of Labor's Office of Federal Contract Compliance Programs. Issues such as the accuracy and appropriateness of data obtained through various job analysis techniques and the role of computers in facilitating the use of job analysis data are discussed. The likely impact of the changing work force composition and interests, and job comparability issues (particularly in the areas of pay equity and layoffs) are explored.

2. A Survey of Job Analysis Methods

There are many job analysis methods and variations on the basic methods. This chapter outlines and briefly discusses only the following ten:

- Department of Labor (DOL) method
- Functional Job Analysis (FJA)
- the Critical Incident Technique (CIT)
- the Job Element method
- the Position Analysis Questionnaire (PAQ)
- the Task Inventory/Comprehensive Occupational Data Analysis Program (TI/CODAP)
- the Health Services Mobility Study (HSMS) method
- Guidelines Oriented Job Analysis (GOJA)
- the Behavioral Consistency method
- the Factor Evaluation System (FES).

Several of the methods—the DOL, the FJA, and the PAQ—are well known and have been widely applied. By contrast, the HSMS method is relatively unknown, the Job Element method has been the subject of litigation, and the GOJA method was developed specifically in response to legal and regulatory requirements. The TI/CODAP, previously used primarily in the military, has recently been applied to jobs in other public sector organizations. A long-established method, the CIT has attracted new interest for its potential applicability to performance appraisal. The Behavioral Consistency method is relatively new as is the FES, an example of a classification or job evaluation method.

Each of the methods, in some way, contributed to the development of the Versatile Job Analysis System. Just as researchers and developers of these methods drew on the work of others, so were the principles, techniques, and concepts of these methods reviewed, applied, accepted, rejected, modified, and incorporated into the VERJAS approach presented in Chapters 3 and 4.

This chapter is intended to provide a broad overview of selected job analysis methods. For additional information and more detailed descriptions of specific methods, the references included in the Bibliography should be consulted.

Job analysis methods are dynamic. They have been developed to address various problems and to meet the specific needs and requirements of diverse situations. As situations change, as new needs arise, these methods are often modified or supplemented, or new methods, such as VERJAS, are developed.

Diversity is reflected in the differences in purpose, scope, terminology, and procedures of the various job analysis methods. The categorization and differentiation of job-related information in terms of *content, requirements,* and *context,* explained in Chapter 1, provide a common framework for discussing the job analysis methods included in this chapter. Briefly, job-content data describe the actions workers perform on the job, the products they produce, or services they provide; job-requirements data describe the areas of knowledge, skills, abilities, physical or other characteristics, or competencies needed; and job-context data describe the environment or the conditions under which the job is performed and the competencies applied.

It is not surprising that there is some overlapping in terminology among the various methods, since their common objective is to describe jobs. But while some of the same terms may be used by various methods, the definitions of these terms are often different. This is most evident in the use of the terms "task" and "element." For example, the definition of a "task" differs slightly in DOL, FJA, HSMS, TI/CODAP, GOJA, and Behavioral Consistency—as well as in VERJAS. (Exhibit 2 shows examples of tasks written according to the definitions of the various methods.) Further, an "element," according to the HSMS method, is a step in the performance of a task, a unit of job content; an "element" in the Job Element method is a knowledge, skill, ability, interest, willingness, or personal characteristic which is an example of a job requirement; and the 194 "elements" of the Position Analysis Questionnaire variously describe job content, job requirements, and job context.

Department of Labor Job Analysis Method

The Department of Labor (DOL) job analysis method was originally designed to gather, document, and analyze information about jobs throughout the economy for inclusion in the third edition of the *Dictionary of Occupational Titles (DOT)*, published in 1965. The method was also used to develop the data for the fourth and current edition of the *DOT,* published in 1977.

As outlined in the *Handbook for Analyzing Jobs*, the method provides for the systematic study of jobs and occupations. Jobs are described in

Exhibit 2. Examples of Tasks As Described By Various Job Analysis Methods

DEPARTMENT OF LABOR JOB ANALYSIS METHOD

Answers inquiries and gives directions to customers: Greets customers at Information Desk and ascertains reason for visit to Credit Office. Sends customer to Credit Interviewer to open account, to Cashier to pay bill, to Adjustment Department to obtain correction of error in billing. Directs customers to other store departments on request, referring to store directory as necessary. (Information Desk Clerk) (*Handbook for Analyzing Jobs*, p. 39)

Administers current programs: Establishes operational policies and procedures and insures conformance by extension service personnel. Reviews programs to determine monetary needs and approve or disapprove budget. Reviews all phases of current programs such as course content and determines if intended audiences are being reached. Oversees program publicity and recording, and approves specific courses and teachers. Awards scholarships for disadvantaged persons to enroll in extension courses. (Director, University Extension) (*Handbook for Analyzing Jobs*, p. 48)

FUNCTIONAL JOB ANALYSIS METHOD

Types/transcribes form letter, including specified information from records provided, following S.O.P. for form letters, but adjusting standard form as required for clarity and smoothness, etc., in order to prepare letter for mailing. (Typist) (National Task Bank)

Evaluates/assesses urgency of client's presented problem, judging circumstances reported and client's behavior/emotional state in relation to general agency guidelines in order to decide whether case requires emergency or routine handling. (Social Service Worker) (National Task Bank)

TASK INVENTORY

From handwritten material, type drafts of correspondence. (Clerical) (Gandy and Maier, p. 63)

File, shelve, or store items (such as orders, books, or other items) in accordance with file codes or classification symbols. (Clerical) (Gandy and Maier, p. 41)

HEALTH SERVICES MOBILITY STUDY METHOD

Taking plain film radiographs of abdominal contents on non-infant patient by reviewing request; reporting observed contraindications; reassuring patient; positioning patient and equipment for erect or recumbent exposure; having radiographs processed and reviewed; repeating for full set of views or as ordered; having patient returned; placing radiographs for use; recording examination. (Radiologic Technologist) (Gilpatrick, 1977 b, p. 4–27)

BEHAVIORAL CONSISTENCY METHOD

Conducts on-site inspection and record check in order to ensure that company policies and procedures are consistent with FAA safety regulations, operating certificate manuals and operating specifications, using knowledge of those documents and knowledge of flying. (Aviation Safety Inspector) (*BRE Manual,* Tab II-41)

Examines qualifications of applicants for professional and technical positions in the administrative field in order to determine grade and series eligibility using X-118 standards and classification standards. (Personnel Staffing Specialist) (*BRE Manual*) (Tab II-41)

GUIDELINES ORIENTED JOB ANALYSIS METHOD

Interprets and applies eminent domain and uniform assistance law in performing value estimates, Relocation Assistance Program supplements and negotiations for property rights. (Associate Real Property Agent) (Biddle, 1978 p. 6-39)

Manages property, as the lessee or lessor, in the day-to-day problems of real property leaseholds. (Associate Real Property Agent) (Biddle, 1978 p. 6-44) terms of "work performed" (job-content data), and "worker traits" (job-requirement data with some contextual information). Within each of these broad categories, more specific information is provided by several subcategories. The subcategories under "work performed" are:

Worker Functions—What workers do in the performance of a job with regard to three categories: (1) information and ideas (*Data*), (2) interpersonal communication (*People*), and (3) using tangibles (*Things*).

Work Fields—The characteristics of the machines, tools, equipment, and work aids used and the techniques employed in the performance of a job (e.g., accounting-recording, painting).

Machines, Tools, Equipment, and Work Aids—The devices and instruments used in performing the job.

Materials, Products, Subject Matter, and Services—The basic materials used (e.g., fabric or metal), the final product made (e.g., carpets or automobiles), the subject matter applied (e.g., insurance or pharmacology), and the service provided (e.g., education or dentistry) in terms of 55 groups with 580 categories.

Tasks—The specific descriptions of job content. A task is defined as "one or more elements and one of the distinct activities that contribute logical and necessary steps in the performance of work by the worker. A task is created whenever human effort, physical or mental, is exercised to accomplish a specific purpose" (*Handbook for Analyzing Jobs*, p. 3).

The subcategories under "worker traits" are:

General Education Development—Those aspects of education which contribute to a worker's reasoning development and ability to follow instructions (*Reasoning*), and the acquisition of "tool" knowledges such as mathematics and language skills (*Mathematics* and *Language*).

Specific Vocational Preparation—The amount and kind of preparation required to learn the techniques, acquire the information, and develop the facility needed for average successful performance in a specific job situation.

Aptitudes—The specific capacities or abilities required of an individual to facilitate the learning of some task or job duty.

Temperaments—The adaptability requirements made on the worker by specific types of job situations.

Interests—The worker's preference for certain kinds of experiences and job situations.

Physical Demands—The physical capacities required of workers to enable them to perform in specific job situations.

Environmental Conditions—Those physical surroundings of a job situation that make specific demands upon workers' physical capacities (*Handbook for Analyzing Jobs*).

In the DOL method, job analysis data are collected, recorded, and rated by trained analysts, based on a review of written materials, observations, and interviews with workers and supervisors. The method provides specific procedures, instructions, and forms for these activities. The data are presented in a job-description format. (Exhibit 3 shows a completed DOL Job Analysis Schedule for "Dough Mixer.")

The procedures and techniques of this method were developed to provide occupational information needed by the various programs of the federal and state employment services. The introduction to the *Handbook for Analyzing Jobs* states that the method is equally applicable to any job analysis project regardless of the intended utilization of the data. Included are recruitment and selection, job restructuring, vocational counseling, identification of training needs, development of training curricula, performance evaluation, and plant safety.

Despite its intended applicability, the method does not provide sufficient job-related information for all of these purposes. It is particularly inadequate with regard to selection and selection-related applications, given the current legal, judicial, and regulatory climate. The method does not provide a means for clearly linking and documenting the relationship between job requirements and specific examples of job content. Although tasks are identified, they serve only as the basis for whole job ratings on the various scales used and are not rated individually. This also lessens the utility of the method for effective structuring and restructuring of jobs. The DOL method is not intended to provide sufficient contextual information for classification or job evaluation purposes. In fact, the analyses are generally conducted with an existing job classification structure.

The General Education Development Scales describe reasoning, mathematical and language skill, and knowledge levels independent of years of education. When applied to specific examples of job content such as manuals, forms, or equipment used, they provide an alternative to the traditional means of describing job requirements. The Language Scale, which combines descriptions of the use of language for reading, writing, and speaking, would be more useful if it were applied as three separate scales. A job, or the various tasks of a job, may require very different levels of language skill for reading, writing, and speaking.

Exhibit 3. A DOL Job Analysis Schedule

JOB ANALYSIS SCHEDULE

1. Estab. Job Title   DOUGH MIXER
2. Ind. Assign.   (bake. prod.)
3. SIC Code(s) and Title(s)   2051 Bread and other bakery products

Code   520.782
WTA Group   Oper. Control p. 435
DOT Title
Ind. Desig.

4. JOB SUMMARY:

Operates mixing machine to mix ingredients for straight and sponge (yeast) doughs according to established formulas, directs other workers in fermentation of dough, and cuts dough into pieces with hand cutter.

5. WORK PERFORMED RATINGS:

Worker Functions	Data D	People P	Things (T)
	5	6	2

Work Field 146 - Cooking, Food Preparing

M.P.S.M.S. 384 - Bakery Products

6. WORKER TRAITS RATINGS:

GED　　　　　1 (2) 3 4 5 6

SVP　　　　　1 2 3 (4) 5 6 7 8 9

Aptitudes G 3 V 3 N 3 S 3 P 3 Q 4 K 3 F 3 M 3 E 4 C 4

Temperaments D F I J (M) P R S (T) V

Interests　　　(1a) 1b 2a 2b 3a 3b 4a (4b) 5a (5b)

Phys. Demands S L M (H) V 2 (3)(4) 5 (6)

Environ. Cond. (I) O B 2 3 4 (5) 6 7

Exhibit 3. A DOL Job Analysis Schedule—*continued*

7. General Education

    a. Elementary __6__ High School_____ Courses_____

    b. College __None__ Courses_____

8. Vocational Preparation

    a. College __None__ Courses_____

    _____

    b. Vocational Education __None__ Courses_____

    _____

    c. Apprenticeship __None_____

    _____

    d. Inplant Training __None_____

    e. On-the-Job Training __six months_____

    f. Performance on Other Jobs __DOUGH-MIXER HELPER --- One year_____

9. Experience __One year as DOUGH-MIXER HELPER_____

10. Orientation __Four hours_____

11. Licenses, etc. __Food Handlers Certificate issued by the Health Department____

12. Relation to Other Jobs and Workers

    Promotion: From __DOUGH-MIXER HELPER__ To __BAKER_____

    Transfers: From __None_____ To __None_____

    Supervision Received __By BAKER_____

    Supervision Given __DOUGH-MIXER HELPER_____

    _____

13. Machines, Tools, Equipment, and Work Aids — Dough-mixing machine; balance scales; hand scoops; measuring vessels; portable dough troughs.

14. Materials and Products

    Bread dough

Exhibit 3. A DOL Job Analysis Schedule—*continued*

15. Description of Tasks:

    1. Dumps ingredients into mixing machine: Examines production schedule to determine type of bread to be produced, such as rye, whole wheat, or white. Refers to formula card for quantities and types of ingredients required, such as flour, water, milk, vitamin solutions, and shortening. Weighs out, measures, and dumps ingredients into mixing machine. (20%)

    2. Operates mixing machine: Turns valves and other hand controls to set mixing time according to type of dough being mixed. Presses button to start agitator blades in machine. Observes gages and dials on equipment continuously to verify temperature of dough and mixing time. Feels dough for desired consistency. Adds water or flour to mix measuring vessels and adjusts mixing time and controls to obtain desired elasticity in mix. (55%)

    3. Directs other workers in fermentation of dough: Prepares fermentation schedule according to type of dough being raised. Sprays portable dough *Trough* with lubricant to prevent adherence of mixed dough to trough. Directs DOUGH-MIXER HELPER in positioning trough beneath door of mixer to catch dough when mixing cycle is complete. Pushes or directs other workers to push troughs of dough into fermentation room. (10%)

    4. Cuts dough: Dumps fermentated dough onto worktable. Manually kneads dough to eliminate gases formed by yeast. Cuts dough into pieces with hand cutter. Places cut dough on proofing rack and covers with cloth. (10%)

    5. Performs miscellaneous duties: Records on work sheet number of batches mixed during work shift. Informs BAKE SHOP FOREMAN when repairs or major adjustments are required for machines and equipment. (5%)

16. Definition of Terms

    Trough — A long, narrow, opened vessel used for kneading or washing

         ingredients.

17. General Comments

    None

18. Analyst   Jane Smith   Date 3/21/70   Editor John Rilley   Date 3/30/70

    Reviewed By   Alexandra Purcey   Title, Org.   Foreman, Bake Shop

Source: U.S. Department of Labor, Manpower Administration. *Handbook for Analyzing Jobs*. Washington, D.C.: U.S. Government Printing Office, 1972, pp. 42–45.

The DOL method is significant not only as a method in and of itself but also because much of the original research contributed to the formulation of other job analysis methods including FJA and PAQ. Further, because it is the method used to develop the *Dictionary of Occupational Titles,* an understanding of its concepts allows the practitioner to use an extensive body of general occupational information that includes jobs throughout the economy.

Functional Job Analysis

The fundamental concepts of Functional Job Analysis (FJA) are based on the research conducted as part of the Functional Occupational Classification Project, which resulted in the third edition of the *Dictionary of Occupational Titles.* This project was conceived and designed by Sidney A. Fine and carried out under his direction during the years 1950–1959. The concepts were subsequently expanded and the specific methods and techniques were refined by Fine and colleagues at the W. E. Upjohn Institute for Employment Research. During the late 1960s, they applied FJA to the analysis of work in human service organizations to create job and career opportunities for minority and disadvantaged workers.

FJA is a comprehensive job/task analysis approach which focuses on interactions among the work, the workers, and the work organization (Fine, Holt, and Hutchinson, 1974). It involves the following five components:

1. *Identification of Purpose, Goals, and Objectives*—An organization's overall purpose, mission and maintenance goals, resources and constraints, and objectives are identified. This analysis provides the basis for describing "what should be" as well as "what is."

2. *Identification and Description of Tasks*—Tasks describing "what a worker does" and "what gets done" are identified and defined to reflect the systems orientation. A task is defined as "an action or action sequence grouped through time designed to contribute a specified end result to the accomplishment of an objective and for which functional levels and orientation can be reliably assigned" (Fine and Wiley, 1971, p. 9). Task statements describing the content of the job are then written in a standardized format.

3. *Analysis of Tasks*—FJA provides a means of assessing and describing the level and orientation of what workers do. Each task is analyzed according to seven scales—the three Worker Function Scales of Data, People, and Things; the Worker Instruction Scale; and the three General

Education Development Scales of Reasoning, Mathematics, and Language.*

- The *Data Scale* describes the worker's involvement with information and ideas in the performance of a task.
- The *People Scale* describes the worker's involvement in the performance of a task that requires communication and interaction with other people such as clients or co-workers.
- The *Things Scale* describes the worker's involvement in the performance of a task with tangibles—machines, tools, equipment, and work aids.
- The *Scale of Worker Instructions* describes the relative amount of prescription and discretion assigned or allowed to the worker in the performance of the task.
- The *Reasoning Scale* describes the requirements of the task in the use of concepts, problem solving, making judgments, and carrying out instructions.
- The *Mathematics Scale* describes the requirements of the task in the use of arithmetic, algebra, geometry, and mathematical principles and techniques.
- The *Language Scale* describes the requirements of the task in the use of language for reading, writing, and speaking.

Orientation percentages are also assigned to describe the worker's relative involvement in the performance of a task with data, people, and things. "Relative involvement" essentially means relative emphasis on performance standards.

4. *Development of Performance Standards*—Task statements and orientation percentages provide the basis for determining descriptive as well as numerical performance standards which define the criteria for assessing the results of a worker's tasks.

5. *Development of Training Content*—FJA distinguishes among three types of skills—functional, specific content, and adaptive—in identifying job requirements.

1. *Functional,* "how to," skills or competencies enable an individual to relate to data, people, and things. They are generally acquired in formal education or training situations and are reinforced through on-the-job experience, e.g., "how to type letters."

---

*While the DOL and the FJA Worker Functions and General Education Development Scales share the same basic concepts and titles, there are significant differences in level definitions.

2. *Specific Content*, "know-how," skills or competencies enable an individual to perform tasks according to the standards or specifications of a particular organization or market. They are acquired on the job or in situations oriented to specific outputs, e.g., "knowledge of standard format for letters."

3. *Adaptive*, "enabling," skills or competencies enable individuals to use content skills and to manage themselves in either a constant or changing job context (physical, social, and environmental conditions), e.g., "punctuality and self-pacing" (Fine and Wiley, 1971).

Job requirements, the functional and specific content skills and knowledge needed to perform a task, are identified through inference, drawing directly on information in the task statement with the scale ratings serving as reference points for consistency and standardization. Adaptive skills are not identified for specific tasks as part of the standard analysis (Fine and Wiley, 1971). When the task analysis is completed, it must conform to the paradigm: "To do this task to these standards, the worker needs this training" (Fine and Bernotavicz, 1973, pp. 11–14). (Exhibit 4 shows an example of a completed Task Analysis Worksheet.)

FJA data is developed by trained analysts and is based on a review of background and reference material, interviews with workers and supervisors, and direct observation of the work as it is performed. The technique includes procedures for group review and for "editing" of the task data by subject matter experts as well as by analysts to assure its validity and reliability (Fine, Holt, and Hutchinson, 1974).

FJA provides data for a range of human resource management applications, including job and career design, development of selection and evaluation instruments, identification of training needs, and design of training and educational curricula. Although FJA does not yield sufficient data for classification or job evaluation, it can be readily used in conjunction with a method designed for these purposes. FJA has been applied to the analysis of work on every level (managerial, professional, clerical, craft) and in a broad range of fields including human services, banking, housing management, construction, marine, electrical, computer, and steel manufacturing.

One of the most comprehensive applications of FJA was a project undertaken by Fine and his associates in collaboration with the International Union of Operating Engineers in response to charges of racial discrimination in selection for apprenticeship training. The project involved describing the work of an operating engineer; identifying the requisite skills, knowledges, and abilities; defining detailed standards of performance; determining the training needed to achieve the specified

Exhibit 4. An FJA Task Analysis Worksheet From the Job of Social Service Worker

W.F. - LEVEL			W.F. - ORIENTATION			G.E.D.				TASK NO.
Data	People	Things	Data	People	Things	INSTR.	Reas.	Math.	Lang.	
3B	2	1A	45%	50%	5%	3	3	2	4	SW.D.2

GOAL:

OBJECTIVE:

TASK: *Talks with client, gives general explanation of particular agency services, answering questions about procedures and policies from knowledge of and experience in agency, in order to inform client about specific agency service.*

PERFORMANCE STANDARDS	TRAINING CONTENT
Descriptive: · Explanation is thorough, clear, accurate, and concise. · Worker shows patience and interest in client. *Numerical:* · Less than x% of clients over x period of time complain of unclear, inadequate information or worker's manner.	*Functional:* · How to explain/describe information to a specific audience. · How to establish rapport with clients. *Specific:* · Knowledge of specific program information.

Source: U.S. Department of Health, Education, and Welfare, Educational Resources Information Center (ERIC). *National Task Bank,* 1st ed. Prepared by the W.E. Upjohn Institute for Employment Research, 1973.

levels of performance; and finally, developing nondiscriminatory work sample performance tests based on the performance standards.

The data were also used as the basis for developing the curriculum for an apprenticeship training film. The methodology designed for this project is a model which can be applied to other types of jobs (Fine et al. 1978).

Functional Job Analysis represents a significant advancement of the basic Department of Labor method. The DOL method was designed primarily for collecting and recording occupational information. FJA was designed to be applied to improving the human resource management functions of organizations.

FJA is a rigorous method requiring an investment of time and effort. Some criticize the technique for requiring too much time, particularly in the identification of an organization's purpose, goals, and objectives. Although components of the method can be used separately, doing so lessens the applicability of the data. For example, it is difficult to identify the appropriate level of detail for a task and to develop meaningful performance standards without information about organizational purpose, goals, and objectives.

A number of task banks have been developed using FJA*. An organization can substantially reduce the data collection and analysis effort by using one of them as a starting point, if applicable. Fine agrees that time and effort are initially required to develop the data base or task bank. He stresses, however, that once the information has been developed and is readily available, the investment will be repaid many times. The various applications of the data will increase the efficiency and effectiveness of the organization (Fine, personal communication).

Critical Incident Technique

The Critical Incident Technique (CIT), developed by John C. Flanagan, is a method of defining a job in terms of the concrete and specific behaviors necessary to perform that job successfully. Based on Flanagan's work during World War II to design procedures for selecting and classifying air crews, the method was further developed by Flanagan, with assistance from colleagues while he was at the American Institutes for Research and the University of Pittsburgh (Flanagan, 1954). The technique involves two basic steps:

---

*For example, the *National Task Bank* includes illustrative tasks in social welfare, rehabilitation services, program administration, clerical support, and money payments. It is available on the ERIC (Educational Resources Information Center) system (First Edition Basic Document, 1973-Ed. 078224; Supplement, 1975-Ed. 120519).

1. *Identification of Critical Incidents.* Incidents illustrating behaviors that are observed to be effective or ineffective in accomplishing the aims of a job are collected from supervisors, incumbents, and others in a position to observe and evaluate job behavior. There must be an agreement among the respondents about the aims or primary purpose of the job. Descriptions are collected in individual and group interviews, from observations, or through structured questionnaires or report forms. The descriptions generally include information about the circumstances leading up to a particular incident, what the person actually did, and why the behavior was effective or ineffective.

2. *Classification of Critical Incidents.* The hundreds or even thousands of descriptions of specific behaviors which may be collected for one job are reviewed and grouped into categories or general behavioral dimensions (e.g., "ability to work accurately and neatly" for the job of Clerk Typist) (Mussio and Smith, 1973, p. 82). The framework for grouping the data depends on its intended use. The grouping is generally done by a trained analyst, with some input from subject matter experts (Flanagan, 1954).

Applications of CIT have included identification of training needs and development of curricula, design of jobs, development of operating procedures, design of equipment, and selection and performance evaluation (Flanagan, 1954).

CIT does not provide a complete description of the job but identifies only those aspects of it that illustrate successful or effective and unsuccessful or ineffective performance. These examples may be descriptions of the content of the job, particular knowledges, skills, abilities, or physical characteristics used, or environmental/contextual conditions. The success of the technique depends upon the respondent's ability to identify and/or to recall incidents and on the analyst's skill in classifying the data to meet specific needs.

The technique is useful primarily when combined with other methods to generate information for performance appraisal, test construction, and development and defense of selection processes. The use of CIT to supplement the basic Job Element procedure is described on page 29 in this chapter.

Job Element Method

The Job Element method, developed by Ernest Primoff of the U.S. Office of Personnel Management, focuses on the characteristics or elements a worker uses in performing a job. A job element may be:

- a knowledge, such as knowledge of accounting principles;
- a skill, such as skill with woodworking tools;

- an ability, such as ability to manage a program;
- a willingness, such as a willingness to do simple tasks repetitively;
- an interest, such as interest in learning new techniques; or
- a personal characteristic, such as reliability or dependability. (Primoff, 1975, p.2.)

The Job Element method involves gathering and quantifying the experience or recalled observations of job knowledge experts—workers and supervisors—about the elements used and their importance for successful job performance. The method includes the following steps:

1. *Identification of Elements.* Elements and subelements used in performing a specific job are identified by a panel of workers and supervisors in a brainstorming session.

2. *Rating of Elements.* The panel of job knowledge experts individually rate each item on four factors:

- Barely acceptable—What relative portion of even barely acceptable workers are good in the element?
- Superior—How important is the element in picking out the superior worker?
- Trouble—How much trouble is likely if the element is ignored when choosing among applicants?
- Practical—Is the element practical? To what extent can we fill our job openings if we demand it? (Primoff, 1975, p. 3.)

3. *Analysis of Elements.* Ratings on the above four factors are scored and analyzed to identify those elements, and the subelements which define them, that have the greatest potential for selecting superior applicants. A FORTRAN program is available for computer calculation, or the calculations may be performed manually. (Exhibit 5 shows a copy of a Job Element blank for rating and analyzing the data.)

Job Element data can be used as the basis for developing an examination or a "Crediting Plan" for a specific job. A Crediting Plan describes the levels of skills, knowledges, abilities, and personal characteristics required to perform the job and is used to assess the applicant's qualifications. It is developed from the elements and subelements identified during the rating process, with additional input from job knowledge experts. Information about applicants' qualifications is obtained through a "Self-Report Checklist," which is generally used in combination with other assessment instruments such as written tests, reference checks, interviews, and background investigations. The method also provides procedures for modifying and amplifying the Crediting Plan and Checklist as they are applied in actual selection situations (Primoff, 1975).

Exhibit 5. Sample Job Element Rating Blank

Job:
Grade:

Date:

Rater No. (col. 3 4 5)

Job No. (6 7 8)

Rater Name and Grade:
Title and Location:

Page No. (col. 1 2)

Element No. (Do not Punch)	Barely acceptable workers (B) + all have, ✓ some have, 0 almost none have	To pick out superior workers (S) + very important, ✓ valuable, 0 does not differentiate	Trouble likely if not considered (T) + much trouble, ✓ some trouble, 0 safe to ignore	Practical. Demanding this element, we can fill (P) + all openings, ✓ some openings, 0 no openings	Columns	(These columns for use in hand calculation of values)					
						$S \times P$	T	Item Index (IT) $SP+T$	Total Value (TV) $IT+S-B-P$	P' ($+=0$, $✓=1$, $0=2$)	SP'	Training Value (TR) $S+T+SP'-B$
					9–12							
					13–16							
					17–20							
					21–24							
					25–28							
					29–32							
					33–36							
					37–40							
					41–44							
					45–48							
					49–52							
					53–56							
					57–60							
					61–64							
					65–68							
					69–72							
					73–76							
					77–80							

Note: for all categories except P', + counts 2, ✓ counts 1, 0 counts 0. For category P', + counts 0, ✓ counts 1, 0 counts 2.

U.S. Civil Service Commission
Personnel Research and Development Center
Washington, D.C.

Source: Primoff, E. S. How to Prepare and Conduct Job Element Examinations. Washington, D.C.: U.S. Government Printing Office, 1975, p. 12.

The Job Element method has been used to determine qualification requirements for trade and labor jobs in the federal government. There have been some applications to professional level jobs, particularly in selecting applicants for upward mobility programs.

The Job Element method provides procedures only for identifying job requirements—the knowledges, skills, abilities, and personal characteristics—needed to perform the work, or the content, of the job. The original method does not include either the identification of job content or the linking of the job requirements to existing content data. It does not provide sufficient data to support a content validity claim for personnel-related decisions.

Primoff has drafted a supplemental procedure combining the Job Element method with FJA and CIT, which "results in a complete description of the work behaviors of the job and provides the requisite operational definitions of the knowledges, skills, and abilities required by the job" (Primoff, 1980). The new procedure can be used to develop a new examination or to document an existing one. There are four steps involved:

1. *Classification of Subelements.* Subject matter experts (SMEs) review subelements and determine whether they represent minimum, satisfactory, or outstanding levels of performance.

2. *Description of Subelements.* SMEs write task statements according to the technique prescribed by FJA to define and further describe subelements at the designated levels of performance.

3. *Evaluation of Task Statements.* SMEs analyze each task and assign scale ratings and orientation percentages in accordance with the procedures of FJA. Quality and/or quantity performance criteria are identified for each task/subelement combination, and the training that is provided by the organization is also listed.

4. *Identification and Description of Critical Incidents.* SMEs review each subelement/task combination and describe one or more critical incidents which illustrate what happens when performance standards are not met (Primoff, 1980).

The classification of subelements by levels of performance and their further description by task statements are intended to ensure compliance with the requirements of the Uniform Guidelines on Employee Selection Procedures for content validity. The evaluation of the subelements/task statements and the identification of illustrative critical incidents are designed to provide additional documentation and information useful in preparing crediting plans and measuring instruments and in applying the data to other personnel management purposes, such as identification of training needs, development of promotional criteria, and performance appraisal (Primoff, 1980). The supplemental procedure is further intended to facilitate the development of valid tests that do not have an adverse impact on specific groups of applicants, as Primoff believes that the courts will not accept any methodology if there is adverse impact (Primoff, personal communication, November 13, 1980).

Many concepts and techniques of the Job Element method have been adapted and incorporated into other job analysis methods—specifically, the concept of the crediting plan, the use of expert workers in a brainstorming session to identify data, the concepts included in the four-factor rating scheme, and the use of supplemental application forms. Two methods, Behavioral Consistency and Guidelines Oriented Job Analysis, draw on these concepts and are discussed later in the chapter.

Position Analysis Questionnaire

In developing the Position Analysis Questionnaire (PAQ), Ernest McCormick and associates of the Department of Psychological Sciences at Purdue University hypothesized that "there is some underlying behavioral structure or order to the domain of human work" (McCormick, Jeanneret, and Mecham, 1972). They distinguished between "job-oriented" elements, which describe the technological aspects of work, and "worker-oriented" elements, which describe the human behaviors involved in jobs. McCormick's group selected worker-oriented elements for further research on the premise that elements that are not technologically based would allow for more relevant comparison of jobs in different work fields (McCormick, Jeanneret, and Mecham, 1972).

The PAQ is a structured job analysis instrument used to analyze and describe the job as it is being performed. The method is composed of 194 elements—187 relating to job activities and 7 to compensation. These elements are organized into six categories:

1. *Information Input.* Where and how does the worker get the information used in performing the job? Examples are use of written materials and estimating size.

2. *Mental Processes.* What reasoning, decision-making, planning, and information-processing activities are involved in performing the job? Examples are level of reasoning in problem solving, amount of planning, and use of learned information.

3. *Work Output.* What physical activities does the worker perform and what tools or devices are used? Examples are use of manually-powered precision tools/instruments and level of physical exertion.

4. *Relationship with Other Persons*. What relationships with other people are required in performing the job? Examples are interviewing and contact with professional personnel.

5. *Job Context*. In what physical and social contexts is the work performed? Examples are noise intensity and importance of civic obligations.

6. *Other Job Characteristics*. What activities, conditions, or characteristics, other than those described in the Job Context category, are relevant to the job? Examples are irregular work schedules and repetitive activities (PAQ Form B).

Each item or job element is rated on a specified scale such as "extent of use," "amount of time," "importance to the job," "possibility of occurrence," and "applicability." In addition, there are several specialized scales for use with certain job elements, for example, "degree of responsibility for material assets" (PAQ Form B).

The PAQ can be completed by job analysts, personnel specialists, or industrial engineers by interviewing workers and supervisors and observing the work as it is performed. Supervisors and workers themselves can also complete the instrument if the reading requirements of the job are at least at the college graduate level. It has been suggested that this level of reading skill is necessary to accurately complete the PAQ (Ash and Edgell, 1975).

Data from the PAQ can be analyzed in several ways. (1) For a specific job, individual ratings can be averaged to indicate the relative importance and emphasis to be placed on various job elements; the results can then be summarized as a job description. (2) The elements can also be clustered into a profile rating on 45 job dimensions (described in Exhibit 6) established on the basis of earlier research. This is the primary analysis; the resulting profiles or job dimension scores can be used in subsequent analyses to compare a job to others which are part of a larger data base. (3) Estimates of aptitude requirements can be made by reference to a data base on which both PAQ analyses and General Aptitude Test Battery (GATB) validation studies have been conducted. (4) Job evaluation points, used in establishing compensation rates for jobs, can also be estimated. (5) Although currently available only for research purposes, the elements can also be analyzed and linked to an existing data base to determine the degree to which 76 human attributes are required to perform the job. (6) Finally, an occupational prestige score can also be computed. PAQ data is computer analyzed. A knowledge of inferential and correlational statistics is helpful in interpreting the results. Data processing is available from PAQ Services, Inc., which was established by McCormick, Mecham, and Jeanneret.

Exhibit 6.   Job Dimensions Based on Principal Components Analyses of PAQ Data for 2200 Jobs: System II

NO. TECHNICAL TITLE	OPERATIONAL TITLE

DIVISION DIMENSIONS

Division 1: Information Input

1. Perceptual interpretation	Interpreting what is sensed
2. Input from representational sources	Using various sources of information
3. Visual input from devices/materials	Watching devices/materials for information
4. Evaluating/judging sensory input	Evaluating/judging what is sensed
5. Environmental awareness	Being aware of environmental conditions
6. Use of various senses	Using various senses

Division 2: Mental Processes

7. Decision making	Making decisions
8. Information processing	Processing information

Division 3: Work Output

9. Using machines/tools/equipment	Using machines/tools/equipment
10. General body vs. sedentary activities	Performing activities requiring general body movements
11. Control and related physical coordination	Controlling machines/processes
12. Skilled/technical activities	Performing skilled/technical activities
13. Controlled manual/related activities	Performing controlled manual/related activities
14. Use of miscellaneous equipment/ devices	Using miscellaneous equipment/ devices
15. Handling/manipulating/related activities	Performing handling/related manual activities
16. Physical coordination	General physical coordination

Division 4: Relationships With Other Persons

17. Interchange of judgmental/related information	Communicating judgments/related information
18. General personal contact	Engaging in general personal contacts
19. Supervisory/coordination/related activities	Performing supervisory/coordination/ related activities
20. Job-related communications	Exchanging job-related information
21. Public/related personal contacts	Public/related personal contacts

Division 5: Job Context

22. Potentially stressful/unpleasant environment	Being in a stressful/unpleasant environment
23. Personally demanding situations	Engaging in personally demanding situations
24. Potentially hazardous job situations	Being in hazardous job situations

Division 6: Other Job Characteristics

25. Non-typical vs. typical day work schedule	Working non-typical vs. day schedule
26. Businesslike situations	Working in businesslike situations
27. Optional vs. specified apparel	Wearing optional vs. specified apparel

Exhibit 6. Job Dimensions Based on Principal Components Analyses of PAQ Data for 2200 Jobs: System II—*continued*

NO.	TECHNICAL TITLE	OPERATIONAL TITLE
28.	Variable vs. salary compensation	Being paid on a variable vs. salary basis
29.	Regular vs. irregular work schedule	Working on a regular vs. irregular schedule
30.	Job demanding responsibilities	Working under job-demanding circumstances
31.	Structured vs. unstructured job activities	Performing structured vs. unstructured work
32.	Vigilant/discriminating work activities	Being alert to changing conditions

OVERALL DIMENSIONS

NO.	TECHNICAL TITLE	OPERATIONAL TITLE
33.	Decision/communication/general responsibilities	Having decision, communicating, and general responsibilities
34.	Machine/equipment operation	Operating machines/equipment
35.	Clerical/related activities	Performing clerical/related activities
36.	Technical/related activities	Performing technical/related activities
37.	Service/related activities	Performing service/related activities
38.	Regular day schedule vs. other work schedules	Working regular day vs. other work schedules
39.	Routine/repetitive work activities	Performing routine/repetitive activities
40.	Environmental awareness	Being aware of work environment
41.	General physical activities	Engaging in physical activities
42.	Supervising/coordinating other personnel	Supervising/coordinating other personnel
43.	Public/customer/related contact activities	Public/customer/related contacts
44.	Unpleasant/hazardous/demanding environment	Working in an unpleasant/hazardous/demanding/environment
45.	Unnamed	Unnamed

Source: McCormick, E. J., Mecham, R. C., and Jeanneret, P. R. *Position Analysis Questionnaire (PAQ) Technical Manual (System II).* Logan, Utah: PAQ Services, Inc., 1977. Reprinted with permission.

The PAQ has been used primarily for the development of job evaluation and compensation programs. Organizations which have applied the PAQ in this way have included those in public utilities, finance, insurance, service industries, health care, manufacturing, and transportation, as well as state and local governments (McCormick, Mecham and Jeanneret, 1977, a). The PAQ also generates data which can be applied to employee selection and placement, performance appraisal, assessment center development, determining the similarity of jobs, grouping jobs into families, vocational counseling, career development, identifying training needs, and developing training curricula (McCormick, Mecham and Jeanneret, 1977, b). The method has also been used for job design or restructuring purposes (Jeanneret, personal communication, October 10, 1980).

The PAQ is a combination of content, requirements, and contextual information (defined in Chapter 1). It does not explicitly identify or differentiate among these three categories of information and it may be difficult to perceive the linkage between job content and job requirements and to understand how the data can be used for multiple applications. The lack of differentiation also precludes easily updating the information to reflect changes in the organization. For example, if there is a change in some of the tasks or job content because a new piece of equipment is being used, it is not possible to identify and correct only the relevant information as can be done with a data bank developed using a task-based method, such as FJA or HSMS. Rather, the PAQ must be completed and analyzed anew. Depending on the rate of change within the organization, this could be expensive. According to McCormick, this has not been a serious problem. Further, PAQ data is computer analyzed with data processing being provided by PAQ Services. The lack of involvement in, and understanding of, the analysis process may affect an organization's ability to use the data effectively. However, McCormick noted that most organizations work closely with someone who is familiar with PAQ (McCormick, personal communication, October 12, 1980).

McCormick and his associates have recently developed another questionnaire for use with professional, managerial, and related jobs. The Professional and Managerial Position Questionnaire (PMPQ) is composed of 98 items divided into three categories: Job Functions, Job Requirements, and Other Information. Items are rated for various factors, including whether or not the item is part of the job, the item's complexity, the impact of inadequate performance, the degree of the worker's responsibility, and on various scales unique to specific items (Mitchell and McCormick, 1980). Data from the PMPQ has been used to develop classification and job evaluation systems for several organizations (PAQ Newsletter, No. 2-81, September 1981).

Computer Analyzed Task Inventory Approach

This approach, frequently referred to as "CODAP," has been developed by Dr. Raymond E. Christal and his associates at the U.S. Air Force Human Resources Laboratory. An outgrowth of the U.S. Air Force Occupational Research project, which began in 1958, it reflects the Air Force's need to collect data from very large populations of workers in scattered locations. There are two basic components in the approach.

1. *The Task Inventory* (TI) is a data collection instrument that includes a list of tasks for a particular job or occupational area grouped into duties or activities. Tasks are defined so that the final list will have approximately

1,000 or fewer tasks. The length of the task list, of course, depends upon the scope and variety of work to be described and the intended use of the data (Christal, personal communication, January 8, 1981). Each task is rated in relation to other tasks of the job on a 7-, 9-, or 11-point "relative time spent" scale with end points of "very much below average" and "very much above average." The inventory also includes a section with questions about the worker's job and background, such as previous education, time on the job, tools used, and attitude toward job (Christal, 1974). (Exhibit 7 shows an example of a portion of an inventory.)

2. *The Comprehensive Occupational Data Analysis Program* (CODAP) is a series of interactive computer programs used to analyze, organize, and report on data from the task inventory. The programs are designed to provide information for a variety of applications. There are over 50 programs covering five basic processes: data preparation and validation, selection of individuals to form potentially useful groups, computation of summary information, comparison of summary information, and prediction (Thew and Weissmuller, undated). For example, CODAP can identify and describe the types of jobs which exist in an occupational area, identify and describe the types of jobs performed by specified groups of workers, such as women or minorities, compare the work performed at various locations or by various levels of personnel, and produce job descriptions (Christal, 1974).

The construction of a task inventory generally involves (a) an initial identification and listing of tasks from a review of available literature by individuals trained in task statement writing, and (b) a review and modification and/or expansion of the basic list by supervisors and others, for example, by technical school instructors who have detailed knowledge of the job or occupational area. The inventory is then administered to, and completed by, incumbents. Supervisors rate tasks on factors such as "training time to reach proficiency," "consequence of inadequate performance," or "criticality of immediate performance." These ratings provide a means for addressing multifaceted factors such as "importance" or "criticality" (Christal, 1974). The data are then automated, processed, organized, and reported by CODAP. This phase requires an understanding of project objectives and an ability to communicate with both producers and users of the data, as well as expertise with CODAP.

Versions of the CODAP system are available for use on UNIVAC, CDC, and IBM compatible equipment. The system has the capacity to process data on 1,700 tasks for each of 20,000 workers (Thew and Weissmuller, undated). Christal has reported that the Air Force attempts to obtain 100 percent samples in occupational areas having 2,000 or fewer workers. Stratified samples are employed with larger population groups

Exhibit 7. Portion of a Task Inventory

DUTY A. ARRANGING FOR APPOINTMENTS, MEETINGS OR EVENTS

Scale for Time Spent

1 = Very much below average
2 = Below average
3 = Slightly below average   (Part III) Time Spent
4 = Average
5 = Slightly above average   (Part II) ✓ If Performed
6 = Above average
7 = Very much above average

A1. Coordinate or* prepare agenda items (prior to typing) for meetings and conferences.			5
A2. Distribute agenda or minutes of meetings.			6
A3. Maintain either personal diary or appointment schedule for others.			7
A4. Make physical arrangements for meetings after being given time and place (such as scheduling rooms, reserving public address equipment and other equipment).			8
A5. Make travel arrangements (such as transportation and hotel arrangements).			9
A6. Notify participants of time and place of meetings as directed.			10
A7. Remind meeting or conference participants of required action.			11
A8. Schedule appointments for either supervisors or others in your office.			12
A9. Schedule events such as court hearing dates or surgery.			13

*The word "or" is used to mean either coordinate or prepare. If you do either of these two things, you ✓ the task as performed. This same meaning is used throughout the task inventory. If you do any part of a task with "or" in it, ✓ the task as performed.

Source: Gandy, A. J., and Maier, W. *Utah Clerical Linkup Study: Comparison of Federal and State Jobs.* Washington, D.C.: Office of Personnel Management, 1979.

and data may be collected from as many as 5,000 workers (Christal, 1974). Clearly, CODAP is most useful for projects involving large populations and may not be feasible or cost effective for smaller groups. It has been suggested that organizations not intending to use CODAP on a recurring basis contract for the required data processing, as there can be substantial computer costs associated with trial and error familiarization and identification of useful programs (Gandy and Maier, 1979).

The TI/CODAP approach develops job content information—descriptions of the work performed—with some contextual information collected on the background section of the inventory. The approach does not identify job requirements, or the knowledges, skills, abilities, physical and other characteristics necessary to perform the work. This information, however, can be inferred from the task data base. For example, an Electronic Principles Job Inventory composed of knowledges and skills that could be used by electronic technicians was used to assess directly the application of these skills and knowledges by job incumbents. In addition, CODAP is being used to establish strength, stamina, and aptitude requirements for Air Force occupations (Christal, personal communication, January 1, 1981). Data developed using this method have been used to identify training needs and design training programs, to validate successful completion of training as a selection criterion, to structure or restructure work assignments, to derive a classification structure and to classify jobs, and to generalize or extend the validity of a selection procedure to a wider range of jobs. TI/CODAP is used in all branches of the military and more recently by other federal agencies and local governments.

As outlined, there are two basic components to the approach—the task inventory and the computer analysis package. The majority of problems with the method result from poorly constructed task inventories. Users should be alert to a potential "garbage in, garbage out" problem, because the computer analysis cannot correct or compensate for inaccurate or incomplete information. To deal with this, Christal recommends using trained personnel to develop inventories and writing specific rather than broad task statements (Christal, 1974).

The TI/CODAP approach was used in a validity generalization study of state and federal clerical jobs to determine if they were sufficiently similar to be treated the same for selection purposes (Gandy and Maier, 1979). In another study, the CODAP program was used to analyze the data from an inventory of work behaviors rather than tasks. Twenty-eight different aide jobs were studied to see if the same selection procedure could be used for all of them (Lilienthal and Rosen, 1980).

Health Services Mobility Study Method

The Health Services Mobility Study (HSMS) methodology evolved in response to a concern in the late 1960s about personnel shortages in the health services field. Conceptually, the methodology is based on the premise that prior education and experience—existing skills and knowledge—can be built upon to facilitate the upward mobility and progression of individuals in a work field or occupational area. The 10-year research and development effort was funded by the Office of Economic Opportunity, the Department of Labor, and the Department of Health, Education and Welfare, and sponsored by Hunter College and the Research

Foundation, City University of New York. It was directed by Eleanor Gilpatrick.

It is a comprehensive, behaviorally oriented, task-based approach involving three operations—task identification and description, rating of tasks by identification and description of skill and knowledge requirements, and grouping of tasks into interrelated hierarchies.

1. *Task Identification and Description.* The method employs a specific task definition oriented to output or result. The output of each task is a complete and separate unit of work and can therefore be used as a "building block" in designing various staffing patterns. Tasks can describe what "should be" by incorporating the results of a literature review with data from incumbents' descriptions of "what is."

A task is defined as "a series of work activities (elements) which are needed to produce an identifiable output that can be independently consumed or used, or that can be used as input in a further stage of production by an individual who may or may not be the performer of the task" (Gilpatrick, 1977, a, p. 2–1). (Exhibit 8 shows a completed task description worksheet.)

2. *Skill and Knowledge Identification and Description.* The method includes a set of skill scales, a knowledge classification system, and a knowledge scale which provides an underlying taxonomy and allows for comparison of skill and knowledge requirements between various tasks and jobs. There are 16 skills:

Three *manual* skills deal with precision and coordination in the use of the body or its parts: (a) *locomotion* deals with the body's movement through space; (b) *object manipulation* deals with the movement, control, and placement of objects; and (c) *guiding or steering* deals with the control of objects moving in space in relation to external stimuli.

There are two *interpersonal* skills: (a) *human interaction* is involved whenever a task requires the performer to communicate, cooperate, or come into contact with other people; and (b) *leadership* is required in a task when a performer must relate or interact with subordinates to influence their work behavior in order to accomplish objectives or tasks.

Three *language* skills deal with the performer's precision in using relevant language to convey or comprehend meaning: (a) *oral use,* (b) *reading use,* and (c) *written use.*

There are two *decision-making* skills: (a) *decision making on method* involves the extent of the performer's choice in how to perform the task and/or what machines, tools, equipment, and work aids to use; and (b) *decision making on quality* involves the amount of latitude the performer

Exhibit 8. HSMS Patient Care Task Description

<u>TASK DESCRIPTION SHEET</u>

Task Code No. <u>182</u>

This is page <u>1</u> of <u>2</u> for this task.

1. What is the output of this task? (Be sure this is broad enough to be repeatable.)	List Elements Fully
Patient and suction machine readied for suctioning; tracheal passageway cleared; machine turned on/off as ordered; patient and/or machine cleansed; matter removed; shown to MD	*Performer uses suction machine for purposes such as gastric lavage (when MD inserts catheter) or with patient who has had a tracheostomy performed for the insertion of a tube for breathing. Performer uses suction machine as result of:*
2. What is used in performing this task? (Note if only certain items must be used. If there is choice, include everything or the kinds of things chosen among.)	*a. Verbal or written request of physician.* *b. Own decision based on observation of patient's need.*
MD's orders; patient's chart or checklist; suction machine; antiseptic soap, water; tubing and sterile catheter(s) for suction machine; trap and drainage bottles; cup; gauze, saline solution; sheet; clock or watch	*1. Performer reads physician's orders on chart or checklist, listens to verbal orders, or considers own decision.*
3. Is there a recipient, respondent or co-worker involved in the task? Yes..(x) No..( )	*2. Obtains necessary materials from storage area or checks that these are with machine. If obtained separately, performer places on table near patient or machine.*
4. If "Yes" to q 3: Name the <u>kind</u> of recipient, respondent or co-worker involved, with descriptions to indicate the relevant conditions; include the kind with whom the performer is not allowed to deal if relevant to knowledge requirements or legal restrictions. *Any patient to be treated with use of suction machine; physician; co-worker*	*3. Performer wheels suction machine near patient or wheels patient to machine if stationary wall unit. (May check that machine is clean; may decide to clean or have cleaned.) If not already done, plugs machine's cord into wall outlet.* *4. Performer may explain to patient what will be done. May drape patient with sheet.*
5. Name the task so that the answers to questions 1-4 are reflected. Underline essential words. <u>*Setting up and using suction machine to clear airway or to assist with gastric lavage*</u>*, by obtaining materials and machine, preparing patient, checking machine, turning machine on and off as ordered for gastric lavage, or inserting catheter into tracheal opening and clearing airway; cleaning up afterwards*	*5. Performer checks machine by turning on suction and checking suction outlet with finger to feel suction. If machine is not functioning, decides to report; obtains another (portable) machine or wheels patient to another machine.* OK-RP:RR:RR
	6. Check here if this is a master sheet..(X)

Exhibit 8. HSMS Patient Care Task Description—*continued*

TASK DESCRIPTION SHEET (continued)

Task Code No. 182

This is page 2 of 2 for this task.

List Elements Fully	List Elements Fully
6. Attaches prepackaged tubing and catheter set to machine by connecting tubing to machine and catheter to tubing.	12. Records what was done and time on patient's chart or checklist, or informs physician that task is completed.
7. If gastric lavage, performer turns machine on and off at physician's orders after he or she has inserted catheter. Stands by during process.	
8. If patient has had a tracheostomy and needs passage cleared, performer inserts the suctioning catheter with appropriate force to enter the tracheal opening. When inserted to appropriate level, performer turns on suction and attempts to clear mucus from the passageway. Turns off machine when done.	
Performer may reassure or comfort patient during process; determines whether passage has been cleaned.	
If not, performer uses fresh catheter(s) and repeats suctioning until the airway is clear.	
9. Performer may clean the area surrounding the tracheal opening with gauze and saline solution.	
10. After use, performer discards the tubing and catheter(s). May place some of the matter removed from the patient in a cup, pouring it from the drainage bottle or glass, and may show to physician (if requested to do so).	
11. Discards cup or matter in bottle; may decide to wash machine and bottles or have subordinate wash (using antiseptic soap and water). Returns machine or has it returned (if portable).	

Source: Gilpatrick, E. *The Health Services Mobility Study Method of Task Analysis and Curriculum Design—Writing Task Descriptions and Scaling Tasks for Skill and Knowledge: A Manual.* Research Report No. 11, Vol. II. Springfield, Va.: National Technical Information Service, 1977.

has over the quality of the task output within the framework of acceptable standards.

There are four *general intellectual* skills: (a) *figural* skills are involved when the performer must deal physically or mentally with the figural properties of visual or mental images and relationships when some predetermined singular standard or objective must be achieved; (b) *symbolic* skills are involved if the performer must use or mentally manipulate abstract symbols; (c) *taxonomic* skills are involved if the performer must apply existing organizing or classifying principles or create new principles to accomplish the task; and (d) *implicative* skills are involved when the performer must come to nonroutine conclusions or draw nonroutine inferences.

There are two *consequences of error* skills: (a) *financial consequences of error* describe performer's awareness of the potential amount of financial damage to the institution; and (b) the performer's awareness of the *consequences of error to humans,* or the potential seriousness of mental or physical harm.

3. *Grouping of Tasks.* Tasks are arranged into interrelated hierarchies using a form of factor analysis by which tasks are grouped on similarities and differences in the skill and knowledge requirements. There are five computer programs used to design job structures and job ladders (Gilpatrick, 1977, a, b, c).

The HSMS methodology utilizes various data-gathering techniques. Individuals trained in the methodology collect and analyze information about tasks and about skill and knowledge requirements during a series of interviews with, and observations of, job incumbents. Relevant literature is reviewed to obtain information on what is desirable in terms of task performance as well as skill and knowledge requirements. In addition, all data are reviewed by experts in the work field for technical accuracy and completeness, and by the project director for methodological accuracy and rigor. There is an abbreviated version of the method which involves identifying "model tasks" and then writing task summaries for those additional tasks which are similar, with the summaries describing only what is different.

The method provides specific processes for using the data to design job ladders and lattices, to develop curriculum objectives and educational ladders for human resource planning, and to devise performance evaluation instruments and proficiency tests. The method is not designed for classification or job evaluation purposes, but much of the data collected could supplement an approach selected for this purpose. Although the pilot testing and initial applications have been in the health field, the methodology is believed equally applicable to other occupational areas (Gilpatrick, 1977, a, b, c). Depending upon how closely the job or occupation is related to the health services field, the Knowledge Classification System would require additional work to expand and refine its coverage.

The HSMS method is rigorous and yields detailed and precise information about job content, job requirements, and how the two are linked. Some contextual information (for example, "consequences of error") is also generated, although, as noted previously, it is not sufficient for classification or job evaluation purposes. Because of this rigor and the time and effort needed to develop the data base, the method may be most practical or cost effective when the data can be used, as was intended by the designers, for various purposes by different organizations. For example, it could be used by an operating institution to structure staffing patterns, select workers, provide on-the-job training, or evaluate performance; by educational institutions to develop curricula and provide education and training; or by certifying or licensing boards to develop criteria and examining procedures.

The method appears to be particularly applicable to projects that cross organizational boundaries, for example, the analysis of work performed by personnel in different states to develop a national selection procedure, or by personnel at various locations within a state to develop a centralized training program or academy. The HSMS method can also be used to analyze and describe the work of a specific organization or operating unit.

The casual reviewer often perceives the HSMS method as overwhelming in its coverage and cumbersome in its detail. Certainly, the method is complex, when compared to more structured, ready-to-use methods, such as the Position Analysis Questionnaire, or to less comprehensive approaches, such as the original Job Element method that develops only job requirements data. The HSMS method, however, proceeds logically, and the potential for confusion is lessened by a series of manuals which detail the method step-by-step (see Gilpatrick, 1977, a, b, c).

Guidelines Oriented Job Analysis

Guidelines Oriented Job Analysis (GOJA) was developed by Richard E. Biddle and associates in the early 1970s in response to new and emerging legislation, regulations, and judicial decisions concerning fair employment practices. It is a step-by-step procedure for describing the work of a specific job classification, for developing standardized employment tools, and for providing the required documentation. There are currently three versions of GOJA: Full GOJA, Brief GOJA, and Simplified GOJA. Although the versions are conceptually related, there are distinct differences among them.

Full GOJA

Full GOJA, the original method, is very detailed and requires approximately 20 hours to complete for the average job. It is used primarily for jobs, such as police and fire, where there is a high probability of employment discrimination suits (Biddle, personal communication, December 19, 1980).

The basic documentation of the GOJA procedure is a job-related job description. The job analysis to develop this documentation involves the following steps:

1. *Task/Domain Identification and Description.* Tasks are identified and described by a group of incumbents and supervisors who are knowledgeable about the work of the job classification. Task statements begin with an action verb, describe what workers do on the job at the acceptable level of performance, and include the difficulty and complexity of the task. Tasks are then grouped into domains and a statement defining each domain is written.

2. *Task/Domain Rating.* Each task is rated on how frequently it is performed, how important or critical it is, and whether it can be learned in a brief orientation period. Ratings on the individual tasks provide the basis for the ratings of each domain. In addition, the reasons why the task is important or critical (e.g., consequence of error) are also listed.

3. *Knowledges, Skills, Other Characteristics, and Physical Characteristics Identification.* The knowledges, skills, other characteristics, and physical characteristics necessary to perform tasks are identified by incumbents. Each task is also rated for frequency, importance, and whether it is generally learned in a brief orientation. Each knowledge, skill, other characteristic, or physical characteristic is also linked back to the task(s) for which it is needed (Biddle, 1976).

Information from the job description can be used to develop a content-valid selection procedure. A Selection Plan identifies those knowledges, skills, other characteristics, and physical characteristics that are needed at the time of selection and are minimum qualifications; those that may be taught on the job if a sufficient number of applicants who already possess them cannot be found; and those that will be taught on the job. The Plan further identifies the practices, procedures, and tests that will be used and describes how they will be used. A Supplemental Application Form can be developed to obtain information on applicants' qualifications for the specific job. This form can be used as a written application or as the structure for an oral interview. The job description also provides information that can be used to develop a Performance

Appraisal Form for evaluating incumbents' performance on relevant tasks. Full GOJA also includes procedures and forms to ensure that appropriate validation information is documented (Biddle, 1976).

Full GOJA focuses equally on developing job content and job requirement data and ties them directly together. Contextual information is included only indirectly to the extent that the environment in which the job is performed results in physical or other characteristics as job requirements. Full GOJA is designed and presented as a selection-oriented job analysis method. The data can also be used for performance appraisal, for the identification of training needs, and for the development of training curricula. Full GOJA does not provide sufficient data for job restructuring or for classification or compensation decisions.

Brief GOJA

Brief GOJA was developed because of the amount of time required to complete the Full GOJA procedure. This abbreviated version takes from four to six hours to complete for the average job. It was developed in 1977 and updated in 1978 after the Uniform Guidelines were published (Biddle, personal communication, December 19, 1980).

In Brief GOJA, incumbents write their own job descriptions using Instruction and Worksheet Booklets. The following steps are involved:

1. *Domain/Duty Identification and Description.* The domains of the job are identified and each is further described by important or critical duties. A good duty statement is defined as telling *"what* is done, *how* and *why* it is done, and what products are obtained. It includes examples to help explain the duty" (Biddle, *Instruction Booklet,* p. 15).

2. *Duty Ratings.* Each duty is rated on how often it is performed and how important it is to the job.

3. *Knowledges, Skills, Physical and Other Characteristics Identification.* The knowledges and skills needed to perform the job are identified, linked back to the duties/domains, and a determination is made as to whether the skill or knowledge can be learned in 8 hours or less. Physical and other characteristics of the job are also listed and referenced back to the duties/domains that require them (Biddle, 1978).

The Brief GOJA procedure yields sufficient information to develop Supplemental Application and Performance Appraisal forms and written tests. The data are not, of course, as detailed as those provided by the Full GOJA method. The applications of the Brief GOJA method are the same as those of the Full GOJA procedure, including selection, performance appraisal, identification of training needs, and development of training curricula (Biddle, personal communication, December 19, 1980).

While this streamlined version can be more efficient and less time consuming in initial data collection, the data from incumbents must still be reviewed and inconsistencies identified. Analysts must determine if incumbents in the same job are describing the same information in different ways or if the information reflects real differences in the work aerformed. It may be necessary to conduct audits or individual interviews with a large percentage of incumbents to confirm or clarify the data.

Simplified GOJA

A third version of GOJA, developed in 1980, is designed to further reduce the amount of time required to gather basic content and competency data. Additional information is also collected for wage and salary and for selection purposes. On the average, two to four hours are required to complete the Simplified GOJA procedures/forms (Biddle, personal communication, December 19, 1980).

Incumbents complete a semistructured Job Analysis form that is reviewed and modified as necessary by the supervisor for coverage and correctness and by a job analyst for clarity and completeness. (Exhibit 9 shows portions of a completed form.) The form requests the following information:

Machines, Tools, and Equipment. Office equipment, manual and power handtools, machines, light and heavy equipment, are listed and rated for frequency of use.

Supervision. Titles and number of people directly and indirectly supervised are listed, and the supervisory tasks performed are checked on a prepared list. A statement describing the amount and kind of supervision received is also checked from a prepared list.

Contacts. Types of people dealt with in the performance of the job and the frequency of contacts are checked.

Duties. Descriptions of the work performed are written and the work products are identified. Each duty is rated for frequency of performance, and its importance to the job is determined.

Knowledges, Skills, and Abilities. Knowledges, skills, and abilities needed to perform the duties of the job are listed and further described by identifying the major parts of each which are needed. For example, the major part of "math skill" needed might be "adding, subtracting whole numbers" (Biddle, *Forms for a Simplified Job Analysis*, p. 11). The knowledges, skills, and abilities are referenced back to the relevant duties to document how they are used.

Exhibit 9. Portion of a Completed Form of Simplified GOJA

SECTION 5a: JOB DUTIES

Use this page to write your job duties. Be sure to:

1) tell how often you do each duty -- Daily, Weekly, Biweekly (every other week), Monthly, Semiannually (twice a year), Annually (once a year). NOTE: Sometimes a duty is performed daily but on a seasonal or quarterly basis. For example, leaves are raked daily but only in the fall; or budgets are prepared daily, but only on a quarterly basis. In these instances, put "Daily" in the "How Often" column, but indicate in your duty statement that the task is performed "periodically," "seasonally," "quarterly," etc.

2) tell whether each duty is critical or important. A critical duty is one which you must do to do your job right. An important duty is one which you usually do, but is not necessary in order to do your job right.

3) list any work products you get when you do the job duty. For example, the work products when you type might be "letters, memos, and reports." The work products when you operate a computer might be "computer printouts."

IMPORTANT NOTE: This is where you tell us what you do on your job. Make sure you list all your duties here. Read over what you have written. If something you do hasn't been listed, ADD IT.

JOB DUTY	HOW OFTEN	CRITICAL/ IMPORTANT	WORK PRODUCT
1. Develop job analyses for a full range of job classifications which address UGESP* requirements, using employer's methodology.	BW	Critical	Completed job analysis
2. Review and critique job analyses developed by others for completeness and compliance; offer written or oral review comments.	BW	Critical	Written review comments
3. Develop employment tools and tests for a full range of classifications which address UGESP requirements, using employer's methodology.	BW	Critical	Application forms, oral interviews, written exams skills tests, performance appraisal
4. Review and critique employment tools and tests developed by others for completeness and compliance; offer written or oral review comments.	BW	Critical	Written review comments

*UGESP = Uniform Guidelines on Employee Selection Procedures, 8/25/78.

**Exhibit 9. Portion of a Completed Form of Simplified GOJA—
continued**

Knowledges, Skills, and Abilities	Major Parts of Knowledges, Skills, and Abilities	Important and Critical Job Duties*
I. Supervision in accordance with EEO guidelines and employer's policies and procedures	-Interviewing applicants -Assigning/delegating -Monitoring -Evaluating -Positive and negative feedback -Discipline	19
J. Evaluation/analysis	-Identifying relevant information -Determining its importance/impact -Applying it appropriately -Making recommendations	2, 4, 6, 8, 13, 14, 21
K. Decision making	-Identifying/defining the problem -Identifying alternatives -Weighing the pros and cons according to existing prob -Selecting & justifying the alternative	2, 4, 6, 8, 14, 15, 16, 17, 18, 19, 20
L. Time management	-Planning/organizing -Scheduling -Prioritizing -Timely completion -Effectiveness & efficiency with changes in workloads, tight deadlines, etc.	9, 15, 16, 18, 20
M. Administration	-Coordination/liaison -Monitoring -Budgeting -Implementing -Efficiency -Deadlines met	16, 17
N. Employer's EEO software -- operation and interpretation	-Adverse impact -Utilization -Goals and timetables -Cut-off -Rater Reliability -Interpret results -Make recommendations	5, 7, 8
O. Record keeping	-Complete and accurate -Easily accessible -Date, time, person, details, decisions -Efficient	11, 12, 16, 19
P. Office machines	-Tape recorder -Photocopier -PET computer	2, 4, 6, 7, 10, 12, 14, 16

*Paraphrase or numerically code duties described in Section 5a.

Exhibit 9. Portion of a Completed Form of Simplified GOJA— continued

SECTION 8:   DIFFERENTIATING REQUIREMENTS

Of the knowledges, skills, abilities, physical or other requirements listed in Sections 5, 6, and 7, list those which are linked with differences in levels of job performance.

Knowledge, Skill, Ability, Physical or Other Requirement	Describe how having more of the knowledge, skill, ability, physical or other requirement is likely to result in better job performance, i.e., doing more difficult tasks, or avoiding some errors or consequences (be specific). It is important to be clear and specific. Use examples.
1. EEO laws, guidelines, and court cases	More in-depth knowledge helps insure advice/recommendations to clients are accurate and defensible; job analyses and tools/tests are in compliance; a wider variety of tools/tests can be developed; job analysis and tool/test review can be completed more quickly and thus more cost-effectively.
2. Evaluation/Analysis	A higher level of skill helps insure that the process can be completed more quickly and thus, more cost-effectively; the analysis/evaluation is accurate, resulting in appropriate responses to clients; the work can be completed more independently, freeing up supervisor time; more complex issues can be tackled.
3. Decision making	A higher level of skill helps insure the process can be completed more quickly and thus more cost-effectively; the work can be completed more independently, freeing up supervisor time; the decisions will be more likely to be appropriate, avoiding costly mistakes.
4. Time management	A higher level of skill helps insure that deadlines will be met, avoiding breach of contract; that other employees won't have to work (and be paid for) overtime; that costly mistakes will be avoided; that more work can be completed within given time constraints; that less supervision will be needed.
5. Administration	A higher level of skill helps insure that projects will be properly/realistically budgeted; project deadlines will be met, avoiding costly breaches of contract; that more complex projects can be undertaken; that the work can be completed more independently, freeing up supervisor time.
6. Affirmative Action Planning Development	A more in-depth knowledge helps insure the compliance of AAP's developed; that the work can be completed more independently, freeing up supervisor time; that more complex AAP's can be handled.

Source: Copyright 1980, R. E. Biddle. Reprinted with permission.

Physical and Other Requirements. Physical capabilities and other requirements (such as licenses or travel necessary to perform the job) are checked on a prepared list, and a notation is made about how the requirement is used or why it is needed.

Differentiating Requirements. Knowledges, skills, abilities, physical, and other characteristics which differentiate between levels of performance are listed. A description is also written of how having more—or a higher level—of the specific requirement can result in better job performance. (Biddle, 1980).

As with the Full and Brief GOJA procedures, Simplified GOJA provides data to develop Supplemental Application and Performance Appraisal forms and written tests. The additional information on those knowledges, skills, abilities, physical, and other requirements which differentiate among levels of performance can be used to develop ranking procedures for selection. Simplified GOJA also lends itself to point-factoring and job-slotting techniques for wage and salary purposes (Biddle, personal communication, December 19, 1980).

As with Brief GOJA, analysts must review the completed Job Analysis forms to determine the reliability of the data. Individual interviews with incumbents may be needed to obtain additional clarifying data.

General Comments

GOJA in its various versions is unique in its adherence and responsiveness to changes in the legal and regulatory requirements. The basic method, Full GOJA, was designed specifically to meet the Equal Employment Opportunity Commission's Guidelines on Employee Selection Procedures. As noted previously, changes were recently made in the Brief GOJA procedure to conform it to the Uniform Guidelines. The "Differentiating Requirements" section of Simplified GOJA is an attempt to respond to the legal and practical problem of ranking job candidates.

The quality of the data from Brief and Simplified GOJA depends upon the ability of the incumbents to read and to follow the instructions and to write clear and concise descriptions of their job and its requirements. These versions may not be appropriate for analyzing jobs which do not require the same levels of reading and writing ability as those necessary to complete the job analysis form.

GOJA is copyrighted by R. E. Biddle. One user noted that it would be difficult for an organization to implement the approach, even if versed in other job analysis techniques, without some training and assistance from someone experienced with the method (Sturm, 1979). These factors must be taken into account by the potential user and weighed against the needs of the organization.

Behavioral Consistency Method

The Behavioral Consistency Method is a selection-oriented job analysis approach developed by Frank Schmidt, James Caplan, Stephen Bemis, and others at the U.S. Office of Personnel Management. It was designed to identify worker competencies for the selection of experienced professional and managerial applicants for mid-level government jobs. The method has also been used to identify competencies needed for private sector managerial and blue-collar jobs.

The method is based on the psychological principle that future behaviors of a given kind can be predicted by measuring past behaviors of a similar nature. In addition, the method encompasses the following principles: (a) applicants should be evaluated only on those behavioral dimensions that demonstrate large differences between superior and minimally acceptable performers, and (b) these maximally differentiating behavior dimensions can be accurately determined only by consulting people who have known and observed superior and marginal performers (Schmidt, Caplan, and Bemis, 1979).

The Behavioral Consistency Method involves the following four components:

1. *Identification and Description of Job Activities/Tasks.* Job activities/tasks are identified and described by personnel specialists trained in the method, on the basis of a review of classification and qualification standards, recent position descriptions, and occasionally, on-site visits. An activity is defined as "an action or sequence of actions that contribute significantly to the accomplishment of a work objective. Activities may be physical, mental or interpersonal" (*BRE Manual*, p. 7). An inventory of activity statements is reviewed by subject-matter experts for accuracy and completeness of coverage.

2. *Identification of KASOs.* Subject-matter experts (SMEs)—supervisors who have themselves performed the work and who have dealt with experienced incumbents and with both superior and inadequate performers—generate information about the knowledges, abilities, skills, and other characteristics (KASOs) required to perform the work. The KASOs are identified in structured group meetings in which SMEs compare successful and unsuccessful employees they have known. The objective or goal is to identify those "ranking" KASOs which best distinguish superior from inadequate performance. A second group or category of "self-screening" KASOs are also identified. These KASOs are necessary to job per-

formance and most applicants will have them. It is important, however, to consider in the selection process those self-screening KASOs which are conditions of employment, such as "willingness to travel."

3. *Evaluation of KASOs*. SMEs independently rate each item on six scales: *Scale 1* evaluates the importance of the KASO in preventing job failure (if this factor is not considered in selecting workers, will it lead to increased failure to meet minimum performance standards?) *Scale 2* determines whether the KASO is nearly universal among incumbents (what percentage of present workers meet minimum performance standard of this KASO?). *Scale 3* determines the generality of the KASO (is this KASO required for all positions?). *Scale 4* evaluates the usefulness of the KASO in differentiating between superior and minimally acceptable workers (how will this KASO help to distinguish superior from barely acceptable workers?). *Scale 5* identifies the extent of variability of the KASO in the applicant pool. *Scale 6* is used only when there are subspecialties in the occupation to which the ranking KASOs apply.

4. *Analysis of SME Ratings to Evaluate KASOs*. Average values and ratings of SMEs are computed to identify self-screening KASOs and to identify and order ranking KASOs. SMEs are then asked to identify which ranking KASOs are related to the performance of each activity (*BRE Manual*.)

The resulting data can be used to design a tailored application blank to solicit relevant information from applicants on past achievements. Exhibit 10 shows a portion of a Supplemental Application Form for the job of Budget Analyst. A Crediting Plan and Rating Sheet can also be developed with additional information from SMEs. The Crediting Plan scales applicants' achievements rather than their credentials in order to make selection decisions (*BRE Manual*).

Both content and requirements data are obtained and linked together by the Behavioral Consistency approach. The method does not focus on job context factors and, in fact, the analysis is conducted within the confines of existing job evaluation or classification systems. It has been used to develop assessment procedures for aviation safety inspectors, budget analysts, veterans' claims examiners, training instructors, equipment specialists, counseling psychologists, economists, position classification specialists, quality assurance specialists, and criminal investigators. Variants of the procedures have been used with a number of private sector jobs including general managers, sales managers, division dispatchers, layout technicians, sales personnel, and project managers (Bemis, 1978). Even where a special application form is not needed, the job analysis procedure can be useful in identifying dimensions that should be covered

52   JOB ANALYSIS

Exhibit 10. Portion of a Behavioral Consistency Method Supplemental Application Form for the Job of Budget Analyst

4. Writing Ability

Budget analysts must be able to communicate well in writing. Can you write clearly and
concisely? On a separate sheet of paper describe your past achievements demonstrating
your writing ability.

DO NOT COMPLETE the following rating until after you have described your achievements rele-
vent to this factor. Remember to use a separate sheet of paper to describe these achievements. Do not forget to include, for each achievement:

    1. What the problem or objective was.
    2. What you actually did, and when (approximate date).
    3. What the outcome or result was.
    4. The estimated percentage of this achievement
       which you claim credit for.
    5. The name, address and telephone number of somebody
       who can verify the achievement.

The statements I have provided on this factor are accurate descriptions of my own achievements and the above rating reflects what I believe to be a fair evaluation of the achievements described.

Signature: _____Date: _____

5. Oral Communication Ability

Budget Analysts must be able to react quickly, confidently, and with composure in stressful,
interpersonal situations and present ideas or information in an organized manner on short
notice. How successful are you in this type of oral communication? On a separate sheet
of paper, give examples of your past achievements demonstrating your ability to communicate
effectively in such situations.

DO NOT COMPLETE the Following Rating until after You Have Described Your Achievements Relevant to this Factor. Remember to use a separate sheet of paper to describe these achievements. Do not forget to include, for each achievement:

    1. What the problem or objective was.
    2. What you actually did, and when (approximate date).
    3. What the outcome or result was.
    4. The estimated percentage of this achievement which
       you claim credit for.
    5. The name, adress and telephone number of somebody
       who can verify the achievements.

The statements I have provided on this factor are accurate descriptions of my own achievements and the above rating reflects what I believe to be a fair evaluation of the achievements described.

Signature: _____ Date: _____

Source: The Behavioral Consistency Method of Unassembled Examining.
Technical Memorandum 79-21. Washington, D.C.: U.S. Office of Personnel Management, Personnel Research and Development Center, 1979, p. 55.

in interviewing for a specific job, and in identifying the knowledges, skills, and abilities which should be sought in the selection process. The method also provides some information useful in identifying training needs for "average" workers.

It provides data only on those KASOs which distinguish superior from unacceptable performance, however, and not on the full range of KASOs necessary to perform the job. The Behavioral Consistency approach does not provide data for classification or job evaluation or for job restructuring.

The Behavioral Consistency method shares two basic concepts with the Job Element examining procedure developed by Primoff: that it is most useful to assess applicants on those dimensions which differentiate between superior and minimally acceptable performance, and that subject-matter experts are the best source of that information. There are also significant differences between the two methods. The Behavioral Consistency method relates KASOs to the activities which require them, tying job requirements to job content. The basic Job Element procedure does not. The Behavioral Consistency method does not include information on traits while the Job Element procedure does (Schmidt, Caplan, and Bemis, 1979).

The Behavioral Consistency approach is presented as a significant breakthrough in unassembled examining—the paper review of applicants' qualifications as opposed to a test which requires applicants to assemble as a group. It appears to be more valid, as well as more reliable, than traditional approaches such as education and experience ratings. The Behavioral Consistency method is also, at least initially, more costly and time consuming. In one study, the approach required more than twice the time as did other more traditional methods (Schmidt, Caplan, and Bemis, 1979). In the long run, the Behavioral Consistency method will probably be more cost effective in generating more reliable and useful data.

Factor Evaluation System

The Factor Evaluation System (FES) is a method for assigning grades (which equate automatically with salary levels) in the classification of nonsupervisory positions, GS-1 through GS-15, under the General Schedule (GS) of the Federal Government's classification system. Jobs are described and placed in grades on the basis of their duties, responsibilities, and the qualifications required to perform them as evaluated by nine factors:

1. *Knowledge Required by the Position*—the nature and extent of information or facts which the worker must understand to do acceptable

work, and the nature and extent of the skills necessary to apply these knowledges

2. *Supervisory Controls*—the nature and extent of direct and indirect controls exercised by the supervisor, the worker's responsibility, and the review of work completed

3. *Guidelines*—the nature of available guidelines and the judgment needed to apply them

4. *Complexity*—the nature, number, variety, and intricacy of tasks, steps, processes, or methods in the work performed; the difficulty the worker faces in identifying what needs to be done; and the difficulty and originality involved in performing the work

5. *Scope and Effect*—the relationship between nature of work, e.g., the purpose, breadth, and depth of the assignment, and the effect of work products on services both within and outside the organization

6. *Personal Work Contacts*—the face-to-face contact and telephone and radio dialogue with persons not in the supervisory chain

7. *Purpose of Contacts*—the purpose of contacts which range from the factual exchange of information to situations involving significant or controversial issues and differing viewpoints, goals, or objectives

8. *Physical Demands*—the requirements and physical demands placed on the worker by the work assignment

9. *Work Environment*—the risks, hazards, and discomforts imposed upon the worker by various physical surroundings or job situations (*Instructions*, 1977).

A primary "standard of standards" describes levels of each of the nine factors in terms common to all GS occupations and gives point values for each level. Classification standards for specific occupations describe the application of the primary standard to the occupation as well as provide information on coverage, titling practices, and benchmark descriptions of typical or representative work. Position descriptions are written in the FES format by supervisors who have received training in the method. The descriptions are reviewed and positions are classified by personnel specialists also trained in the method. (Exhibit 11 shows a copy of an FES position description for Mail Clerk.)

There seems to be a close correspondence between the Factor Evaluation System and the Hay Guide Chart-Profile method, widely used for job evaluation in the private sector as well as by state and local governments. This is evident in the following comparison of factors as outlined by Michael Bronson:

FES	HAY
Knowledge Required by the Position	Know-How (depth)
Supervisory Controls	Freedom to Act; Freedom to Think
Guidelines	Freedom to Act; Freedom to Think
Complexity	Problem Solving
Scope and Effect	Know-How (breadth); Impact on End Results
Personal Contacts	Human Relations Skills
Purpose of Contacts	Human Relations Skills
Physical Demands	Physical Effort
Work Environment	Working Environment

The apparent similarity is reinforced by the results of a study in which jobs were evaluated by both FES and the Hay method. There was a high correlation between the points assigned to jobs by the two systems (Bronson, 1980).

There are four basic types of job evaluation systems or methods: (1) ranking, in which jobs in an organization are hierarchially ordered according to their worth or value to the organization; (2) classification, in which jobs are compared to factors in a preestablished ideal structure; (3) factor comparison, in which jobs are assessed in terms of specified factors and then compared to a set of benchmark jobs about which there is some consensus of worth; and (4) point method, in which a job is reviewed in relation to established factors with specified levels and where the ratings on each are totaled for a job worth score. FES is an example of a point factor system. The Hay method is a modified factor-comparison approach.

The methods differ primarily in the way in which jobs are evaluated for worth, specifically the selection and weighting of factors and how the resulting data is used in determining wages and salaries. They are generally similar in regard to their descriptive or job analysis component (Treiman, 1979). Job evaluation methods emphasize contextual factors and describe job content broadly in terms of duties and responsibilities. Job requirements are generally only briefly described in terms of the knowledges and skills needed at the full performance level or by the more traditional evidences of education and experience.

Job evaluation methods have been designed specifically to address the worth or value of jobs for compensation purposes. Data from a system which assesses jobs in terms of job context/contextual factors can provide input in identifying and establishing career paths, in identifying training needs, or in grouping similar jobs for selection and performance appraisal as well as for pay. However, a job evaluation system method, for example,

Exhibit 11. Sample FES Position Description for Mail Clerk (marked to show subfactors)

Major Duties

Performs mail duties in the central mail processing office of the agency:

—Sorts incoming mail and issuances, including packages, telegrams, and special messages. Selects and time-stamps designated mail items. Verifies or secures enclosures. Sorts and racks mail by file designations or subject-matter categories for attachment of required background information by the files section. Loads incoming mail on delivery cart and delivers it.

—Picks up outgoing mail, checks for attachments and calls attention of sender to obvious discrepancies. Sorts mail picked up enroute for immediate delivery to succeeding mail stops. Checks outgoing mail for completeness and conformance to applicable instructions and regulations, and sorts into various categories *(e.g., chain mail, stop mail, air mail, registered, certified, foreign, etc.)*. Wraps packages and separates different classes of mail for delivery.

—Detaches file copies from outgoing mail and routes to appropriate sources.

—Makes special messenger trips as requested.

Factor 1. Knowledge Required by the Position

—Knowledge of the functions, locations, and organizational components of the agency *(to sort and deliver mail.)*

—Knowledge of mail handling procedures *(to time-stamp, obtain background information; sort by category, file desigation, or subject matter; wrap for mailing and detach file copies.)*

Factor 2. Supervisory Controls

The mail supervisor makes assignments, giving specific instruc-structions on new or revised procedures to be used. *(The incumbent performs routine work on own initative.)* [Work is reviewed for conformance to established requirements. Promptness and accuracy of mail distribution is spot-checked.]

Factor 3. Guidelines

Mail distribution points and delivery schedules are preestablished and are updated frequently with changes in organizational

Exhibit 11. Sample FES Position Description for Mail Clerk—
          continued

designations. Mail-handling instructions are specific. *(The employee uses some judgment in expediting delivery to avoid undue
delays, e.g., sorting and delivering enroute.)*

Factor 4. Complexity

The work involves recurring mail processing tasks, i.e., sorting,
seeing that background material is attached or detached, and
delivering mail to approximately 45 delivery points. *(Considers
the category of mail or subject matter, identifies obvious discrepancies.)* [Different categories of mail receive different treatment.]

Factor 5. Scope and Effect

Accuracy and reliability in the processing and flow of mail
(facilitates work accomplishment in the agency.)

Factor 6. Personal Contacts

Contacts are with employees in the immediate office and people within the building who are designated to receive and send
mail.

Factor 7. Purpose of Contacts

Contacts are for the purpose of exchanging factual information,
reporting problems, making special or routine deliveries, and
picking up mail.

Factor 8. Physical Demands

The work involves considerable walking with pushing or pulling
of delivery carts. Packages lifted onto the carts occasionally
weigh up to 25 pounds.

Factor 9. Work Environment

The incumbent observes normal safety precautions while working in the mail room and delivering mail throughout the office
building.

Source: U.S. Office of Personnel Management. *How to Write Position Descriptions Under the Factor Evaluation System.* Washington, D.C.: U.S. Government Printing Office, 1979, pp. 31-32.

FES, must be combined with a task-based method such as FJA, DOL, or HSMS to produce a comprehensive and exhaustive description of a job sufficient for the full range of personnel functions.

Conclusion

While the purpose of job analysis is to describe objectively the content of jobs, their requirements or competencies, and the context or environment in which they are performed, there are clearly various approaches to achieving this purpose. This chapter presented and discussed only ten. There are many other job analysis methods available including the Physical Abilities Analysis approach (Fleishman, 1975), the Skills and Attributes Inventory (Baehr, 1971), and the Occupational Analysis Inventory (Cunningham et al., 1970).

It should be clear that there is no one right or best job analysis method, although in presenting the Versatile Job Analysis System which follows, the authors express their preference for a comprehensive approach which develops a data base that can be applied to the full range of personnel functions. Still, the characteristics, strengths, and weaknesses of specific methods, including VERJAS, must be assessed in relation to the needs and constraints of a particular situation.

3. Assembling VERJAS Data

Introduction

This chapter is directed specifically to the manager—the person most likely to be responsible for, and affected by the job analysis. As a manager you are a primary source of job information and an important user of it. Within the constraints imposed by the employing organization, union agreements, higher level managers, and regulatory authorities, you determine what activities are performed by your immediate subordinates. Many people believe the manager is also in the best position to know what it takes for a worker to do the job.

VERJAS does not demand that the analysis be done totally by the manager, however, or by a single type of staff person. In the pages that follow, the overall instructions assume that the manager is responsible for documenting information with little or no staff assistance. Jobs may be "analyzed" by any number of different staff people, or outside consultants, and these "job analysts" may document and store the resulting information. Thus, several sections contain supplementary instructions (where instructions differ) for those who are not managers themselves but whose job it is to accomplish the job analysis, when the manager's role is limited to that of responding job specialist or "subject matter expert." These supplementary instructions are in italic type with the heading *"Notes to Job Analyst."* The term job analyst refers to an administrative or personnel staff employee, or an outside consultant, who is responsible for gathering and documenting job facts. The term does not necessarily imply extensive job analysis training or experience. In general, the job analyst should read all of the instructions, adapting procedures where necessary.

There are some exceptions to the statement that the manager is in the best position to know what is done on the job and what it takes to do it. For instance, employees may operate a piece of machinery on which the manager is not experienced and/or qualified. The procedures in this chapter take into account one of these exceptions, where the manager is not particularly knowledgeable about *how* a job is done, but only about the goal or objective achieved. For these situations, you are asked to supplement your information with information obtained directly from the employee, using one or more of the techniques for gathering data described in Chapter 1 and in this chapter.

Some organizations may use job analysts exclusively while others may depend on managers to implement the system. Most will find that a combined approach is most compatible in their organization, with manager(s) and other job analyst(s) dividing and sharing the responsibilities of data gathering. Different parts of the same organization may decide to implement these procedures in different ways. Assuming such adaptation, the basic procedures are versatile enough to be applicable across a broad spectrum of situations and organizations.

When a new job is created in an organization, you will not be in a position to conduct a job analysis as described in the body of this chapter. In these situations, external experts, professional associations, design engineers, human factors experts, or others will have to be consulted in order to do the initial documentation of job facts. A special section at the end of this chapter discusses the documentation of job facts when new or modified machinery is introduced into the organization.

Recognizing that such exceptions exist and that the amount of assistance or guidance given to the manager by job analysts or consultants will vary from organization to organization, this chapter focuses on the majority of situations where the manager is the best source of job information. The system presented here balances the pragmatic use of organizational resources with the dictates of legal acceptability.

A Note on Terminology

In Chapter 1, we defined job analysis as a systematic procedure involving gathering, documenting, and analyzing information about job content, job requirements, and/or the context in which the job is performed. While this definition is broad, we believe that most personnel professionals and writers in the area of job analysis would embrace the definition after some consideration. There is not the same likelihood, however, that the terms used to define content, requirements, or context would be similarly accepted. The term "element," for example, refers to job requirements in the Job Element Method (see page 26), but refers to job content where used in the Civil Service Reform Act. At the 1980 convention of the American Psychological Association, one job analysis expert defined "activities" as subsets of "tasks," while another psychologist referred to "tasks" as subsets of "activities." The authors themselves have used the terms interchangeably in other work.

In other parts of this book, we use terms as they are used in the particular method under discussion. In explaining our own method—VERJAS—and its uses, however, the following definitions have been used for job analysis terms:

Task: Something that workers perform—an action they take—in order to create a product or service that, theoretically, someone else can use. (Tasks describe job content.)

Task statement: A statement describing specified aspects of a task in a prescribed format.

Duty: A collection of tasks that recur and are nontrivial. (Duties relate to job content.)

Job: A group of positions that are identical or very similar in their duties and required competencies. "Parts Manager" is an example of a job.

Position: A group of major tasks performed by one individual (or two or more part-time individuals working on a "shared position" basis). "Eastern Regional Parts Manager" is an example of a position.

Competency: A knowledge, skill, ability, or other job-related characteristic or circumstance. (Competencies describe job requirements.)

Basic competency: A knowledge, skill, ability, or other characteristic that an individual must possess or obtain (or circumstance that must exist) in order to perform one or more tasks in a particular job context.

Special competency: A knowledge, skill, ability, or other characteristic that an individual must possess or obtain (or circumstance that must exist) in order to perform one or more tasks in a superior manner in a particular job context.

*Knowledge:** A body of information applied directly to the performance of a function.

*Skill:** A present, observable competence to perform a learned psychomotor act.

*Ability:** A present competence to perform an observable behavior or a behavior which results in an observable product.

*Other job-related competency:*** These are either characteristics of an individual (e.g., tact) or circumstances in the environment of an individual

---

*These definitions are given in the Uniform Guidelines on Employee Selection Procedures. In practice, the terms "ability" and "skill" are sometimes used interchangeably.

**Even though competencies are "job related," they are sometimes challenged when viewed as a pretext for race or sex discrimination.

(e.g., ability to work a shift because he/she has a car). Circumstances are more likely to change (e.g., worker might lose his/her license or car) than characteristics. An individual may be unwilling to travel either because of a fear of flying (characteristic) or because of responsibilities to an invalid spouse (circumstance).

Job context: Degree of accountability, responsibility, and supervision, and the physical, personal, or emotional demands of the job.

Job description or position description: A record of the job content, requirements, and/or context. Most existing job or position descriptions reflect information collected only for the purposes of job evaluation or classification. The record of results of a more comprehensive job analysis (such as those spelled out in this chapter) is also referred to as a job description in this book. (This use of the term implies a comprehensive analysis and thus differs from the formal definition in the Uniform Guidelines.)

Summary of the Method

There are five steps for you to follow in the system. Each of the steps, and its origin and purpose, is summarized here in order to give a clear picture of VERJAS. Each step is described in detail later in this chapter.

1. *Write an overview of the job describing the purpose for which the job exists and the primary duties involved in accomplishing that purpose:* This step takes a fresh look at the job and its reason for being. This step also helps the manager or analyst to keep the total job in mind through the rest of the steps. It provides the information which appears on a typical organization's job description.

2. *Describe the action, purpose, and result of each task involved in carrying out job duties, and then identify the training mode and rate its relative importance.* This step utilizes concepts in the DOL method (see page 14). The specific format for writing task statements closely parallels FJA (see page 21). This step provides a description of specific expected job behavior. This data base is invaluable in identifying basic worker competencies, developing performance standards, and defending personnel practices as job related.

3. *Describe the context of the job; its scope, effect, and environment:* Factors considered in a number of popular job evaluation systems for exempt, nonexempt, and skilled jobs, as well as the FES (see page 53), are identified in VERJAS. The purpose of this step is to assure documentation of information needed to determine the value of a job.

4. *Identify basic worker competencies needed for minimum acceptable performance of job tasks:* This step currently exists in one form or another in many job analysis systems. It is a critical step in deciding what kind of workers to recruit, where to recruit them, and what qualification requirements may be established for the job.

5. *Identify the special worker competencies that make for successful job performance:* These are the factors that can be of most value in identifying the best candidate from among a group of basically qualified candidates, and in identifying overlooked training needs. This step closely parallels procedures in the Behavioral Consistency method (see page 50), which, in turn, was built on concepts in the Job Element Method (see page 26).

The Need for Review

Whenever job facts are documented, it is desirable to have an independent review of what has been done to make sure that provincialism or bias has not inadvertently crept into the process. Such reviews carry considerable weight with judges and arbitrators, especially when conducted by the representatives of a group likely to be affected by job requirements, e.g., minorities, women, handicapped persons (see Chapter 5). Therefore, we strongly encourage that you arrange for a review in all situations. If you are a manager doing the job analysis completely unassisted, we consider such reviews to be essential to meet judicial concerns.

Using Forms to Do Job Analysis

Throughout this chapter and Chapter 4, we have provided sample forms which were developed by the authors and which have already been used successfully in many job analyses of this type. They may be reproduced as they are or adapted to a particular situation. Consistent and replicable documentation is not only useful in the day-to-day implementation of job analysis purposes, but also necessary if and when proof of the basis of past decisions is demanded.

Documenting the Content and Context of the Job

Managers usually know very well what needs to be done on the jobs they supervise and the context in which the jobs are performed. The procedures described in this chapter assure that this information is documented and available to be acted on. Clearly identifying what is done on the job involves breaking the job into large components—duties. These duties are then divided into their component parts—tasks. The procedure for determining job context (degree of accountability; responsibility and supervision; and personal, physical, or emotional demands of the job) involves systematically considering a number of aspects of the job.

This section provides details on how to document the content and contextual aspects of the job. A later section provides details on how to document job requirements.

Job Content

Job Duties. The procedures described in this section will help you to organize your thinking about job duties and tasks and to document this information for your own use and the use of others.

In using the Duty Worksheet, Exhibit 12, you are encouraged to follow these guidelines:

1. Find a time and a place to spend 10 to 15 minutes thinking about the job in question without distraction.

2. Avoid reference to existing documentation (such as job descriptions) during this period. Most managers consider this a silly prohibition when they first begin to gather job facts. Once they start to think about the job without reference to notes or to a position description, however, they frequently get a fresh perspective on the job and become comfortable with the process. The objective of this step is to allow you to take a fresh look at the job and to identify its major duties at the full performance or journey (journeyman/woman) level. (Of course, if this is a new job, existing information such as training manuals and/or the task analysis conducted by the human factors engineer will need to be referenced to get an understanding of the job.)

3. Write a one-sentence statement describing the purpose of the job and the reason it exists. This step helps to focus your attention on the nuts and bolts of the job. This statement may be written on a blank piece of paper, or at the top of the Duty Worksheet. The job title and position number should also be written down.

4. List the large chunks or duties of the job, making notes of each duty.

5. After making a note of all of the job duties that come to mind, look at the official job description and other published information on the job or occupation to see if there are any additional duties. *Duties from the job description should not be added to your list unless you consider them part of the job.* On the other hand, don't overlook important duties that are not presently performed by incumbents but that will be as soon as the incumbents reach the full performance level. (For instance, duties involved with a large, demanding client in a sales job, a complicated piece of

Exhibit 12. Duty Worksheet

Job Title: __Clerk Typist/Receptionist__   Position No.: __327__

Use this worksheet to describe the duties of a job and to list the tasks associated with each duty, as well as to make any notes that might be helpful. Assign sequential numbers to the duties of each job. Use a separate copy of the worksheet for each duty.

Purpose of the Job (Record on the first page only):
Greet visitors, direct calls and visitors to proper person, type, and answer telephones.

Duty No.

[1] Duty: _Typing_

Notes on Tasks:
1. _Types letters, etc._

2. _Transcribes_

3. _Types forms_

4. _Proofreads_

5. _____

6. _____

equipment in a maintenance job, or a multiproblem family in a social work job, may be reserved for more experienced staff members.)

6. After you have identified the duties of the job, use your own words to write a one-sentence description of each duty. Use a separate Duty Worksheet for each. (Normally, a job will have three to seven major duties; however, it is quite possible that you may identify only two duties, or, alternatively, you may identify eight or more.) Do not concern yourself

ˌᴇᴛ with the "Notes on Tasks" section which follows each duty description on the Duty Worksheet.

> *Notes to Job Analyst. Review existing job descriptions and other documentation to gain a general familiarity with the occupation. Then go to the workplace and observe the incumbent at work. Such a worksite visit will help you to understand the context of the job and in many cases (more often in physical than in nonphysical jobs), will also help you to understand the job content. At the job site, it may be desirable to interview the incumbent and/or the manager to help you to understand what you are seeing and to get information on job content not performed during your visit. Ask questions about tasks performed at other times of the year, or after further training or experience. Appendix I contains guidance for the conduct of such job site interviews. Make notes on duties, tasks, and environmental factors uncovered.*

Job Tasks. All duties are composed of tasks. These are activities that workers perform to create a product or a service that they will use in performing another task or that someone else will use. Normally, each duty will include at least two tasks. For instance, the duty "typing" usually includes a task involving the typing of drafts from handwritten copy or dictation and another involving typing of final copy from an edited draft. To describe a job fully and without unnecessary detail, it is useful to construct a formal task statement. The four parts of a task statement used in VERJAS are:

(a) the action performed (e.g., types)

(b) what is acted upon (e.g., letters)

(c) the purpose or expected output of that action (e.g., in order to produce final copy)

(d) use of which machines, tools, equipment, manuals, laws, rules, and work aids (e.g., electric typewriter and organization style manual)

A completed task statement would read:

"Types[a] letters[b] in order to produce final copy[c] using electric typewriter and organization style manual[d]."

Two other task statements might read:

"Adjusts[a] internal combustion engines[b] in order to keep them running efficiently[c] using small hand tools (e.g., screw drivers, wrenches), electronic testing equipment (e.g., sun tester, timing light), and specification manuals[d]."

"Writes[a] vacancy announcements[b] in order to advise employees of requirements of vacant positions[c] using job descriptions and company employment procedures manual[d]."

The instructions in the following sections describe in detail how to identify job tasks and write the task statements.

A. *Getting information to describe tasks.* (If you are working with a few employees, use Duty Worksheets for this purpose. If it is a larger group, transfer the information to a chalkboard or flip chart. A flip chart is preferable because it provides unlimited space and a permanent record.) You should involve one or more of your employees in the identification of job tasks. If you supervise only a few people in the occupation, it is suggested that you work with all of them in doing this. If the work group is large, you should try to include several representative employees in the process to make sure you do not overlook important activities performed by some employees and not by others. (If you have one or more handicapped employees, include them if their method of performing the job differs from that of other employees. For similar reasons, include minority-group employees, and both male and female employees, if they are in the work group.) While you can gather this information in individual interviews, it is more productive and time efficient to meet with employees in a group.

When you conduct your meeting, proceed in the following manner:

1. Outline for the employee(s) the duties you have identified and allow them to make comments or suggestions.

2. Next, go through each duty and have the employee(s) assist in identifying the important tasks, including the four parts of each. (Note this information on the Duty Worksheets, chalkboard, or flip chart as you go along.) The information will be used after the meeting to write Task Statements.

Notes to Job Analyst. You should obtain information on tasks as well as duties during the on-site visits. Reexamination of job descriptions or training materials should be helpful in obtaining the detail necessary for the writing of task statements. Do not add duties or tasks simply because they are on the job descriptions. If they are on the job descriptions, question the manager or incumbent about them to determine if they are performed but were overlooked. Then decide whether to include them. Do not be concerned at this point if there are duties you find are performed but are not on the job description.

B. *Writing task statements.* The Task Worksheet (Exhibit 13) can be useful in helping to structure your thinking about the four components of a job task. Once you have written several statements, you may no longer need the worksheet, but you are urged to use it when you begin to write task statements. Always write in the identifying information at

Exhibit 13. Task Worksheet

Job Title: _Clerk Typist/Receptionist_   Position No.: _327_   Duty No.: _1_   Task No.: _1_

Part I. As the first step in preparing the task statement, respond to the following four questions.

1. What action(s) is (are) performed? _Types_

2. What is acted on? _Letters, memos, and reports_

3. What is (are) the purpose(s) or expected output? IN ORDER TO _produce final copy_

4. What machines, tools, equipment, manuals, laws, rules, or other work aids are used? USING _Electric typewriter,_
Organization style manual

Write a task statement in this space, using the above responses.

Types letters, memos, and reports from handwritten material according to standard formats in order
to produce final copy using an electric typewriter and organization style manual.

Part II. Task Evaluation

Perf. at Entry?	Training Mode						Importance Level			Reason for Important/Critical Ratings				
	Brief Orient	How Long?	O-J-T	How Long?	Class Trng.	How Long?	Not Imp.	Imp.	Crit.	Prop. Time	Lev. Diff.	Cons. Err.	Freq.	Other
Yes	Yes	1 Day	No		No				✓	✓				

Division W, XYZ Corp.
Organization

Joanne Margolis
Signature

_6-11-83_
Date

the top of the Task Worksheet. From your notes on the Duty Worksheet or flip chart, construct a task statement by responding to the specific questions in the top box of the Task Worksheet. The four basic processes are:

1. Describe the action: What is the action performed *in this specific* task? Try to use one or more "action" verbs that are meaningful and descriptive. ("Types letters" is more concrete than "communicates.") "Prepares," "reviews," and "assists" are also not sufficiently descriptive and should be avoided where possible. Write single verbs (e.g., "types") or compound verbs (e.g., "composes and types") on line 1 of part 1, section 1 of the worksheet. Sometimes the initial action verb(s) will need to be expanded upon or clarified by additional phrases. In these phrases, use the "ing" form of the verb, preceding or following the object. For example, "Role-plays sales presentation *demonstrating product and answering questions* in order to provide on-the-job training to sales staff using promotional materials."

2. Describe the object of that action: That is, answer the question, "What is acted upon?" (In a previous example, "letters" were acted upon.) Write single objects (e.g., "letters") or compound objects (e.g., "letters, memos, and reports") on line 2, part I of the worksheet.

3. Describe the purpose or expected output of this task: What is (are) the purpose(s) or expected output(s)? All tasks have some mental or physical output which can be acted on by somebody else. Write this purpose on line 3, part I of the worksheet. (Note that the purpose is always preceded by the phrase "in order to.") For example, "produce final copy" is the purpose or expected output of typing letters.

4. Describe the machines, tools, equipment, manuals, laws, rules, or other work aids used to accomplish the activity. Most tasks involve some work aids, such as rules or simple tools. Some tasks will involve a significant man/machine interface. Write the description of these machines and/or work aids on line 4, part I of the worksheet. (Note that this description is always preceded by the word "using.") In the above example, the equipment used was "electric typewriter" and the manual used was the "organization style manual."

Once you have fully completed each of the four processes, you should be able to use the answers (and the preprinted capitalized words) to write a grammatical task statement. Write this complete task statement in the space provided in the middle of the worksheet. Clarify the statement as necessary by the addition of modifying phrases. In the typing example, the phrase "from handwritten material according to standard format" would help the reader visualize the process of typing in this organization.

C. *Evaluating tasks.* After writing the task statement, you need to evaluate it in terms of (a) when it is first performed; (b) what training, if any, is provided; and (c) its importance to the job. This evaluation should be recorded in part II at the bottom of the Task Worksheet according to the following procedures:

1. In the first column, indicate whether workers need to be able to perform the task upon entering into the job (yes or no).

2. In the next set of columns labeled "Training Mode," indicate with a check mark whether the task is learned in a brief orientation to the work unit and its organizational procedures, or if on-the-job training and/or classroom training are provided either within the organization or at a separate site (write yes or no in each subcolumn). If there is orientation or training, also write in the boxes provided the approximate amount of time it takes.

3. The last set of columns is used to indicate the importance of this task to the job. Use a check mark to rate each task as "Not Imp." (not important), "Imp." (important), or "Crit." (critical). Under "reason," mark one or more of the following reasons, as appropriate, for any task you mark as important or critical: "Prop. Time" (proportion of time spent on this task), "Lev. Diff." (level of difficulty of the task), "Cons. Err." (consequences of error in performing this task), or "Freq." (frequency with which the task is performed). If there are other reasons why the task is important or critical, note those reasons in the "Other" box.

> *Notes to Job Analyst. Have the task statements reviewed by the manager for accuracy. Provide the manager with the Task Worksheets (if used) and instruct him or her to edit the statements as necessary to better reflect the job. At this time, you should obtain the manager's evaluation of the task statements. If you believe that you know the job well and the manager's time is severely limited, you can do the evaluation and have the manager review the evaluation along with the task statements. However, it is preferable for the manager to do this evaluation rather than the job analyst. The name and position of the person doing the evaluation should be recorded at the bottom of the Task Worksheet.*
>
> *If there are a number of employees in similar positions, you should consider listing all your task statements in a Task Inventory and getting them evaluated by some or all of the incumbents or supervisors. Use of such a Task Inventory is a particularly efficient approach when there are a number of employees in similar positions under different supervisors or at geographically separated locations (see Appendix 1).*

Job Context

As we have noted before, the term "job context" refers to the degree of accountability and responsibility the employee has in the job, the amount of supervision he or she exercises, as well as the kinds of physical, personal, and emotional demands he or she will sustain. To determine the job context, consider the environment in which the work is performed and make notes on unique aspects, independence involved, and supervision exercised. (Managers might do this at the session where they first note job duties.)

The factors considered, your perception of the relationship of each of the factors to this job, and the tasks associated with each factor should be documented in a consistent way. We recommend the use of a Job Context Worksheet such as that shown in Exhibit 14.

(Note: The questions in the next section relate to classification and job evaluation factors commonly used in determining compensation for jobs. You should expand this list of questions and the Job Context Worksheet if there are additional factors considered in the job evaluation system used by your organization. A common job evaluation factor, "knowledge and skills requirements," will be documented at a later point in the job analysis process.)

Identifying the Job Context. Consider these questions as you document the job context:

1. How much and what kind of *supervision is received?* How are assignments given? What kind of assistance is available? When is work reviewed—in progress, at completion, or in the course of another's work? Is the employee physically separated from supervision? What is the frequency of contact? How much decision making is left to the incumbent? What freedom does the employee have to act? Mark the appropriate boxes on proximity and frequency, and note relevant facts in row I of the worksheet.

2. What *guidelines*—manuals, policies, procedures, forms—are available? What judgment is needed to apply them? What is prescribed and what is left to the workers' discretion? What responsibility does the workers have for decision making? Does equipment require the operator to make independent judgments based on fine discriminations? The fourth part of the task statements should provide the information needed for this factor. Indicate whether the factor is applicable and, if so, note relevant facts in row II of the worksheet.

3. To what extent are *research and analysis*—fact finding, interpretation, investigation—required by the position? What *reports* are prepared? Who receives the reports? Is information compiled, studied, reported, and used as a basis for deciding on a plan of action? To what extent is complex interpretation required? Task statements should provide data for this factor. Indicate whether the factor is applicable and, if so, note relevant facts in row III of the worksheet.

Exhibit 14. Job Context Worksheet

PART A—SCOPE AND EFFECT   Clerk Typist/Receptionist   Page ___1___ of ___2___   Position No.: ___327___

			TASKS WHICH REQUIRE THIS FACTOR
I.	SUPERVISION RECEIVED	NOTES Sits in reception room but can be seen from manager's office. Sometimes may go for several days without supervision during heavy travel periods for manager.	
	Proximity: [X] Visual [ ] Physical Sep. [ ] Geog. Sep.	Frequency: [ ] Constant [X] Hourly [ ] Daily [ ] Weekly [ ] Less Than Weekly	
II.	GUIDELINES [ ] Not Applicable [X] Applicable	NOTES Style manual. Much of guidance is oral. Some areas of work not covered by guidelines -- must exercise judgment.	1, 2, 5, 6, 7
III.	RESEARCH ANALYSIS REPORTS [X] Not Applicable [ ] Applicable	NOTES	
IV.	ACCOUNTABILITY CONSEQUENCES OF ERROR [ ] Not Applicable [ ] Life [ ] Injury [X] Monetary [X] Applicable [ ] Property [ ] Inconvenience	NOTES Contracts can be lost.	
V.	PERSONAL CONTACTS [ ] Not Applicable [X] Applicable	NOTES (INTERNAL) Does typing for 5 people. NOTES (EXTERNAL) Key source of contact with clients and other outsiders.	1, 2, 3 5, 6

Exhibit 14. Job Context Worksheet—continued

	NOTES	TASKS WHICH REQUIRE THIS FACTOR
VI. SUPERVISION EXERCISED ☒ Not Applicable ☐ Applicable Number Supervised: Nature: ___ Skilled/Semi-Skilled ☐ Hire/Fire ___ Clerical ☐ Train ___ Prof./Technical ☐ Assignments ___ Other ☐ Review Work ☐ Eval. Perf.		
PART B—ENVIRONMENT		
VII. PHYSICAL DEMANDS ☐ Not Applicable ☒ Applicable Lifting: Mobility: ☒ 10 Lbs. Max. ☐ Standing ☐ Kneeling ☐ 20 Lbs. Max. ☒ Walking ☐ Crouching ☐ 50 Lbs. Max. ☒ Sitting ☐ Crawling ☐ 100 Lbs. Max. ☒ Stooping ☐ Climbing ☐ Over 100 Lbs. ☒ Reaching	NOTES *Mostly sitting -- some walking.* *Stooping and reaching required when filing or retrieving materials.*	1, 2, 3, 4, 6 7, 8
VIII. WORK HAZARDS ☒ Not Applicable ☐ Applicable ☐ Mechanical ☐ Explosives ☐ Electrical ☐ Radiation ☐ Fire ☐ Atmospheric ☐ Chemical ☐ Height	NOTES	
IX. PERSONAL DEMANDS/STRESS ☐ Not Applicable ☒ Applicable ☒ Overtime ☐ Climate ☐ Shift Work ☒ Stress ☐ Split Shift ☒ Repetitious Operations	NOTES *Some overtime.* *Can be stressful when proposal must get out by deadline and there are phone calls.* *Repetitious during periods of heavy typing*	1, 2, 5

4. What is the degree of *accountability* and potential *consequence of error*, or both? Is the employee responsible for the security of, or maintaining records on, money or other valuables? Is the employee responsible for the operation or maintenance of expensive equipment? To what extent is the employee responsible for the accomplishment of a goal or profit? Could others be threatened by injury or loss of life? Could others be inconvenienced, and face loss of time, money? Indicate whether the factor is applicable, and if so, indicate the nature of consequences of error and note relevant facts in row IV of the worksheet.

5. What *personal contacts* are required by the job? What internal contacts are involved—co-workers, other departments, upper levels of management? What external contacts are required—customers, representatives of regulatory agencies, job applicants? What is the purpose of these contacts—to provide information, to obtain information, to persuade? Task statements should provide data for this factor. Indicate whether the factor is applicable in row V of the worksheet. If it is applicable, make a note of the kinds of internal and external contacts in the space provided.

6. What *supervision is exercised?* What is the complexity of supervision—train, hire/fire, assign work, review work, evaluate performance? How many employees of what kind are supervised—skilled or semiskilled, clerical, professional or technical? Task statements should be reviewed for references to this factor. Indicate in row VI of the worksheet whether supervision is exercised, and if it is, indicate the number of people supervised and the nature of this supervision. Also make a note in row VI about information relevant to supervision exercised.

7. What are the *physical demands* of the job? What are the mobility requirements of the job—standing, walking, sitting, stooping, kneeling, crouching, crawling, climbing? What are the lifting requirements—is the work sedentary, light, medium, heavy, or very heavy? Is vertical or horizontal reaching required? Indicate in row VII of the worksheet whether the job has any physical demands. If it does, indicate the nature of any lifting or mobility requirements in the spaces provided and note any other physical demands.

8. What are the *work hazards?* These might be mechanical, electrical, fire, chemical, explosive, or radiation. The source of hazards might be equipment operated or the physical environment in the work place. Is the work done at heights or underground? Are there bad atmospheric conditions (i.e., fumes, odors, dusts, mists, gases, stagnant air)? Indicate in row VIII of the worksheet whether the job has any work hazards, and if so, the nature and severity of those hazards.

9. Does the job make *personal demands* in addition to work hazards? Does the job involve work in heat, cold, dampness, confined space, or

around noise or vibration? Does the job involve shift work, availability for call out during nonworking periods, or mandatory overtime during emergency situations? Are there *stress* factors built into the job, such as interruptions for a typist in a reception area, demanding customers in a sales clerk situation, or competing demands, such as in a dispatcher or control operator position? Indicate in row IX of the worksheet whether the job imposes any personal demands, and if so, the nature of those demands.

Considering Tasks. Context factors II–IX should all be related to job content factors. Certain duties may require the job incumbent to establish personal contacts outside of the organization (e.g., "arrange press conferences"). Certain tasks may place the employee in the vicinity of work hazards (e.g., "trims tree branches from area of high tension wires"). Look at each of the job context factors identified as applicable and determine which tasks are associated with the context factor. Make a note of the relevant tasks. Write the task numbers from the Task Worksheet in the box on the right side of the appropriate row.

Now, review all the tasks to see if you are reminded of any additional context factors that have not been noted. If more are identified, add them to your list and show the associated tasks.

Additional Documentation

Creating a Job Description. Many organizations require a formal description of all their jobs. The data assembled at this point and documented on duty and task worksheets are ideal for creating a comprehensive job description. Since the forms are too bulky for job description purposes, it is recommended that the results of those analyses be summarized in one place as described below.

Begin by recording the purpose of the job (from the Duty Worksheet). Then document the content of the job by writing the first duty on a clean sheet of paper. Under this duty, write each of the associated task statements as a complete sentence. After all of the tasks for a duty have been recorded, write out the next duty and its associated task statements. Continue this process until all of the job content has been recorded. Exhibit 15 shows a sample job description prepared in this way.

Some organizations may have interactive computer systems or sophisticated word processing systems that allow for easy storage and easy retrieval of job content and context data. Where such facilities exist, their use is recommended.

Creating an Individual Position Summary. The job description that has been constructed can be used to create a position summary sheet

Exhibit 15. Job Description for Clerk Typist/Receptionist

Greet visitors, direct calls and visitors to proper person, type, and answer telephones.

I. TYPING/PRODUCING FINAL COPY

1. Types letters, memos, and reports from handwritten material according to standard formats in order to produce final copy, using an electric typewriter and organization style manual.
2. Types/transcribes letters, memos, and reports from dictated copy according to standard formats in order to produce final copy, using an electric typewriter, transcribing equipment, and organization style manual.
3. Types forms and form letters, filling in specified information from handwritten or typed material in order to produce final copy, using an electric typewriter.
4. Proofreads typed copy and corrects spelling, punctuation, grammatical, and typographical errors in order to produce final copy, using an electric typewriter, dictionary, style manual and correcting fluid.

II. ANSWERING TELEPHONE AND GREETING VISITORS

5. Answers telephone in order to connect callers to appropriate parties or records messages, using multiline telephone, office directory, and "while you were out" forms.
6. Greets office visitors, inquiring as to nature of business or appointment in order to direct visitors to appropriate office, using office directory.

III. FILING

7. Files correspondence, memos, reports, and other documents chronologically, alphabetically, and by subject-matter in order to provide records and facilitate retrieval of information.
8. Searches alphabetical, chronological, or subject matter file in order to locate and pull requested documents.

for each of your employees in the job. In some situations, you may have a slightly different grouping of duties and tasks for each employee, while in others, the prepared job description will be precise for several employees. When employees are at different levels, there will probably be some variation in the duties and/or tasks performed.

1. For each of your employees in the occupation, consider such duty and whether it has been assigned to the employee.

2. If the employee *has* been assigned the duty, check the tasks to be certain that they are all pertinent to that position.

3. If the employee *has not* been assigned that duty, and will not be, then go on to the next duty.

4. If the duty has not been assigned to the employee, but definitely will be (through correction of oversight or when the incumbent reaches a certain level of development in the position), then make specific plans for that assignment and check the tasks to be certain that they will all be pertinent to that position.

For these determinations, you can create an individual position summary by marking up a copy of the job description for the particular employee, or by using a form such as that shown in Exhibit 16 (Individual Position Summary Form). A copy of the job description should be attached to the form unless the task and duty summaries recorded on the form are descriptive.

Exhibit 16 shows an Individual Position Summary Form with columns 1 and 2 completed. The use of columns 3, 4, and 5 will be discussed in Chapter 4.

*Identifying Critical Elements.** One or more of the duties (or an associated task) may be "critical" to performance in positions. These critical elements are of sufficient importance that poor performance in one will require corrective action on your part even if the employee is performing all other aspects of the job well. The importance of understanding the concept of critical element cannot be emphasized too strongly.

Accurate identification of the critical elements of each job is the key to shaping an effective workforce. If you do not identify all the critical elements of a job, the job may not be fully done. If you label noncritical parts of the job as critical, the employee may be treated unfairly. For instance, there may be one physical element in an otherwise sedentary job. If the element could be absorbed by other employees, if necessary, it should not be labeled as critical. If it is identified as critical, an employee who performed all other elements well would still have to be considered unsatisfactory because of this element.

To identify critical elements, consider each of the duties and tasks and determine which ones would have the most severe impact if performed poorly. While all of them are *important* parts of the job, noncritical elements are those where poor performance can be tolerated if balanced by outstanding performance on another element. Critical elements are those where such compensation *is not* possible. Duties and tasks related to direct contact with the public frequently fall into this category. Maintaining customer good will would be an example of such a critical element in certain jobs. Duties and tasks that cannot be performed by others in the work group might also fall into this category.

Use an asterisk to identify the duties and/or tasks on the Individual Position Summary Form which you consider to be critical (see Exhibit 16).

Determining Job Requirements

There are two kinds of requirements associated with most jobs: basic competencies and special competencies. *Basic compentencies* are those knowl-

---

*Managers in the Federal Government are required by instructions implementing the Civil Service Reform Act to identify critical elements of jobs. The instructions in this paragraph will help federal managers meet these requirements. Other managers are also urged to identify the critical elements of the jobs they supervise.

Exhibit 16. Individual Position Summary Form

Job Title: _Clerk Typist/Receptionist_   Position No.: _327_   Page No.: _1_

1. Duties	2. Tasks	3. Performance Criteria	4. Performance Standards	5. Indicators of Performance
I. Typing*	1. Types letters, memos, and reports*			
	2. Types/transcribes letters, memos, and reports*			
	3. Types forms and form letters*			
	4. Proofreads and corrects			
II. Answering telephone/ greeting visitors*	5. Answers telephone*			
	6. Greets visitors*			
III. Filing	7. Files			
	8. Searches files/ pulls documents			

Signature--Supervisor: _Joanna Margolis_   Signature--Employee: _Roberta Ward_

Date: _6-11-83_

edges, skills, abilities, or other worker competencies necessary to perform *at least minimally* on a job. These are frequently referred to as qualification factors, "minimum quals" or "MQs." *Special competencies* are knowledges, skills, abilities, or other worker competencies necessary to perform a job in a *superior* manner. (These are the factors used to compare two or more basically qualified job candidates.) This section outlines procedures for identifying the most important basic competencies and special competencies from the nearly infinite number of competencies that may bear on performance of a specific job.

Suggestions for Writing Competencies

The wording of a competency has an important bearing on its understandability and usefulness. If it is written too broadly (e.g., "knowledge of the law") or too narrowly (e.g., ability to operate Dictaphone Model X"), the competency will be of relatively little value for many potential human resource management purposes. Below are suggestions to help guide you in writing competencies.

Format. When the competency is a skill, ability, or area of knowledge, use the following format:

- skill to _____
- ability to _____
- knowledge of _____

When the competency is an "other characteristic or circumstance," try to start the phrase with the key word, such as:

- pride in _____

Broadness. A balance must be found between the too broad or too narrow competency. Rather than the broad phrase, "knowledge of the law" mentioned above, or the restrictive one "knowledge of Title 27 of the State Labor Act," it would be better to say "knowledge of federal and state labor laws."

Normally it is better to identify generic (e.g., manual typewriter, electric typewriter, word processing equipment) rather than brand names for machines and equipment (e.g., IBM Selectric). This assumes that the transfer of skill or ability will occur easily after a short orientation. If a piece of equipment is so different from others in the same category that its use requires considerable training, it may be desirable to identify the equipment. While it would not be appropriate to say "ability to drive a

Ford," it would be appropriate to say "ability to drive four-wheel vehicle with manual transmission."

Level. The level of a competency needed should be specified. Frequently this can be done by adding "sufficient to" or "as demonstrated by" after the general ability statement. For instance, "knowledge of correct English language usage sufficient to identify and correct errors and type dictated copy."

"Ability to read" has no meaning without detailed knowledge of the job content. Perhaps 90 percent of the adults in the United States can read at some level, but many may not be able to read at the level needed on a particular job. It would be much better to define the level needed, as in the following examples:

- ability to read at the sixth grade level on a standardized reading test
- ability to read safety signs and labels
- ability to read instruction manuals for transformer repairs
- ability to read court decisions to identify key issues and precedents
- ability to read English language sufficient to understand style manual and instructions for typed copy and to file documents by subject.

Operational Definition. Write the competency so that its application to the performance of the job is clear. This suggestion is closely related to level. For instance, the last four examples of ways to modify a reading ability requirement have been operationally defined.

Basic Competencies

New workers must possess or obtain basic competencies in order to perform the job. These competencies can usually be identified from the task statements.

Look at each of the task statements prepared for the job you are analyzing and think about the skills, abilities, areas of knowledge or special qualifications required to perform that task. These should be *minimum* requirements you consider necessary to permit satisfactory job performance. They should also be competencies that the majority of incumbents now at the journey level of the job possess. (As a guide, you might consider two workers out of three to be a "majority.") Each time you think of a new knowledge, skill, or ability which is basic to task performance, make a note of it on the Basic Competency Worksheet (see Exhibit 17) and show which task it is associated with. If you think of

Exhibit 17. Basic Competencies Worksheet

Job Title: _Clerk Typist/Receptionist_   Position No.: _327_

Organization: _Division W, XYZ Corp._   Supervisor: _Jones_   Page _1_ of _2_

Competencies	Tasks Which Require This Competency	Authority
1. Knowledge of typing format.	1, 2, 3	
2. Ability to type final copy from handwritten material.	1, 3	
3. Eye-hand dexterity to operate electric typewriter.	1, 2, 3	
4. Ability to type forms.	3	
5. Eye-hand-foot coordination to simultaneously operate typewriter and transcribing equipment.	2	
6. Ability to use standard references (dictionary, style manual).	1, 2, 3, 4, 5, 6	
7. Ability to speak/understand spoken English language sufficient to answer telephone, greet visitors and transcribe dictated copy.	2, 5, 6	
8. Knowledge of organizational filing procedures and system.	7, 8	
9. Knowledge of correct English language usage (grammar, spelling, punctuation) sufficient to identify and correct errors and type dictated copy.	2, 4	

Signature: _S. E. Jones_   Date: _6/19/83_

Exhibit 17. Basic Competencies Worksheet—*continued*

Job Title: _Clerk Typist/Receptionist_   Position No.: _327_

Organization: _Division W, XYZ Corp._   Supervisor: _Jones_   Page _2_ of _2_

Competencies	Tasks Which Require This Competency	Authority
10. Ability to proofread and correct own work.	4	
11. Ability to operate multi-line telephone (hold, transfer, and connect calls).	5	
12. Ability to read English language sufficient to understand style manual and instructions for typed copy, and to file documents by subject.	1, 2, 3, 4, 7	
13. Ability to alphabetize sufficient to file and retrieve material.	7, 8	
14. Ability to recognize and differentiate between numbers and series of numbers sufficient to file and retrieve material.	7, 8	
15. Ability to use English language; to read/write/type specified information on forms.	3, 5	
16. Ability to compare and perceive differences between two sets of copy.	4	

Signature: _S. E. Jones_   Date: _6/19/83_

this basic competency again when you are considering another task, be sure also to list or to mark the number of that task next to the basic competency on your list.

The following questions should be helpful in identifying basic competencies.

1. What knowledges, skills, or abilities are workers expected to bring to the occupation as a result of their training, education, or ex-

perience (e.g., knowledge of advanced calculus)? Do *not* record the training, education, or experience as a requirement (e.g., B.S. in mathematics
or engineering). It is the knowledge, skill, or ability acquired through
training, education, or experience that is important. A formal degree may
not mean that the competency is possessed, and conversely, there may be
other indicators that an individual has the basic competency (see Chapter
5).

2. Are there any legal or regulatory requirements for the job? For
instance, is there a requirement to be a licensed civil engineer or to be
licensed by the U.S. Department of Transportation to transport hazardous
material? (Note the authority which is the source of this requirement in
the last column of the Basic Competency Worksheet.) *Caution*: Some
license and other "legal" requirements have been challenged in court, as
in the case of citizenship; careful thought should be given, therefore, to
what is really required (see Chapter 5).

3. Are there any special technologies or other developments which
create additional worker requirements? Are there tools, machinery or other
equipment which require specialized skills which must be brought to the
job (e.g., operation of electric arc welding equipment)?

Look over your list of basic competencies to make sure that the list
makes sense as a whole. You might want to discuss the list with job
incumbents and other managers.

Special Competencies

When managers think about employees they have known in a job
and consider why some employees were successful while others failed (or
were not as successful as managers would have liked), they can usually
identify important knowledges, skills, abilities, or other special competencies of the workers that were key to their success or failure. Some of
these may have contributed to superior performance in the job, while the
absence of others detracted from the employee's ability to perform the job
in a superior way. Occasionally, the special competencies involved in
superior performance of the job are a different level of the basic competencies for the occupation identified at an earlier time. For instance,
minimum typing ability might be required for acceptable performance
in all typing jobs in an organization, but above minimum typing ability
might be a special competency in the word processing unit. More often,
however, the competencies critical to superior performance are not the
same as the basic competencies. For example, ability to type is a basic
competency for the Clerk Typist/Receptionist but it does not differentiate
between acceptable and superior performance. Factors such as ability to

work with interruptions and ability to format typewritten material are the ones which distinguish the superior worker.

Identifying and Documenting Special Competencies. To help stimulate your thinking, remember the five best employees you have supervised in this occupation over the years. If you are a relatively new manager, or if you have not supervised very many employees, think of employees in the occupation whose performance you are familiar with. Perhaps they were fellow employees at one time in the past. If you cannot think of five that fall in the superior category, think of as many as you can who were superior. Write down their names on the left side of a blank sheet of paper.

Think about some people who were successful even if you or other managers did not think very highly of them on a personal basis. Perhaps they had personal habits that were offensive or they stayed aloof from the social activities of the organization. Try to identify at least one person who falls in this category but objectively must be considered a good performer and add this person to your list.

Now think of about five unacceptable or barely acceptable employees in this same occupation at similar grade levels. Once again, you may consider employees you have known but did not supervise as well as those you have supervised. Write their names on the right side of the paper. (This is a working paper that only you will see, and you should destroy it when you finish this exercise.) Try to add at least one person to this list who was liked personally by management and/or fellow workers, but who could not perform the work adequately.

Now think about the major differences between the two groups. What kept the barely acceptable employees from being better performers? What did the best employees have that made them superior? List those special competencies associated with successful performance on the Special Competencies Worksheet (see Exhibit 18). The competencies you list can be, among others, knowledges, abilities, skills. Write down all the special competencies that you think of on the left side of the Special Competencies Worksheet. If you have trouble thinking of special competencies, ask yourself the following questions:

1. What characteristics might a worker show that would prove he or she is superior?

2. If you wanted to give an award, what might you say about a worker to show why he or she gets the award?

3. What else would really show that a worker is outstanding?

4. If you had to pick one person to get a special bonus for outstanding work, what might you look for?

5. What made the poor workers weak?

Exhibit 18. Special Competencies Worksheet

Job Title: __Clerk-Typist/Receptionist__   Position No.: __327__

Organization: __Division W, XYZ Corp.__   Supervisor: __Jones__   Page __1__ of __1__

Competencies	Ratings Import.	Ratings Avail.	Tasks Which Require This Competency
1. Ability to work with interruptions (e.g., phone or visitors) when typing.	++	S	All
2. Ability to format or layout handwritten dictated material on typed page.	+	H	1, 2, 3
3. Ability to work with minimal supervision/ instruction.	++	L	All
4. Ability to identify and correct grammar, spelling, and punctuation errors in original copy.	++	S	1, 2, 3
5. Ability to apply/adapt instructions or procedures from one assignment to another.	++	S	All
6. Social skills as demonstrated by pleasant handling of callers and visitors.	++	S	5, 6

Signature: _S. C. Jones_   Date: _6/19/83_

CODE: Important -- ++ = Extremely useful; + = Considerably useful (strike if average or less)

Avail.   -- H = Most fairly high; S = Spreadout; L = Most fairly low

Notes to Job Analyst. The manager is the key person in the identification of special competencies. Your role is to structure a situation which allows you to get this information from one or more managers in the most efficient way. In general, there are two ways to do this. If there are several managers, they can be brought together for a brainstorming session. Frequently, this is a more reliable and worthwhile way to identify special competencies.

The alternative is for the job analyst to guide the individual manager through the steps necessary to identify special competencies. Do this by getting the manager in a one-on-one situation, away from job distractions, and ask him or her to go through the procedures and answer the questions in the preceding paragraphs. Your job is to record the special competencies as the manager identifies them.

Evaluating Special Competencies. Each of the special competencies that you have placed on the worksheet should be looked at critically to find out which ones should really be considered. Ask yourself the following questions and then put your responses in the appropriate columns on the worksheet.

Notes to Job Analyst. Each of the special competencies that you have placed on the worksheet should now be looked at critically to find out which ones should really be considered. Ask the manager the following questions and then put his or her responses in the appropriate columns on the worksheet.

Correctness. Is the competency stated positively? Frequently when one thinks of unsuccessful people one thinks of negative things. It is important that these be stated in terms of what we want people to possess. List competencies, not incompetencies. If the factor is written negatively, strike it out and write it positively. For instance, should somebody not perform well because of frequent tardiness, the special competency that you note on the worksheet might be "promptness."

Clarity. Is the competency stated clearly? Is it definitive? Frequently we use terms in a number of different ways. "Dependability" might mean good attendance, promptness, working without supervision, or follow-through on projects. Be sure that the word or phrase used communicates what you have in mind. If it does not, amplify the phrase or strike it out and rewrite the competency.

Operational definition. Is the competency stated in a way that makes it clear what specifically is required on the job? Refer to paragraphs on "Suggestions for Writing Competencies" (page 79), specifically the suggestion on level and operational definition. Modify competencies as needed by using such techniques as the "sufficient to _____ " or "as demonstrated by _____ " phrases described earlier.

Importance. In your experience, how useful is this special competency in distinguishing superior from barely acceptable employees in this job?

1. If you consider it to be of *average usefulness*, or less, strike the factor (i.e., if the competency is no more useful with this job than it is with many other jobs).

2. If you think that it is *considerably useful*, put a " + " in the "importance" rating column (i.e., it is more useful with this job than it is with most other jobs).

3. If you think it is *extremely useful*, one of the best for this purpose, put a " + + " in the "importance" rating column (e.g., this is a key competency for distinguishing levels of employee performance).

Availability. In your best judgment, how much will the people who apply for this job vary on this special competency? Be sure to think about likely *applicants* for the job (either current employees in other jobs or new hires), not job incumbents. Do this rating only for special competencies which remain on the worksheet (those you did not strike).

1. If you think that *most applicants* will be *fairly low* on this special competency, put an "L" in the "availability" rating column.

2. If you expect that *applicants* will be considerably *spread out on levels* of this competency (that is, some will be high, some low, and some in the middle) put an "S" in the "availability" rating column.

3. If you think *most applicants* will be *fairly high* on this competency, put an "H" in the "availability" rating column.

Special competencies that you rated as important (" + " or " + + ") and rated "S" on this scale, are prime areas to consider when comparing basically qualified candidates. Important ones (" + " or " + + ") that you rated "L" are suggestive of areas where the employer should provide training, but these competencies will have little value in most selection situations. On the other hand, those rated "H" will not be of much use for either purpose. They should be looked at closely if rated important (" + " or " + + "), however, to see if they might more appropriately be considered basic competencies.

Relationship to tasks. For each of the special competencies which remain on the worksheet (those you did not strike), determine which tasks are not performed well when workers do not have that special competency or, conversely, which tasks are performed very well if the individual does have the special competency. There may be more than one task for each special competency. It may involve all of one duty or tasks from two or more duties. Further, a task may require more than one special competency. For each special competency, write the number(s) of the associated tasks to the right of the special competency in the last column of the worksheet.

The steps described in this chapter result in the documentation of the important content, context, and requirements of a job. The next chapter will show how this information can be of help in effectively utilizing human resources. Before discussing the uses of this valuable job analysis information, there is a critical job analysis topic to consider.

Keeping the Data Current

Most organizations are dynamic. New responsibilities and equipment are introduced into work units, while others are removed; responsibilities are rearranged, new procedures introduced, or priorities modified. Incidents may bring safety or equal employment issues to the attention of managers or investigators. These activities, which are normal in a dynamic organization, can cause changes in the content, competencies, and context of a job. For instance, the installation of a platform or catwalk to correct a safety concern may cause the tasks involved in machine feeding to change, and thus change some of the competencies needed to perform the job. The introduction of new equipment may reduce or change the physical requirements of a job.

The effort expended in documenting job information will be wasted if the data are not kept current and usable. To fail to do this would be much like buying a car and failing to replace worn points and plugs or to change a flat tire. A change of parts, and the car would be functional again—a change of tasks, and job information will be functional again.

There are two major sources of change that require an update in the job data documentation:

1. Significant changes that take place over a short time period. For example, when (a) major new responsibilities are added to a job, (b) new or greatly modified equipment is introduced, (c) a consent decree or affirmative action plan mandates changes, or (d) there is a major organizational change, job descriptions should be reviewed and necessary modifications made as soon after the change occurs as possible.

2. Changes in jobs that occur subtly, over time, and which are not immediately noticeable. At least once a year the manager must look at the duties and tasks assigned to each job to be certain that they are current and still accurately reflect the job. It is suggested that this review be done in conjunction with the performance appraisal, if this is done at least annually.

Man/Machine Situations

Rapid technological growth is affecting all aspects of the economy. New equipment is being introduced into factories, offices, and retail establishments. While the equipment may eventually abolish jobs, it also creates new jobs and significantly modifies others. Once the equipment has been introduced and operated for a period of time, the man/machine interactions can be described and analyzed by the manager and worker in the manner described in this chapter. Unfortunately, decisions on the selection and training of workers must be made before this experience is gained. This section describes some of the ways that job facts can be gathered from other sources, and analyzed for their selection and training implications.

The workers' advocate in the design of equipment is the human factors engineer. The possibility of getting equipment which real people can operate or maintain is greatly enhanced and the task of selecting and training such people is greatly eased if a human factors engineer was involved from the preliminary planning or principal design stage. It is during this stage that the human factors engineer does the detailed staffing study. The decisions made at this stage about the skills needed to operate or maintain the equipment are reality-tested during the prototype or mock-up state. The "validity" of these decisions is tested when the equipment is finally put into operation.

There are two major differences between the job analysis data documented by the human factors engineer and the job analysis data described earlier in this chapter. First, the job content analysis done by the human factors engineer is much more detailed. Frequently tasks identified in these analyses are narrower than those described in this chapter, and therefore, many more tasks are needed to describe the job. Further, the tasks are divided into elements that describe exactly what actions the worker must take, with what control, based upon what stimulus. This elemental analysis is needed to prepare operations and maintenance manuals, and to make sure that worker and machine interact in the most efficient and safest way possible. It is more detailed than the manager needs, or should be expected to document.

The other major difference is that the human factors engineer infers knowledges, skills, abilities, and other worker requirements (competencies) from the content of the job. Thus the derived competency data tend to be what are described as basic competencies in this book. The special competencies—those that distinguish the superior from the acceptable employee—are not as likely to surface in the human factors-oriented job analysis process as they are when workers in the operational setting are compared using the VERJAS procedures detailed in this book.

The manager should become familiar with the overall aspects of the task analysis performed by the human factors engineer, the inferences about basic competencies, and the resulting staffing decisions. As long as the manager does not get lost in the elemental details, this information should help to give the manager and worker a running start on the use of equipment, and help managers to spot work performance problems early. The data may also help the manager to identify training needs that go beyond the "how to" of machine operation and repair.

If you are analyzing a new job that involves machinery, you should obtain the task analysis conducted by the human factors engineer to supplement your understanding of the job, as a basis for identifying job duties. You should then use this information to write out task statements, describe the job context, and verify basic competencies using the forms and procedures outlined in this chapter. (The delineation of special competencies will have to await operational experience.) Training, evaluation, and restaffing decisions then can be based on these documented job facts using the forms and procedures described in the next chapter.

4. Using VERJAS Data

Accurate and detailed information about the content of jobs; about the skills, abilities and areas of knowledge required to perform them; and about the context in which they are performed is essential to effective human resource management. This was outlined in Chapter 1 and will be reinforced by the discussion of legal issues in Chapter 5.

This chapter is intended to help the manager to understand the various applications of job analysis data, and more specifically, to use the data developed using the VERJAS procedures outlined in the preceding chapter. In discussing job analysis applications, we will talk about three illustrative jobs: Clerk Typist/Receptionist, Plant Sales Manager, and Line Repairer. The VERJAS data base for the clerical job is shown in Chapter 3 and will not be repeated here. The data base for the latter two jobs is shown on appropriate forms (Exhibits 19–22 and 23–26 respectively) on the following pages. These examples will be discussed as we explain the applicability of job analysis data to

1. job design
2. classification and evaluation
3. recruitment
4. selection
5. training
6. performance appraisal.

Several examples of actual applications are also discussed, and specific instructions for applying VERJAS data are included, as appropriate.

Depending upon the size and structure of your organization, a personnel specialist may develop many of these job analysis applications. Even if managers are not directly responsible, however, it is critical that they understand how information about the job is translated into personnel decisions. First, of course, they must be able to communicate their needs and problems to the personnel specialist. Second, managers are a primary source of information about the job and will be working closely with

91

others who will use these facts for various purposes. Finally, managers must accept and work with decisions concerning classification, pay, selection, training, and performance appraisal which affect the jobs for which they are responsible.

Job Design

The first application we will discuss is job design. Job analysis data can be used to structure or to restructure the work of an organization or unit for various purposes. These data are used in combination with other job data about the flow of information and materials, the location and layout of the workplace, and available tools and equipment. There are a number of reasons why this might be done, for example:

- to meet organizational production or mission goals, utilizing available skills,
- to accommodate new technologies,
- to remove barriers to employment opportunities for groups with special employment problems, such as handicaps, and
- to respond to the concerns of workers for increased job satisfaction and alternative work patterns, including flexitime and job sharing.

Organizational Goals and Available Skills

It may be difficult for an organization to fill several full-performance level positions. The manager may want to consider restructuring the work by grouping tasks that require complex or scarce skills into one or two positions and by designing some combination of entry-level and support positions for remaining tasks. This approach has several advantages. First, the work will be performed. Second, the skills of the staff will be used more effectively—perhaps with some saving of salary costs, although cost saving may be offset by additional training and supervisory expenses. Third, new job opportunities will have been provided to applicants with different qualifications. This may also be a way for organizations to begin to improve their affirmative action profile.

The job of Line Repairer provides an illustration of how this might be done. The job of Cable Splicer is similar in many respects to Line Repairer, and in many electric utilities the functions are combined into one job. The major difference between the two jobs is that Cable Splicers do not have to climb poles. An organization with these functions combined might have some female candidates with all of the needed competencies except the ability to work at heights. The organization could separate the

Cable Splicer responsibilities out of the Line Repairer job and hire some women to perform the Cable Splicer's functions. This use of job analysis information would allow the company to utilize an available human resource and take affirmative action to get women into physical jobs at the same time.*

Exhibit 19. Job Description for Plant Sales Manager

To direct the activities of the plant sales force in promoting and obtaining profitable sales of Company's products.
I. SUPERVISORY

1. Interviews and assesses qualifications of applicants for job in the department in order to select person for the job using applicants' resumes, job description and company personnel policies and procedures manual.
2. Evaluates qualifications and availability of staff in relation to requirements of specific project in order to assign work to staff using project calendar and personnel files as necessary.
3. Role-plays sales presentation demonstrating product and answering questions in order to provide on-the-job training to sales personnel using promotional materials.
4. Reads production reports, project files and/or observes sales presentations and compares actual achievement to preestablished objectives in order to evaluate employees' performances using records, files, and performance appraisal forms.

II. SALES

5. Meets with potential customers, explaining benefits and cost of product in order to make a sale using sample products, promotional material, and order forms.
6. Meets with potential customers in order to obtain information regarding their interests/needs concerning company product using marketing questionnaire.
7. Assesses market conditions as they relate to specific products in order to develop marketing strategy and plan specific sales program using company planning objectives, economic forecast, and past sales reports.

III. PLANNING

8. Evaluates market conditions in relation to specific product in order to develop plant sales goals for the coming year using company market research and financial reports, and trade and journal publications.
9. Discusses sales goals with Plant General Manager in order to jointly agree on goals for the coming year using company market research and financial reports, and trade and journal publications.
10. Reviews quarterly sales objectives in order to assess actual progress/performance and identify problems using monthly sales and financial reports and annual goals.

IV. FINANCE

11. Evaluates credit applications in order to approve/disapprove request for credit using corporate procedures and criteria.
12. Reviews accounts receivable identifying past due accounts in order to ensure collections of delinquent accounts using accounts receivable printout and corporate policies and procedures regarding delinquent accounts.

---

*This is a realistic example in that it reflects physiological differences between men and women. For a number of reasons, however, the problem is not as simple as spelled out here: (1) some organizations with these functions separated find that they need to require climbing ability for purposes of job bidding or emergency repairs during power outages, (2) smaller companies may find they need the flexibility of combined jobs, and (3) this could become an undesirable way to stereotype jobs and keep qualified women out of the "macho world" of Line Repairer, and pay them less.

Exhibit 20. Job Context Worksheet

PART A—SCOPE AND EFFECT   Plant Sales Manager   Page   1   of   2   Position No.: 164

			NOTES		TASKS WHICH REQUIRE THIS FACTOR
I.	**SUPERVISION RECEIVED**		Line supervision is from Plant Manager but technical supervision is from Director of Marketing at corporate office.		
	Proximity:	Frequency:			
	☐ Visual	☐ Constant ☒ Weekly			
	☒ Physical Sep.	☐ Hourly ☐ Less Than Weekly			
	☒ Geog. Sep.	☐ Daily			
II.	**GUIDELINES**	NOTES			5, 11
	☐ Not Applicable	Company guidelines on stock rotation.			
	☒ Applicable	ABC standard general procedures on credit.			
III.	**RESEARCH ANALYSIS REPORTS**	NOTES			7, 8
	☐ Not Applicable	Conduct market surveys.			
	☒ Applicable				
IV.	**ACCOUNTABILITY CONSEQUENCES OF ERROR**		NOTES		9, 12
	☐ Not Applicable	☒ Applicable	Key responsibility for profitability of plant.		
	☐ Life	☐ Property	Responsible for collection of accounts.		
	☐ Injury	☐ Inconvenience			
	☒ Monetary				
V.	**PERSONAL CONTACTS**	NOTES (INTERNAL)			1, 2, 3, 4, 9
	☐ Not Applicable	Sales force. Product supervisors.	Plant Manager.		
	☒ Applicable	NOTES (EXTERNAL)			5, 6
		Customers.			

Exhibit 20. Job Context Worksheet—continued

		NOTES	TASKS WHICH REQUIRE THIS FACTOR
VI.	**SUPERVISION EXERCISED** ☐ Not Applicable ☒ Applicable **Number Supervised:** Nature: __ Skilled/Semi-Skilled ☒ Hire/Fire __ Clerical ☒ Train __ Prof./Technical ☒ Assignments _13_ Other _Sales_ ☒ Review Work ☒ Eval. Perf.	Supervision of sales force is key aspect of job.	1, 2, 3, 4
	PART B—ENVIRONMENT		
VII.	**PHYSICAL DEMANDS** ☐ Not Applicable Mobility: ☒ Applicable **Lifting:** ☒ 10 Lbs. Max. ☒ Standing ☐ Kneeling ☒ 20 Lbs. Max. ☒ Walking ☐ Crouching ☐ 50 Lbs. Max. ☒ Sitting ☐ Crawling ☐ 100 Lbs. Max. ☒ Stooping ☐ Climbing ☐ Over 100 Lbs. ☒ Reaching	NOTES Must visit retail establishments with sales force and on own.	7
VIII.	**WORK HAZARDS** ☒ Not Applicable ☐ Applicable ☐ Mechanical ☐ Explosives ☐ Electrical ☐ Radiation ☐ Fire ☐ Atmospheric ☐ Chemical ☐ Height	NOTES	
IX	**PERSONAL DEMANDS/STRESS** ☐ Not Applicable ☒ Applicable ☐ Overtime ☐ Climate ☐ Shift Work ☒ Stress ☐ Split Shift ☐ Repetitious Operations	NOTES Considerable pressure for sales and meeting promises to clients.	5, 10, 11

Exhibit 21. Basic Competencies Worksheet

Job Title: _Plant Sales Manager_   Position No.: _164_

Organization: _AJAX_   Supervisor: _S.K._   Page _1_ of _1_

Competencies	Tasks Which Require This Competency	Authority
1. Ability to speak/understand English language sufficient to obtain/convey information with customers and sales force.	1, 5, 6	
2. Ability to read English language sufficient to understand letters, memos, and reports.	2, 4, 7	
3. Ability to use English language to write letters, memos, and reports.	8, 11, 12	
4. Knowledge of company products (e.g., characteristics, cost of producing, marketing, and selling).	5, 6, 7, 9	
5. Knowledge of company policy and operating procedures.	5, 6, 7, 8, 9	
6. Knowledge of direct sales techniques.	5, 6, 7	
7. Knowledge of company's personnel policies and procedures	1, 2	

Signature: _Stan King_   Date: _6-11-83_

Exhibit 22. Special Competencies Worksheet

Job Title: __Plant Sales Manager__   Position No.: __164__

Organization: __AJAX__   Supervisor: __S. K.__   Page __1__ of __1__

Competencies	Ratings Import.	Ratings Avail.	Tasks Which Require This Competency
1. Ability to deal with people (motivate, train, command respect) in order to get sales results.	++	S	3, 5, 6
2. Ability to evaluate costs to differentiate those with a payoff from those that are unnecessary.	++	S	8, 9, 10, 11, 12
3. Ability to establish rapport and maintain communication with client.	++	S	5, 6
4. Ability to analyze market conditions and sales patterns.	+	S	7, 8
5. Ability to make decisions to act on market conditions and sales patterns in a timely way.	+	L	7, 8, 9
6. Ability to plan, execute the plan, and evaluate its effectiveness	+	H	8, 9, 10
7. Ability to explain assignments to staff, suggest ways of carrying out, available resources, etc.	+	S	2
8. Ability to plan work of sales department considering goals, resources, constraints.	++	S	8, 9, 10
9. Ability to monitor work performance, to identify problems and inefficiencies, and to develop solutions.	++	S	2, 11

Signature: _Stan King_   Date: _6-11-83_

CODE: Important -- ++ = Extremely useful; + = Considerably useful (strike if average or less)

Avail.   -- H = Most fairly high; S = Spreadout; L = Most fairly low

Exhibit 23. Job Description for Line Repairer

Install and repair electrical distribution lines and equipment to meet current and future energy needs of customers.

I. INSTALLS, REPAIRS, AND REMOVES PRIMARY WIRING

1. Constructs rigging, ties knots, and splices, in order to raise transformers and equipment, using information on mechanical advantages of different types of knots, splices, and sling loading.
2. Erects, removes, or replaces construction in order to maintain electrical service, using information obtained from company work orders and construction standards.
3. Refuses cutouts, ties circuits, or operates substation breakers on callouts working from ground, pole, or bucket, in order to restore electrical service, using circuit maps, body belt, safety strap, and climbers.
4. Repairs or improves energized circuits to 600 volts in order to fulfill work order without loss of service, using rubber gloves and protective equipment, hand tools, and construction standards, while working from pole or bucket truck.
5. Repairs or improves energized circuits to 12,500 volts in order to fulfill work orders without loss of service, using rubber gloves and sleeves, blankets and pole guards, and hot sticks, while working from pole or bucket truck.
6. Splices aluminum and copper conductors by removing insulation, roughening surface, and installing connector in order to make repairs or for new installations, using Burndy Hy-press Pump and proper size dies.
7. Reviews conditions at trouble site in relation to own or crew's equipment capabilities in order to determine and inform dispatcher whether additional crews and equipment are needed, using mobile radio.

II. INSTALLS, REMOVES, AND REPAIRS TRANSFORMERS AND CAPACITOR BANKS

8. Changes taps in single phase and three phase transformers in order to accommodate load and voltage changes, using hand tools such as pliers and screw drivers.
9. Installs, replaces, and repairs single and three phase transformers in order to maintain electrical service, using meters, hand tools, rigging, boom truck, body belt, safety strap, and climbers while working from pole or bucket truck.
10. Connects portable transformers (single phase and three phase) to existing construction in order to prevent interruption of service, using meters to phase and rotate banks, hand tools such as socket wrenches, body belt, safety strap, and climbers, while working from a pole or bucket truck.
11. Installs, replaces, and repairs capacitor banks and regulators in order to maintain electrical service, using test equipment, hand tools, boom truck or rigging, body belt, safety strap, and climbers, while working from bucket truck or pole.
12. Tests electrical circuits in order to check output of transformers and capacitors, using meggar, ammeter, phase meter, voltmeter, rotation meter, and fault finder ("thumper"), while working from pole or bucket truck.

III. INSTALLS, REPAIRS, AND REMOVES SERVICE WIRING

13. Installs, replaces, and repairs distribution circuits in order to maintain electrical service using wire-pulling equipment, hand tools, body belt, safety strap, climbers, and rubber protective equipment, while working from bucket truck or pole.
14. Installs and maintains URD (i.e., underground residential distribution facilities) in order to provide electricity to recent residential construction and to make repairs and additions to existing facilities in areas prohibiting above-ground cable, using URD cable splicing kit and hand tools.
15. Transfers conductors of various sizes and types in order to establish new, or to maintain existing, service, using rubber gloves or "hot sticks," body belt, safety strap, climbers, and any rigging required, while working from bucket truck or pole.
16. Installs, removes, and repairs multiple and series street light circuits in order to maintain street lighting, using hand tools, and meters, working from bucket truck.
17. Installs and removes services and secondaries in order to establish, discontinue, or repair service to customer owned properties, using hand tools, Burndy Hy-press Pump, blocks or lug-all, body belt, safety strap, climbers, and rubber protective equipment, working from ladder, pole, and/or bucket.

Exhibit 23. Job Description for Line Repairer—*continued*

IV. OPERATES TRUCKS AND OTHER MACHINERY

18. Drives company trucks and/or automobiles in order to transport equipment and personnel to job site.

19. Operates company lifting equipment (i.e., corner mount boom, Hyster, or bucket) in order to load and unload, or lift to the working level, equipment such as transformers or capacitors.

20. Operates wire-pulling equipment (i.e., tensioner, winch, and capstan) in order to install cable.

21. Operates trenching machine, jack hammer, and/or backhoe in order to remove road surface and/or earth to install underground cable.

V. COMMUNICATION

22. Operates mobile radio in order to call for additional parts, tools, or aid, using company codes and regulations.

23. Talks to customers in order to answer their questions or to tell them of work to be done that will affect them, using work orders and customer-contact standard operating procedures.

24. Signals using hands in order to be understood when noise or distance interfere with voice communication, using prearranged signals and company manual.

VI. EQUIPMENT MAINTENANCE AND SAFETY

25. Tests rubber gloves, sleeves, rubber hose, and insulating blankets before each use, in order to detect leaks, using air hose and company procedures.

26. Makes equipment-related test measurements such as holding valve test or weight test, in order to determine whether equipment is in proper working order, using measuring equipment and manufacturer's procedure manual.

27. Administers first aid (CPR, control of bleeding, or treatment for shock) in order to aid co-worker until medical help arrives, using approved procedures.

VII. COMPLETES PAPERWORK

28. Fills out company forms (e.g., outage reports, tags, and time sheets) in order to record data and maintain records, using pencil and clipboard.

29. Corrects work orders in field, adding, deleting, and modifying information in order to show "as built" conditions.

Exhibit 24. Job Context Worksheet

PART A—SCOPE AND EFFECT   Line Repairer   Page ___1___ of ___2___   Position No.: 233

		NOTES	TASKS WHICH REQUIRE THIS FACTOR
I.	SUPERVISION RECEIVED Proximity: ☐ Visual ☒ Physical Sep. ☐ Geog. Sep. Frequency: ☐ Constant ☐ Weekly ☐ Hourly ☐ Less Than Weekly ☒ Daily	Crew leader provides on-site supervision. Contacts with management are once or twice a day.	
II.	GUIDELINES ☐ Not Applicable ☒ Applicable	NOTES Company, NECA and state rules spell out proper practices.	All
III.	RESEARCH ANALYSIS REPORTS ☒ Not Applicable ☐ Applicable	NOTES	
IV.	ACCOUNTABILITY CONSEQUENCES OF ERROR ☐ Not Applicable ☒ Applicable ☒ Life ☒ Injury ☐ Property ☒ Monetary ☒ Inconvenience	NOTES Constant threat of injury or death to self, co-workers, or customers. Possibility of inconvenience to customers and financial loss.	1-21, 25-27
V.	PERSONAL CONTACTS ☐ Not Applicable ☒ Applicable	NOTES (INTERNAL) Works as a member of a crew. NOTES (EXTERNAL) Contacts with customers when installing services or repairing outages.	1-21, 24 23

Exhibit 24. Job Context Worksheet—continued

		NOTES	TASKS WHICH REQUIRE THIS FACTOR
VI.	SUPERVISION EXERCISED ☒ Not Applicable ☐ Applicable Number Supervised: Nature: ___ Skilled/Semi-Skilled ☐ Hire/Fire ___ Clerical ☐ Train ___ Prof./Technical ☐ Assignments ___ Other ☐ Review Work ☐ Eval. Perf.		

PART B—ENVIRONMENT

		NOTES	TASKS WHICH REQUIRE THIS FACTOR
VII.	PHYSICAL DEMANDS ☐ Not Applicable ☒ Applicable Lifting: Mobility: ☐ 10 Lbs. Max. ☒ Standing ☐ Kneeling ☐ 20 Lbs. Max. ☐ Walking ☐ Crouching ☐ 50 Lbs. Max. ☐ Sitting ☐ Crawling ☐ 100 Lbs. Max. ☒ Stooping ☒ Climbing ☒ Over 100 Lbs. ☐ Reaching	Frequent working from poles and buckets requiring strength in operating tools and equipment. Must use jack hammer.	3-5, 9-13, 15-17, 19-21
VIII.	WORK HAZARDS ☐ Not Applicable ☒ Applicable ☒ Mechanical ☐ Explosives ☒ Electrical ☐ Radiation ☐ Fire ☒ Atmospheric ☐ Chemical ☒ Height		1-21
IX.	PERSONAL DEMANDS/STRESS ☐ Not Applicable ☒ Applicable ☒ Overtime ☒ Climate ☐ Shift Work ☐ Stress ☐ Split Shift ☐ Repetitive Operations	Work in summer provides no protection from sun. Emergency work often occurs in wind, rain, ice, and lightning.	1-21, 24

Exhibit 25. Basic Competencies Worksheet

Job Title: __Line Repairer__   Position No.: __233__

Organization: __WP&L__   Supervisor: __BJS__   Page __1__ of __1__

Competencies	Tasks Which Require This Competency	Authority
1. Ability to work at heights.	3-5, 9-13	
2. Arm, leg, and back strength sufficient to climb, reach, and work from bucket.	15-17	
3. Ability to remain calm during emergency situations.	1-21, 24, 27	
4. Eye-hand coordination to use small tools and hot sticks.	4-6, 8-17, 26	
5. Ability to foresee potential problems.	7, 29	
6. Ability to operate trucks and equipment.	18-22	
7. Ability to write or print legibly.	28, 29	
8. Willingness to work outside in all kinds of weather.	1-21, 24	

Signature: _B. J. Smith_   Date: __6/13/83__

Exhibit 26. Special Competencies Worksheet

Job Title: _Line Repairer_   Position No.: _233_

Organization: _WP&L_   Supervisor: _BJS_   Page _1_ of _1_

Competencies	Ratings Import.	Ratings Avail.	Tasks Which Require This Competency
1. Knowledge of electricity (e.g., understand role of transformers and resistance, prevent shock).	++	L	1-17, 25-26, 29
2. Knowledge of construction procedures and standards so that new/replacement service is installed properly.	++	S	1-17, 19-21, 29
3. Willingness to accept responsibility.	+	S	7, 23
4. Knowledge of test equipment.	++	L	9-12, 16, 25, 26
5. Ability to get into proper work position.	++	S	3-5, 9-13, 15-17
6. Ability to work smart (do work in easiest way and shortest time).	+	S	1-17
7. Ability to read code transfer and Cus sheets.	++	L	1-17, 23, 28, 29
8. Knowledge of current construction standards.	+	L	1-17, 19-21, 29

Signature: _B. J. Smith_   Date: _6/13/83_

CODE: Important -- ++ = Extremely useful; + = Considerably useful (strike if average or less)
       Avail.   -- H = Most fairly high; S = Spreadout; L = Most fairly low

Removing Barriers

Job analysis data can also be used to identify and remove unnecessary barriers to the employment of individuals with handicapping physical or mental conditions. For example, a review of several position descriptions may show that some tasks, such as those involving use of the telephone, can be shifted from one position to another, allowing the work of the first job to be performed by someone with a hearing impairment. A review of job analysis data may also show that while it is not feasible to modify the mix of tasks performed in a position, it might be possible to change the behaviors needed to perform it. For example, information might be recorded rather than written to accommodate a loss of sight, or material might be packed in two 25-pound boxes, which would require less physical strength to lift than one 50-pound box.

The Clerk Typist/Receptionist position described earlier provides a good case example. Look at the job description shown as Exhibit 15 on page 76. A typist with an outgoing personality who is confined to a wheelchair could do most of the tasks shown, but the filing and retrieval of documents would be a problem. Filing is the least important duty in this position, so perhaps it could be removed from the position and assigned elsewhere, for example, to another clerk. The professional staff could also retrieve materials they need and a high school student could be hired for a few hours a week to file and refile. Another possibility would be to get a lateral file cabinet that would make all files accessible to the clerk in the wheelchair.

Currently the job involves some walking when the receptionist delivers visitors to the office of the person they wish to visit. If each of the offices is accessible for wheelchairs, the receptionist could continue the responsibility. However, the receptionist could use the intercom to call the person being visited, who could then come to the reception area to greet their guest. Such a change could have additional benefits in some organizations (e.g., permit the receptionist to continue monitoring telephones). While some alternatives would work in some offices and not in others, job analysis data can be used to identify alternatives that could remove barriers to those with special employment problems.

Accommodating New Technologies

The introduction of word processing equipment into a typical office setting generally results in changes in job content, competency requirements, and the context in which the work is performed. This provides two examples of the use of job analysis to redesign jobs to accommodate new technologies. For instance, various offices of an organization might have clerk typist/receptionist positions similar to the illustrative job (see clerical data base in Chapter 3). With the introduction of word processing equipment, all or most of the typing tasks might be centralized into a specialized unit for greater efficiency and the more expensive equipment would be properly and fully utilized. In this instance, one job (clerk typist/receptionist) would be changed, and a new job (clerk/word processor) created. In another organization, the clerk typist/receptionist may operate the new equipment. In this case, the job will change and training will be needed to give incumbents the additional skills and knowledge to perform the new tasks. The automation of office accounting systems is another common technological trend which necessitates many changes in job design.

Job Satisfaction and Alternative Working Patterns

Jobs can also be analyzed and structured or restructured to provide greater worker satisfaction. The range of tasks performed may be expanded, or more complex tasks added, to provide greater variety in a job. The work of an entire plant—for example, an automobile assembly line—may be analyzed and the jobs restructured so that workers are assembling entire components and performing a range of tasks, rather than just one or two. Probably the best known projects of this type were those undertaken by the Saab and Volvo corporations in Sweden.

More recently, there has been growing interest in developing alternatives to traditional working patterns including flexitime, permanent part-time, and shared jobs. Job sharing, the employment of two people in a full-time position formerly held by one person, is an exciting new option. Effective job sharing opportunities utilize job analysis data. A job may be shared by two people who perform essentially the same tasks with equal responsibility, or by two people with complementary skills who perform different tasks and have different responsibilities. One project to develop strategies and alternatives to standard work scheduling was implemented by the State of Wisconsin. The objective of Project JOIN (Job Options and Innovations) was to increase both productivity and job satisfaction. Fifty-nine full-time or 118 shared positions ranging from Electronic Technician to Attorney to Library Assistant were developed. Project staff noted that "task analysis was an absolutely crucial step in defining the new part-time positions." (Cirilli et al., 1980.)

Job Classification and Job Evaluation

The second application of job analysis data involves the classification and/or evaluation of a job. Once a job has been designed and defined, the information about the content, requirements, and context of the job can be used to classify or to evaluate the job in relation to others or to a preestablished structure so as to determine the job's worth or value.

The VERJAS procedures provide sufficient data for most classification or job evaluation systems. Because VERJAS gathers and documents job facts for a variety of purposes and not just for classification or evaluation, the information required by the factors of a specific evaluation system may be labeled slightly differently. For example, information about the duties and responsibilities of a job is recorded on Duty and Task Worksheets (see Exhibits 12 and 13). Information about knowledge and skill requirements of a job is listed on the Basic and Special Competencies Worksheets (see Exhibits 17 and 18). Since content and requirements data are also used for other purposes, including selection, performance appraisal, and training, the VERJAS worksheets provide more specific and detailed information than is generally gathered for classification or job evaluation. This additional information, however, is useful in clearly distinguishing one job (or class of jobs) from another and in supporting classification, evaluation, or pay decisions. Information about other classification or evaluation factors is listed on the Job Context Worksheet (see Exhibit 14). This worksheet describes the context in which the job is performed in terms of traditional factors including the amount and kind of supervision received and/or exercised, the nature and extent of guidelines available, the extent to which research and analysis is required, the degree of accountability or potential consequence of error, the type and nature of personal contacts made, and the physical demands and working conditions of the job.

VERJAS is applicable to various kinds of jobs or positions—managerial, clerical, trade. The same procedures are followed to collect and to document information about each type. How an organization chooses to evaluate this information, weighing and rewarding more for some job characteristics than for others, is a policy decision involving philosophical as well as business considerations entirely separate from the job analysis.

Recruitment

Job analysis data can also be used to provide applicants and potential applicants with a clear picture and understanding of the job and its requirements. For example, a job analysis utilizing a preliminary version of VERJAS was conducted for an organization interested in improving its method of selecting plant sales managers. The analysis identified a set of "make or break" performance factors.* These were used to develop a

---

*Stephen Bemis; Frank Schmidt, Ph.D.; and James Caplan, Ph.D., using a procedure that was actually a modification of the Behavorial Consistency Method.

self-screening checklist (see Exhibit 27) to be used by persons interested in applying for the job. In another situation, a sign-off sheet (see Exhibit 28) was developed for a public utility company which wanted senior bidders for the job of division dispatcher to be aware of the requirements and personal demands of the job. Too often, applicants do not have sufficient knowledge of the job to make an informed decision about whether to apply. Assessing individuals who do not possess even the minimum qualifications or those who are not interested in the job once they understand its requirements is wasteful for both individuals and the

Exhibit 27. Self-Screening Checklist for Plant Sales Managers

INSTRUCTIONS:

For these first questions dealing with your ability to become a plant sales manager, you will check "yes" or "no" in the appropriate box. These questions represent "minimum qualifications" in the sense that you should be able to answer "yes" to all of them before going on to Part II.

Be sure your answer to each question is sincere, otherwise you could find yourself in a position that you couldn't do or didn't like. If you cannot honestly answer "yes" to all questions, it may indicate that you need further training in order to qualify for a sales manager's position.

A. Are you able to communicate effectively with both superiors and subordinates?
Yes _____ No _____

B. Do you have the strong will and determination necessary to stand up for your ideas?
Yes _____ No _____

C. Are you able to carry out policies willingly even if you don't agree with them?
Yes _____ No _____

D. Do you have the flexibility to adapt to changes and to modify plans accordingly?
Yes _____ No _____

E. Do you have a basic understanding of all aspects and levels of sales operations?
Yes _____ No _____

F. Do you enjoy market evaluations and direct contact work?
Yes _____ No _____

G. Are you profit oriented?
Yes _____ No _____

H. Are you willing and able to work long hours?
Yes _____ No _____

I. Are you a good salesperson?
Yes _____ No _____

J. Are you able to establish priorities?
Yes _____ No _____

K. Are you able to delegate?
Yes _____ No _____

L. Are you able to exercise leadership by setting good examples for subordinates?
Yes _____ No _____

M. Are you able to plan sales programs?
Yes _____ No _____

Exhibit 28. Job Information Form for Division Dispatcher*

The following questions reflect aspects of the Division Dispatcher job. They represent "minimum qualifications" in the sense that you should be able to answer "yes" to all of them before entering the Dispatcher training program.

Be sure your answer to each question is sincere, otherwise, you could find yourself in a position that you couldn't do or didn't like.

QUESTIONS AND ANSWERS	EXAMPLES
1. Are you willing to make decisions on your own even in emergency situations? Yes _____ No _____	1. A Dispatcher might have to cut off the power in one section in order to save the rest of the system.
2. Are you able to apply information to solve a problem in stress situations? Yes _____ No _____	2. Dispatchers have to apply knowledge of the system to decide quickly how to provide service by bypassing a problem area.
3. Are you able to take harrassment without it affecting your judgment? Yes _____ No _____	3. Customers might harass a Dispatcher when they discover their electricity was cut off for nonpayment.
4. Are you able to deal with several problems at the same time? Yes _____ No _____	4. During a storm, a Dispatcher will have a multitude of problems to deal with at the same time.
5. Are you able to apply your technical knowledge to solve a problem? Yes _____ No _____	5. Most of the Dispatcher duties involve the application of technical knowledge.
6. Are you able to decide quickly what to do first when there are several things which must be done as soon as possible? Yes _____ No _____	6. A Dispatcher might be faced with a block of houses which are out of electricity with an iron lung being used in one, while a rescue unit is waiting for a line to be de-energized before they can treat an accident victim.
7. Are you able to act on a decision in spite of distractions? Yes _____ No _____	7. Police and customers may be calling on the telephone and the Line Repairer calling on the two-way radio while the Dispatcher tries to act on the decision described in the example above.
8. Are you able to reason logically? Yes _____ No _____	8. Dispatchers frequently need to track down likely sources of problems—such as a bad transformer—for the Line Repairer.
9. Are you able to get along with people? Yes _____ No _____	9. Dispatchers, like most people, encounter unpleasant people occasionally. Dispatchers may need to continue to talk with such people in spite of their feelings in order to accomplish their job.
10. Can you make common sense judgments? Yes _____ No _____	10. When their electricity is cut off, many people will have reasons that sound good why their bill wasn't paid. A Dispatcher must decide when to call the credit manager at home or when to restore service.

*This form is completed by job bidders.

Exhibit 28. Job Information Form for Division Dispatcher—*continued*

QUESTIONS AND ANSWERS	EXAMPLES
11. Are you willing and able to work shifts? Yes _____ No _____	11. Dispatchers must work shifts. Some find that there are family pressures when they work any shift other than days, and others resent the influence of shift work on their social life.
12. Do you have basic ability in math (i.e., can you add, subtract, multiply, and divide whole numbers, decimals, and fractions)? Yes _____ No _____	12. Dispatchers must make computations based upon electrical formulas.

organization. Frequently, a current and accurate job description is sufficient to help candidates determine whether they are interested in a specific job. Some organizations provide a book of such descriptions for "walk-in" candidates to review before applying for jobs. Having informed applicants apply for jobs in which they are actually interested, and for which they have the basic qualifications, can provide a more realistic base from which to review an organization's applicant/employee profile.

Selection

A fourth application of job analysis data is selection. Selection decisions, for both entry and promotion in an organization, must be based on objective information about the skills, areas of knowledge, abilities, and other competencies required to perform the job, rather than on unrelated characteristics of the applicant(s).*

Detailed information about the tasks and duties of a job, the competencies required, and the context in which it is performed allow an organization to identify job-related selection criteria and to develop job-related selection instruments.

For example, if one job task is to "type graphs, charts, tables, etc.," then one *critical* job requirement would be "skill in formatting graphs, charts, tables"; and it would be relevant to assess whether and to what degree applicants possessed this skill. If the job included only straight copy or form typing, however, this would not be a relevant job requirement.

VERJAS allows you to identify basic and special competencies needed to perform the job. These job requirements are linked back to tasks and

---

*Although the use of job analysis data will help assure job relatedness, the demonstration of validity in court of law, when required, involves additional considerations. For instance, some might argue that some of the competencies shown in the examples in this section are constructs and cannot be justified on the basis of content validity. See Chapters 1 and 5 for a more detailed discussion of the legal issues involved in job relatedness.

can be related to contextual factors to provide examples of how, and in what environment, the competency (knowledge, ability, skill, and other characteristic or circumstance) is used.

There are a number of different selection techniques or instruments— ways of gathering and assessing applicants' qualifications. The specific method or methods used depend on a variety of factors, such as the nature of the job, the number of positions available and the kind and number of applicants expected. This section discusses five selection methods: application forms, interviews, written tests, assessment centers, and work samples.

Tailored Application Blanks

Job analysis data can be used to develop application blanks, to be used along with standard applications, which are tailored to the requirements or competencies necessary for a particular job or occupation. These Tailored Application Blanks (TABs), sometimes called Supplemental Application Forms (SAFs), enable an organization to increase the job relatedness of experience and education ratings or "unassembled examinations" and to assess more accurately applicants' qualifications as described on resumes and applications. This selection procedure is commonly used, particularly for professional and managerial jobs, and provides good data for selection decisions. Ratings of education and experience, however, are liable to charges of bias, subjectivity, and non-job-relatedness. TABs, developed from the job analysis data, ask all applicants to provide the same information or to answer the same questions and thereby assure that all candidates are assessed on the basis of comparable information.

In an example mentioned earlier in this chapter, a preliminary version of VERJAS was used to help a client to improve selection procedures for plant sales managers. Differentiating factors were identified, and then used to develop a tailored application blank. Exhibit 29 shows a page from this application form. (On the actual form, this page is preceded by detailed instructions explaining what activities should be included.) Other pages on this application form cover the following areas:

1. *Ability to deal with people.* Plant Sales Managers must be able to select, train, motivate, and command the respect of people in order to get sales results from the entire department. They must maintain control of the sales operation while encouraging creativity and freedom of thought.

2. *Profit orientation.* Plant Sales Managers must understand the impact of costs on profit. They must be able to differentiate between costs beneficial to profit on a short- or long-term basis and costs that have no

Exhibit 29. Tailored Application Blank for Plant Sales Managers

I. ABILITY TO COMMUNICATE

Plant Sales Managers must be able to establish and maintain communication with customers, subordinates, peers, and superiors. They must be able to speak, to write, and to listen effectively.

In the space below, continuing onto the back of the page, if necessary, describe achievements or accomplishments demonstrating your ability to communicate effectively. *Remember to include for each achievement* (1) what your objective was, (2) what you did and when (approximate date), (3) what the outcome was, (4) the extent to which you were responsible for the achievement (estimate the percent for which you claim credit), and (5) the name and telephone number of somebody who can verify the achievement.

(Continue on the back of this page. You may then use additional sheets of paper if necessary.) *Do not complete* the following rating until *after* you have described your relevant achievements.

My record demonstrates:

no ability	some ability	between 1 & 3	moderate ability	between 4 & 5	exceptional ability
0	1	2	3	4	5

The statements I have provided on this factor are accurate descriptions of my own achievements and the above rating reflects what I believe to be a fair evaluation of the achievements described.

Signature: _____ Date: _____

return. They must know when to spend money to earn money and when expenses are unnecessary.

3. *Management skills.* Sales Managers must be able to develop, execute, and follow up a plan. The planning might be short range, such as planning the content of a sales call, or long range, such as planning holiday sales strategies in advance.

4. *Analysis and decision making.* Plant Sales Managers must analyze details such as market conditions and sales patterns and decide how to solve problems. Plant Sales Managers must also be able to evaluate their staff and act on that evaluation.

In another situation, the manufacturer of large transportation equipment was vexed by an inability to find managers of quality control who could perform successfully at one of the plants. A blue-ribbon committee of subject matter experts (plant manager, vice president of quality control, chief of engineering, and others) were taken through the brainstorming process. They identified a number of elements that were key to success in that particular plant, and less important elsewhere. The differences were related to proximity to corporate offices and a slightly different product line that was of particular interest to inspectors of the U.S. Department of Transportation, who made regular inspections. The important factors were related to the willingness to make tough decisions and the ability to make them stick, rather than to more engineering or quality control knowledge. A tailored application blank eliciting information about these requirements was developed.

Interviews

Interviews are another selection device vulnerable to charges of subjectivity, non-job-relatedness, and ineffectiveness. Interviews can be, however, both nondiscriminatory and effective. Job analysis data can be used to develop structured interview guides, much like tailored application blanks, to ensure that comparable information is obtained from all candidates, to document candidate responses, and to prevent the asking of illegal or inappropriate questions by the interviewer. When the language requirements of a job are lower than those required to read and complete a written TAB, an interview guide is an appropriate alternative for gathering basic information about applicants' qualifications. Interviews also help to differentiate among equally qualified candidates with regard to the basic competency requirements of the job. In addition, a structured interview guide can be developed to elicit information about the extent to which candidates possess the special competencies needed for the job.

The VERJAS brainstorming procedure has been used to identify elusive factors that cause less than successful job placements. In one situation, a public utility company was interested in developing a content-valid test of electrical knowledge for selecting union workers for promotion to the job of division dispatcher. The job analysis showed that although electrical knowledge was an important factor, interpersonal skills and stress tolerance were the real keys to successful job performance, especially in emergency situations. An interviewer checklist (see Exhibit 30) was developed that enabled the supervisor to obtain information for evaluating whether applicants possessed these competencies, and to what extent.

There are a number of advantages to the use of a structured interview. As outlined in *Integrated Job Analysis* (Buckly et al., 1980), such standardization enables one to:

1. obtain information on all competencies identified for assessment with the interview;

2. focus on these competencies and associated tasks rather than irrelevant topics;

3. gain as much information as possible within the given time period of the interview;

4. obtain behavioral information rather than abstract, hypothetical information.

Within the format of the structured interview, a combination of question types should be used. The same evaluation, open-ended, and/or situational questions should be asked of all candidates with appropriate follow-up questions of the direct and yes/no type. This method of questioning is known as "funneling," with the questions going from general to specific. By funneling, interviewers can ensure that they obtain the information necessary to assess applicants on job-related competencies. Furthermore, they can obtain information that applicants may overlook or attempt to hide.

While the format of direct and yes/no questions is known to all, examples of open-ended, situational, and evaluation questions may be helpful.

1. Example of an *open-ended* question for Cafeteria Worker:

"What did you do the last time the grill you were using began malfunctioning and caused you to stop working?"

2. Example of a *situational* question for Labor Relations Manager:

"A supervisor wants to fire a subordinate due to the subordinate's lack of motivation, tardiness, and below-standard work. However, the subordinate has filed a grievance with the union saying she is being harassed by the supervisor because she is the only female in the department. How would you handle this situation?"

Exhibit 30. Interview Guide for Division Dispatcher*

In addition to technical knowledge, a number of worker characteristics have been found to be necessary to successful performance as a Division Dispatcher. You should discuss each of these worker characteristics and the related job duties with candidates for Division Dispatcher positions to make sure that all candidates understand the job fully. This form is intended to serve three purposes:

1. It provides you a list of the important worker characteristics to jog your memory in discussions with candidates.
2. It documents the date when you discussed the item with a candidate.
3. It may be used to record any notes you may want to make about points that come up in the discussion with the candidate.

Candidate: _____

NECESSARY WORK COMPETENCIES	DATE DISCUSSED	NOTES
Ability to apply technical knowledge		
Ability to apply information in stress situation		
Willingness to make decisions		
Ability to accept responsibility for decisions		
Ability to set priorities		
Ability to act on priorities in spite of distractions		
Ability to reason logically		
Ability to take harassment		
Ability to deal simultaneously with several problems		
Knowledge of where to find information		
Ability to get along with people		
Ability to function under pressure		
Confidence in own ability to handle situations		
Ability to consider alternatives when normal solutions do not work		
Adaptability to changing situations		
Ability to communicate effectively (e.g., in dispatching line crews)		
Ability to comprehend complex problems and reach reasonable conclusions		

*To be completed by the job supervisor when interviewing candidates for a Division Dispatcher job.

3. Example of an *evaluation* question for Personnel Analyst:

"A personnel analyst was conducting a meeting and was faced with one job expert who repeatedly complained that he was a busy man and that it was a waste of his time to be sitting in this meeting. After listening to the complaints for about 30 minutes, the analyst told the job expert he could leave if he so desired. How do you feel about the way in which this analyst handled the situation?"

It is important that evaluation questions be carefully worded to make sure that they are not leading. A leading question in the above scenario would be one that asked "you would have handled the situation differently, wouldn't you?"

Reliable assessment through interviewing requires that both the interview questioning and assessment of responses be structured. Rating guidelines serve to focus the rater's attention on the specific competencies being assessed and on specific responses which are acceptable or unacceptable. At a minimum, rating guidelines should include brief descriptions of clearly acceptable (rating value of 2) and clearly unacceptable (rating value of 0) responses. It is desirable to include examples of possible responses at these levels and at two additional levels (3-clearly superior, and 1-marginal) with indications of corresponding benchmarks.

Generally, rating guidelines must be developed for each competency being assessed with each interview question. For certain competencies (usually knowledges), different sets of rating guidelines are needed for each question used to assess the competency. For other competencies (usually abilities), the same rating guidelines can be used for each question assessing the competency. Two examples of rating guidelines are shown below.

1. Example for Examination Analyst

Question: Assume you are conducting a meeting at which you are rating test items. One of the job experts complains about having been asked to such a meeting. This job expert disrupts the meeting and disturbs the other raters. What would you do?

Competency assessed:
Human Relations Ability

Rating guide:
    0—ignore him or do nothing
    0—tell him to leave when he first complains
    0—ask him to be quiet
    1—ask him to leave after about 30 minutes if he is still not cooperating
    2—work with him to obtain cooperation
    3—attempt to use peer group pressure to obtain cooperation

2. Example for Data Processing Supervisor

Question: A box of cards has been punched from a set of data sheets. It is discovered that the numbers in column 78 through 80 on the data sheets are incorrect and therefore the cards are not usable. Explain your solution for this problem and discuss how you arrive at this solution:

Competencies assessed:
> Knowledge of Keypunch Procedures
> Decision-Making Ability

Rating guide:
> 0—have data sheets recoded and cards repunched
> 1—explain error to keypuncher and let keypuncher decide how to handle problem
> 2—have corrections indicated on data sheets, have cards duplicated up to column 78, have columns 78–80 repunched
> 3—have corrections indicated on data sheets, prepare drum card which automatically duplicates cards up to column 78, have columns 78–80 repunched

Written Tests

When there are many applicants for the same job, written examinations are frequently used as an early step in the selection process. If the tests are job related, this is the most efficient and objective way to reduce the number of applicants to a manageable number. Traditionally, many of these examinations were tests of general knowledge possessed by current employees, or needed for higher-level jobs in the organization rather than entry-level jobs. Everyone has many skills, abilities, and areas of knowledge that are not used in performing their job. Good judgment and the prevailing legal climate dictate, however, that when selecting individuals for a job, we assess only those skills, abilities, and knowledge areas required to perform the work.

The basic and special competencies identified through the VERJAS procedures provide data to develop valid (job-related) examinations. For instance, if a trait such as honesty were identified as a critical job requirement, this information would be part of the data needed by a psychologist to develop a construct valid test or assessment of honesty. Similarly, VERJAS provides data needed by those trained to design and to conduct criterion-related validation studies. For instance, job information is essential to the development of useful and defensible criterion measures of job success, such as work performance measures, ratings of job performance, or tenure. Other uses of VERJAS data in a criterion-related validation study are in the identification or development of a battery of experimental tests, identification of an experimental sample, and specification of the positions for which the final battery of selection tests should be used. The VERJAS data also provide guidance on the portability of tests developed for other jobs, locations, and/or organizations to specific situations.

VERJAS data are useful in the development of written examinations through the content sampling approach. In this approach, knowledge or skills required at time of job entry are specified and their level defined. For example, in preparing a content-valid written examination for a clerk typist/receptionist, specific items can be developed from "knowledge of typing format," and "knowledge of correct English language usage (grammar, spelling, punctuation) sufficient to correct errors and to type dictated copy." In developing an examination for Line Repairer, specific questions can be written to assess applicants' understanding of the role of transformers, their knowledge of resistance, of how to prevent shock, and of other aspects of electricity, if it is reasonable for applicants to have this knowledge before selection.*

Work Samples

Job analysis data, such as that developed through the VERJAS procedures, can be used to develop effective content-valid work samples for many jobs. This selection device may require more time, both to develop and to apply, but the close relationship to the job suggests the use of this approach when job relatedness is likely to be questioned. The U.S. Office of Personnel Management has suggested that work samples which closely replicate the work performed on the job appear to be the best alternative to written tests for selection and promotion decisions (U.S. OPM, 1980).

The VERJAS data base provides information on the skills, abilities, and areas of knowledge required to perform the job; it also provides task and contextual data that illustrate how the competencies are used in the job situation. For example, applicants for clerical positions are often given a standardized straight copy, timed typing test which measures speed, accuracy, and basic typing ability. Some clerical jobs, such as the Clerk-Typist/Receptionist, may require additional competencies not assessed by a traditional typing test, but critical to successful job performance. A more effective approach is to use actual material from the job to construct a work sample, or job simulation to evaluate applicants' competencies, such as "ability to type final copy from handwritten material," "ability

---

*Usually such an examination would be given at the conclusion of training, prior to a candidate's actual performance in the field as a Line Repairer. Thus, it would be part of one of the final steps in the selection process.

to use standard reference sources (dictionary, style manual)," and "knowledge of correct English language usage (grammar, spelling, punctuation) sufficient to identify and correct errors and type dictated copy."

Another, more generalized approach to the use of work samples is represented by the work of the Job Trials Research Center of the Jewish Employment and Vocational Service. The work samples developed by this group are oriented to specific jobs, but simulate tasks which cut across organizational lines. For example, the job trials for a bank teller involve counting money, cashing checks, and balancing a cash drawer, all of which would be required of a teller at any bank (Fiks, Bawden, and Gaspair, 1976).

Assessment Centers

Job analysis data can also be used to develop assessment center simulations. This method of selection is frequently used after an initial pool of candidates for managerial or other demanding jobs has been reduced to a manageable number. An assessment center allows a number of evaluators to see the candidates perform such activities as dealing with information in a simulated in-basket. Skills, abilities, and areas of knowledge to be assessed are identified from the Basic and Special Competency data. They can then be combined to form job dimensions. For example, consider the Plant Sales Manager job: the basic competency ("ability to speak and understand the English language sufficient to obtain/convey information from/to customers and sales force") might be combined with aspects of special competencies ("ability to deal with people—motivate, train, command respect—in order to get sales results"), ("ability to establish rapport and maintain communications with client"), and ("ability to explain assignments to staff, suggest ways of carrying out, point out available resources, etc.") to form an "Oral Communication" job dimension. Duty/Task and Context Worksheets provide more specific examples of exactly how, and in what context, a skill or knowledge is used.

Work samples generally replicate actual tasks and are therefore situation specific. Assessment centers, on the other hand, are developed so that they can apply in a variety of settings. This allows for a fair evaluation of candidates, regardless of their knowledge of the organization or job environment. The work sample exercise must fairly simulate the way in which the competency or dimension is applied on the job, however. For example, candidates for the Plant Sales Manager position discussed above might be assessed on how well they performed various administrative tasks of an "in-basket" exercise* for an insurance executive.

---

*An in-basket exercise requires candidates to review a number of issues described in papers, memos, messages, calendars; to establish priorities; and to act upon them (approve, disapprove, delegate) in a specified period of time.

Assessment centers were originally developed as a selection technique for managerial jobs. They have gained popularity for other jobs, such as police, fire, lower level managerial, and supervisory, for which critical requirements are difficult to evaluate by other methods. They have generally been well received by the courts when they were based on job-related data and administered objectively and consistently.

Medical Standards for Physically Demanding Jobs

Some jobs place such physical demands on workers that medical standards are needed to restrict entry into the job. VERJAS identifies the tasks which are critical and also have injury potential characteristics. These are characteristics that have a potential for injury to those individuals who appear healthy from a medical viewpoint, but who are at a low level of the healthy range. Any task which meets both of these criteria should be examined to see if it involves a high rate of injuries and worker compensation claims. As explained by Deborah L. Gebhardt (Gebhardt, 1982), these tasks should then be subjected to an in-depth analysis to determine exactly what movements are taking place and how they affect the muscularskeletal system in the present—and after five or ten years. Such an analysis is the key to successfully determining which physical conditions cause, or have the potential to cause, injury, absenteeism, or poor job performance.

Frequently medical disqualifiers have been applied broadly to "physical" jobs without an appreciation of the different activities involved in each of the jobs. Medical disqualifiers must be legitimate and job related in order to serve the needs of the employer and to be defensible. The two primary concerns are whether (1) the existing medical condition limits or precludes the person's ability to perform the job duties and (2) the presence of the disease creates a health risk for the individual.

The job and physiological analyses provide the data needed for a physician's manual. Such a manual helps the physician do his or her job better and documents the job-relatedness of the medical standards. The manual should include: (1) a brief description of the job, (2) medical disqualifiers detailed in chart form, and (3) information on tests which should be used and the results needed, shown in chart form.

Selection Grid

After a decision has been made as to which competencies will be assessed in the selection process, it is useful to prepare a selection grid to make certain that all critical competencies are addressed at the appropriate step or steps of the process. Competencies which are minimum qualifications should be addressed in the initial stage of the process, perhaps through a review of experience and education as reported on a TAB, or by a written examination. Special competencies should be assessed at the end of the process, when applicants have demonstrated that they possess the minimum qualifications and basic competencies for the job.

Exhibit 31 is one example of a selection grid. Typical components of a selection plan are shown across the top, and the competencies to be evaluated are listed down the side. The grid should be designed to accommodate all steps of an organization's selection plan. The plan may include other components in addition to those discussed in this section, such as reference checks, and review of biodata. It should be noted that VERJAS may not provide appropriate data to support all medical examinations or biodata assessments.

Training

Managers are responsible for assuring that training funds are spent in the development of employee competencies that are currently needed in the organization or will be needed in the future. At the employee level, these may be competencies required on the present job or on the jobs to which the employee aspires. This is the fifth application of job analysis data.

In addition, when new goals, programs, procedures, techniques, or equipment are introduced, changes in the tasks or content of the job and/or the context in which they are performed may result, with consequent changes in the competencies needed. Any of these changes should trigger a review of the job analysis data base, both to ensure that it is current and to identify what additional training is needed. The need for training may also be identified through the performance-appraisal process. Unsuccessful performance *may* be the result of insufficient knowledge, skill, or ability and may be remedied by additional training. Job analysis data such as those developed in VERJAS provide the basis for identifying some of the training needs of an organization and developing a training program to meet them.

Identifying Training Needs

Organizations find training necessary to supplement the competencies workers bring to their jobs. It is not practical or even appropriate to assess whether applicants possess all of the competencies of successful performance at the full-performance level. Competencies that are organizationally based and can be learned through either orientation or on-

Exhibit 31. Selection Plan

Competency	Learned in Brief Orientation	Learned On-the-Job	Self-Evaluation	Training & Exper. Review/ Rating	Written Test	Work Sample	Biodata	Interview	Reference Check	Medical Exam	Assessment Center

the-job training are not appropriate selection criteria. For example, while you can evaluate applicants' "ability to type letters" and "knowledge of typing format," you cannot expect applicants to have knowledge of an organization's specific form or style. Further, within a given labor market, it may not be possible to find sufficient candidates with specific competencies to fill all positions. For example, few candidates in the job of Line Repairer are able to climb poles without steps unless specially trained.

To identify the training needed by a new worker or group of workers: (1) review the VERJAS Task and Competency Worksheets against the selection plan or grid to determine what additional competencies are needed for acceptable performance but were not assessed at selection; (2) note the Basic Competencies specific to the organization and for which orientation, on-the-job, or classroom training must be provided, and (3) review the Special Competency Worksheet that lists those knowledges, skills, and abilities which have been associated with successful workers, particularly noting competencies rated " + + " (extremely useful) on importance, and "S" (spread out), or "L" (fairly low), on availability.

Developing Training Curricula

Specific job-related training curricula can be developed from the job analysis data base. Training objectives can be identified directly from content and contextual data which furnish examples of how, and under what conditions, a competency is used. If more specific information about methods or procedures is needed, it must be obtained from technical manuals. Successful completion of training programs is measured by the ability to perform the tasks.

Performance Appraisal

The sixth application of job analysis data is performance appraisal. In developing and implementing a performance appraisal system, the manager's goal should be to make what can often be a subjective process as objective as possible. Two general judicial principles, derived from laws, regulations, and relevant case decisions, concern the issue of subjectivity in performance appraisal. The first is that performance evaluation must be based on workers' qualifications and not on their race, color, religion, sex, national origin, or age. The second is that criteria for evaluation must be job related and valid when there is a disparate impact on members of a protected group. Both principles necessitate that a defensible performance appraisal system be based on a careful analysis of the job. (See discussion of Feild and Holley study in Chapter 1.)

Job analysis data such as those developed in VERJAS provide the basis for developing performance criteria and standards which are behavior- and result-, rather than trait-oriented and for identifying specific indicators of various levels of performance. Job content (task) data (e.g., types letters) lead directly to the identification of the criteria (e.g., accuracy) for assessing how well a worker is performing a task, to the development of performance standards describing more specifically what will be assessed (e.g., no errors on final copy), to the identification of performance indicators that describe how performance will be monitored (e.g., based on review of copy when signing on periodic "sample" days).

There must be a clear understanding and documented agreement between workers and supervisors about performance standards and how they will be measured. Since the VERJAS procedures require the involvement of both workers and supervisors in identifying duties and tasks, this process can be easily and logically extended to include identification of performance criteria, standards, and indicators. Workers continue to be an important source of information about their jobs and often are more familiar with the specific procedures, equipment, and the day-to-day or hour-to-hour flow of work than is their manager. They may be able to suggest appraisal standards and ways of monitoring performance that are both effective and practical.

Information about performance criteria, standards, and indicators can be documented on the Individual Position Summary (see Exhibit 16). In Chapter 3, in which gathering and documenting content, competency, and contextual information were discussed, only duties and tasks were recorded on the form. The remaining columns provide a means of converting the job analysis data into a useful and defensible performance appraisal system for many jobs (see Exhibit 32).

Begin by reviewing the basic job analysis data (Task, Context, and Competency Worksheets), considering the job actions or behaviors, and the resulting products or services in order to identify appropriate criteria and standards. For example, one criterion for a task of "types letters" might be "speed or timeliness" and the standard applied might be "completion within X period of time." Once a potential standard has been identified, it must be considered in relation to the environment or context in which the task is performed. For example, if the job involves only typing and filing tasks, it might be appropriate to expect and to set a higher standard of speed and timeliness than if the job also involved answering the telephone and greeting visitors, activities which interrupt the typing tasks. Performance criteria and standards are entered in columns 3 and 4 of the Individual Position Summary Form.

Often the most difficult part of the performance appraisal process is identifying and developing indicators of performance and ways of mon-

Exhibit 32. Individual Position Summary Form

Job Title: Clerk Typist/Receptionist   Position No.: 327   Page No.: 1

1. Duties	2. Tasks	3. Performance Criteria	4. Performance Standards	5. Indicators of Performance
I. Typing*	1. Types letters, memos, and reports*	Speed	At least 4 dbl. space new pgs. completed or 15 forms filled in per typing hour.	Difficult to measure due to phone and visitor interruptions.
	2. Types/transcribes letters, memos, and reports*	Accuracy	No more than one uncorrected error per draft page or per 4 forms.	Note weekly the number of draft pages returned for retyping due to copying/transcribing/formatting errors.
	3. Types forms and form letters*			
	4. Proofreads and corrects	Accuracy	No errors on final copy.	Note weekly the number of final products returned for retyping due to typist error.
II. Answering telephone/greeting visitors*	5. Answers telephone*	Quality/Accuracy	All calls answered pleasantly & referred properly. Complete & accurate messages taken.	Randomly choose 6-8 wks. over the course of a yr. and keep track of all messages.
	6. Greets visitors*	Quality	All visitors greeted pleasantly and made to feel welcome.	Make a note any time a visitor comments positively or negatively about their reception.
III. Filing	7. Files	Accuracy	Alphabetical and numerical filings done accurately. 95% accuracy in subject filings.	Spot-check files 3-4 times a year.
	8. Searches files/pulls documents	Timeliness/Accuracy	Requested information found expeditiously at least 95% of the time.	Check files whenever materials cannot be found. Note whether materials are in proper place.

Signature—Supervisor: Joanne Margolis   Signature—Employee: Roberta Wood   Date: 6-11-83 itoring and documenting actual performance in relation to the established standards. The monitoring process should be practical and integrated into on-going operations and should make use of existing forms and reports to the greatest possible extent. The manager will need to draw on information about the checks and balances built into the flow of work and those inherent in some kinds of work, such as bookkeeping. Typically, performance is monitored by the supervisor who reviews work in progress and/or upon completion. Job analysis data—specifically, task and contextual information—should be reviewed to identify additional or alternative sources of information on workers' performance. In some jobs, clients, customers, or other recipients of products or services may be able to provide a better, or at least a different, view of performance. For example, user satisfaction is an important aspect of computer programmers' or system analysts' work. Job analysts should be particularly concerned with obtaining additional sources of information about performance if all or most of the supervisors are white males and the workers are primarily minorities or women or both.

Information about how performance will be monitored is recorded in the last column under "Indicators of Performance" of the Individual Position Summary form. Consider the criticality or importance of each task in determining which standard should weigh most heavily in evaluating overall job performance. (Refer to Part II of the Task Worksheet (Exhibit 13) for information about the criticality and importance of the task.) Finally, note or "star" those standards identified for additional weight.

5. Legal Perspectives

Evolving Standards

After more than a decade of litigation, employers and employees are aware that employment procedures which have an adverse impact on the employment opportunities of a race, sex, or ethnic group, and which are not job related, are illegal. Sophisticated employers recognize that the applicable legal and professional standards for demonstrating job relatedness, including the methods and uses of job analysis, are still evolving. To these, and to most other employers, personnel managers and specialists, psychologists, and other persons involved in human resource management, the extent, direction, and impact of the legal standards for job analysis are still unrecognized and unclear. Even the majority of attorneys are not fully aware of the complexities involved in this particular legal arena.

Judicial interpretations of government regulations and laws relevant to job analysis are particularly unfamiliar and problematic. The recent profusion of information published on the topic has confused rather than clarified the situation. This chapter and other legal information in the book are intended to help remedy this, providing as complete an answer as possible at present to the questions, "What is going on?" and "What can I do?"

This book is not intended to be a legal text or casebook, nor is it intended to cover all the laws, cases, and issues related to employment practices. These are more explicitly addressed by other materials, e.g., Schlei and Grossman's *Employment Discrimination Law* (1983). A basic understanding of the applicable laws is also assumed. More specific information on federal and state fair employment requirements and related court cases is available and routinely updated in *Fair Employment Practice Cases* (The Bureau of National Affairs, Inc.). The aim here is to advise personnel practitioners on the most important laws and court cases where job analysis played a major part in determining the validity of an employment practice or policy.

This chapter also presents a framework which allows employers and personnel practitioners to understand legal guidelines and judicial decisions, to know whether their own practices are meeting legal standards, to assign priorities for making changes in their practices, and to assess their possibilities for surviving and winning litigation. It is the authors' contention that sound job analyses which meet professional and legal standards are cost effective and make good business sense for numerous reasons. This is particularly true today as suits are more likely than in the past, as judges have become more knowledgeable and demanding, and as penalties for not having an adequate system have increased substantially.

Increased Likelihood of Suits

Employees and applicants are becoming more knowledgeable about their rights and more prone to sue (Singer, 1978; Smith, 1978). Over 5,000 employment discrimination cases are filed each year in federal district courts, with 48 percent of the nation's largest companies involved in such litigation. Further, half of the remaining companies not named in these suits admitted that employees had filed formal discrimination charges against them (Business Week).

The majority of the more sophisticated suits brought in the seventies were initiated by private parties and groups; however, tightened rules and regulations, more stringent recordkeeping and reporting requirements, and systematic enforcement procedures evidence the government's awareness and attention to proof of job relatedness in assuring equal employment opportunity. While federal enforcement efforts have varied depending on official priorities and concerns, these efforts have moved toward endorsement of job analyses which make sense pragmatically, socially, and psychometrically. Regardless of federal enforcement efforts, personnel practices based on job-related factors will usually help to insulate an employer from individual and union suits. With this perspective, judicial standards attain additional significance.

Sophisticated Judiciary

The courts are taking a more sophisticated, sterner look at employer's practices than in the past. The last few years have seen dramatic changes in the judicial standards for employment practices, with implications for job analysis. The imposed remedies have been changing dramatically too. For example, in one appellate court case in 1975 (*Shack v. Southworth*), the existence of a "rational" relationship between a hiring preference given to local police officers and job performance was sufficient to reject a black applicant's bias claim; but in 1979 a court barred the further use of a civil service test developed at a cost of over $1.25 million due to improper validation procedures (*U.S. v. State of New York*). A review of the early employment cases reveals that validation was only rarely and briefly mentioned, and the terminology was often conflicting and misused (Horstman, 1977). This is in marked contrast to more recent cases, where judges have rendered sophisticated decisions on complicated psychometric issues of test fairness and differential validity. New areas for litigation, such as the "employment at will" doctrine and layoffs, have yet to focus on job analysis, but have this potential, as described in Chapter 6.

Harsh Penalties

Severe monetary losses, imposed quotas, and loss of normal managerial control over employment practices have made many officials, managers, and personnel analysts painfully aware that previously acceptable practices and job analyses, if challenged, may not meet today's standards (Brady, 1979; Siegel, 1980). The increased likelihood of suit and the associated penalties of new, heightened standards are certain to bring to the attention of more managers and personnel officials the need for valid, nondiscriminatory personnel practices, including job analysis.

Private and public officials can now be held personally financially responsible for assuring nondiscrimination in employment practices. The U.S. Supreme Court first held a manager financially liable for failing to alter a discriminatory employment policy in 1978 (*Monell v. Department of Social Services of City of New York*). Other Supreme Court decisions have made federal officials personally liable for damages for violation of certain constitutional provisions and state and local officials personally liable for damages for violations of any federal law (Schuck, 1980).

Thus, theoretically, an employer could be held liable for discriminatory practices resulting from a poor job analysis system that failed to meet equal employment laws, regulations and guidance such as the Uniform Guidelines. At this writing there have been no such cases, but some relevant suits have been filed. The employer would not typically be insulated from such liability even if the analyses were conducted by an outside firm or individual. This is another reason for the wise manager to pay attention to the quality of the job analyses, whether conducted internally or externally.

Background

Before describing the new legal and professional standards, we provide the following background. Over 25 federal laws and numerous regulations prohibit discrimination in employment (Seberhagen, 1978). These laws all declare, in one form or another, that discrimination against protected classes on the basis of a non-job-related factor is illegal unless expressly provided for by statute. The Supreme Court's interpretation of these laws has established the legal doctrine that one has to measure the person for the job and not the person in the abstract (*Griggs v. Duke Power Co.*). Any test used should measure the requisite knowledges, skills, and abilities for a particular job. No test should be used unless it is demonstrably a reasonable measure of job performance.

Subsequent case law has delineated the standard for proof of non-discrimination and job relatedness and has included standards for job analysis in its considerations. Relevant federal guidance, especially the Uniform Guidelines on Employee Selection Procedures (1978) and the Questions and Answers published six months later to interpret and clarify the Guidelines, have emphasized the need for adequate job analysis to show job relatedness and to demonstrate that a person is not assessed in the abstract. Job analyses have been required, ranging from simple job descriptions to analyses sufficiently complex and detailed to comply with the Uniform Guidelines' technical requirements, depending on the circumstances and the type of employment decision (Greenman and Schmertz, 1979; Powers, 1976; Schlei and Grossman, 1983).

The psychological profession has not developed, nor does it intend to develop, an authoritative set of principles for job analysis; judicial standards, therefore, have assumed additional import (Manese, 1979; *Division 14 Principles*, 1980). The relationship between psychological standards for job analysis and legal standards was aptly summarized by the Chief Psychologist of the Equal Employment Opportunity Commission, Donald Schwartz (Schwartz, 1980), at a conference on job analysis as follows:

> I believe that the psychological profession has the ability to control the use of job analysis so as to differentiate between adequate and inadequate techniques. If it chooses not to do so . . . if it chooses to follow an "anything goes" philosophy that ignores the rights of individuals to be measured for the job and not in the abstract, that ignores the effect of its procedures on the disadvantaged groups in our society . . . then it must accept the fact that Congress and the courts will determine the standards that will govern the proper use of job analysis. (*Daily Labor Report*, 1980.)

Legal Standards

There is no legal requirement for employers to hire or to consider individuals for employment, nor is there a requirement to use or to validate selection measures and practices, unless adverse impact has been proven. Differentiating or discriminating among individuals on the basis of non-job-related factors is prohibited if it results in adverse impact, unless expressly provided for by law (Player, 1976). Title VII of the Civil Rights Act, the primary law affecting employment, permits employers to give and to act upon the "results of any professionally developed ability test." However, seemingly neutral selection criteria having a disparate impact on protected classes give rise to a *prima facie* case of employment discrimination in violation of Title VII. The defendant, generally the employer, must then establish that the selection criterion is a bona fide occupational qualification for the job or that it bears a demonstrable relationship to successful performance of the job for which it was used (Blumrosen, 1972). A professionally unacceptable procedure may be legal under Title VII if the procedure is judicially accepted as relevant and necessary (Koenig, 1974). A more detailed description of the legal standards of proof may be found in Agrid's *Fair Employment Litigation* (1979) or Madjeska's *Handling Employment Discrimination Cases* (1980).

Supreme Court Rulings

The Supreme Court first recognized the criticality of job analysis in 1971 in the case of *Griggs v. Duke Power Co.* In 1975 in *Albemarle Paper Co. v. Moody*, the Supreme Court made it clear that the relationship between selection criteria and job performance was not to be taken at face value, but to be established only after a thorough examination of the employer's operations, the history of the selection criteria under attack, and the validation guidelines promulgated by the EEOC. The Court in *Albemarle* also suggested that less restrictive devices might be required if plaintiffs proved "other tests or selection devices without a similar undesirable racial effect would also serve the employer's legitimate interest in efficient and trustworthy workmanship."

Uniform Guidelines on Employee Selection Procedures

The basic principles established by the Supreme Court in *Griggs, Albemarle*, and subsequent decisions directed the evolution of detailed, comprehensive regulatory standards for selection; most importantly, the Uniform Guidelines on Employee Selection Procedures. These Guidelines and the clarifying Questions and Answers on the Guidelines were issued by the Equal Employment Opportunity Commission, the Office of Personnel Management, the Department of Labor, and the Department of Justice, and were concurred with by the Department of the Treasury. They apply to most public and private employers throughout the United States. These Guidelines, which supersede the 1970 EEOC Guidelines on Employee Selection Procedures (republished in 1976) and the 1976 Federal Executive Agency Guidelines on Employee Selection Procedures, have been given great deference by the courts in evaluating employment practices and policies, especially on selection issues.

The Uniform Guidelines and the Questions and Answers will not be reproduced nor rephrased here. Only those aspects of the Uniform Guidelines and judicial decisions directly relevant to job analysis will be addressed, but employers and personnel analysts are strongly urged to strive for maximum understanding of, and compliance with, these Guidelines (Manese, 1980; Miner and Miner, 1979).

Other important federal mandates establishing standards for job analysis include the Rehabilitation Act of 1973 and the Age Discrimination Act and subsequent amendments, which respectively prohibit discrimination on the basis of handicap or age when these are not related to ability to perform the job. (See Chapter 6 for a discussion of the future impact of these laws.)

Job Analysis Requirements in the Guidelines

As noted previously, when an employment practice has an adverse impact on a protected group, the practice may be justifiably continued only by a showing of job relatedness or business necessity, usually through a formal study evidencing validity for the selection procedure. The Uniform Guidelines emphasize job analysis as one of numerous conditions and requirements for an acceptable validity study.

The most important situations involving the job analysis requirements in the Guidelines, according to one noted authority (Sparks, 1980), are:

1. Defending a selection procedure as content valid, i.e., the test or other evaluative procedure is representative of the job itself, knowledge necessary to performance of the job or a demonstration of the end product of the job.

2. Defending a selection procedure as having criterion-related validity, i.e., the test or other evaluative procedure correlates with or predicts some measure of job performance or other important measure of job success. Here the analysis must provide a rationale for choosing the evaluation measure and evidence that the criterion is important and reflects job requirements. A job analysis should be conducted to assure job similarity when combining employees from different departments to provide an adequate number for a validity study.

3. Transporting validity studies from one employer to another, wherein job analysis is used to demonstrate job comparability.

4. Development of performance appraisal forms.

5. Using training programs as job requirements for selection or promotion. Content of the training program should be based on an analysis of the job to which training will lead; in these situations the difficulty level of the training program should not be higher than that necessary to perform the job. (*Daily Labor Report*, 1979.)

Judicial Rulings on Job Analysis

Judges generally do not comment directly on the value of a specific job analysis approach or strategy. Standards of acceptability for job analysis procedures must be inferred from judicial rulings. Indeed, until 1982 the only job analysis strategy to evoke judicial discussion was the Job Element approach developed by Ernest Primoff and utilized in the development of the New York State Police trooper examination (see Chapter 2 for a fuller discussion of the Job Element Method). The Court declared that "the sole use of the job element method of job analysis and test development for other than blue collar jobs does not comport with generally accepted standards of the psychological profession" (*U.S. v. State of New York*). In *Berkman v. City of New York*, the judge carefully reviewed the methods used to analyze the jobs before ruling that the disputed examination was discriminatory. The ruling partially resulted from the failure of the job analysis methods to provide sufficient information to support the validation strategy. (This case is discussed in Chapter 6.) These decisions are also noteworthy for evidencing increasing judicial sophistication about job analysis methods.

Growing judicial awareness of the effect of seemingly unrelated employment practices on selection and promotion has shifted thinking to focus on numbers, or a "bottom line" mentality. Basically, the theory is that what counts with courts and enforcement agencies is the number of protected class members included in an employer's work force. Statistics have thus become powerful indicators of discrimination. As held in *Teamsters v. United States:*

> [I]mbalance is often a telltale sign of purposeful discrimination; absent explanation, it is ordinarily to be expected that nondiscriminatory hiring practices will in time result in a work force more or less representative of the racial and ethnic composition of the population in the community from which employees are hired. Evidence of long lasting and gross disparity between the composition of a work force and that of the general population thus may be significant even though 703(j) makes clear that Title VII imposes no requirement that a work force mirror the general population. (pp. 339–340 n. 20.)

The job analysis method used to support the employment practice will face much more rigorous scrutiny if the numbers of minority group members and women in the organization are extremely low.

Five Current Judicial Concerns

Judicial attention has been directed recently at five concerns where job analysis plays a significant part.

1. *Generalizability and transportability of studies.* A study is said to be generalizable or transportable when it can be used in a similar job or employment situation which it was not specifically designed to cover, e.g., for police officers in a different city or for a secretary in a company other than the one studied.

2. *Cutoff scores and ranking procedures.* These formalized measures for making selection decisions are frequently used by public and other large employers for reducing the number of applicants or candidates for a job to a more manageable size. For example, only applicants scoring above a 70 percent cutoff score might be considered for employment.

3. *The "inferential leap."* In providing person-job linkage, this refers to the assumptions necessary to establish that a job *behavior* is truly predicted or reflected by testing of *characteristics* such as knowledge or motor skills.

4. *Relevance of criteria.* Criteria such as performance appraisals, training academy scores, or job output data (number of widgets processed per hour) are relevant if they indicate something about performance or success on the job.

5. *Alternative methods of assessment.* Employers whose validated employment procedures have an adverse impact are required by the Guidelines to investigate alternative assessment measures or methods and to use the ones with less adverse impact. "Alternatives" is a term frequently used to refer to tests or selection procedures of equal validity and less adverse impact.

These and other matters concerning the *use* of assessment measures such as written tests are expected to continue to be in the legal spotlight in the near future and merit special attention. They are dealt with in more detail in what follows.

Generalizability

The Supreme Court and others have expressed concern when tests are used for situations based on studies done for other dissimilar situations. In *Albemarle*, an "odd patchwork of results" failed to entitle the company to use its test for either studied or unstudied jobs, as there was no analysis of the "attributes of, or skills needed in the studied job group" and "accordingly no basis for concluding that no significant differences existed" along progression lines. Thus the job analysis did not show sufficient relevance or similarity among jobs to allow the test to be used in the company's employment process.

Other employers have also had difficulty establishing similarity of jobs and the generalizability of test usage. For example, in *U.S. v. City of Chicago*, the defendant's argument that other agencies used similar entry tests was denied by Judge Marshall, who noted that as time passed, these tests were being declared invalid. The judge acridly added that "while the general practice in a trade or industry may be relevant to prove a standard of care, it has never, to our knowledge, been a defense to a charge of discrimination that everyone does it." In *Gosa v. Phelps*, the validation evidence relied on two studies; the primary one, however, was held deficient in several respects, including a failure to consider sample differences between Alabama and California police.

The generalizability of validity evidence to jobs with somewhat different duties was upheld more recently by a district court when empirical research showed that the tests did predict job performance and also showed that the state agency used all reasonable efforts to assure equal employment opportunities (*Pegues v. Mississippi State Employment Service*). Job analysis evidence documenting the general similarity of jobs, and empirical research demonstrating that test "validity is not perceptibly changed by differences in location, differences in specific job duties or applications" were ruled necessary to support generalized use of exams for similar jobs. However, the Court of Appeals held that, since the test in question had not been shown to have an adverse impact, the issue of validity could not have been legally addressed. In the words of the court, "That question remains for another day." Thus, more guidance as to the acceptable demonstration of generalizability of test usage should be forthcoming.

Cutoff Scores and Ranking Procedures

The Uniform Guidelines requirements [Section 5G, 14B(5) and (6), 14C(8) and (9)] to justify cutoff scores and ranking procedures used with written tests have been endorsed by several courts. For example, stronger evidence was ruled necessary for ranking candidates by order of test scores than if pass-fail or categorical ranking were used in *Guardians Association of New York City Police Dep't v. Civil Service Commission* and *Firefighters Institute for Racial Equality (FIRE) v. St. Louis*. In *FIRE*, the Court held, among other things, that because the test was a written multiple-choice examination purporting to select those firefighters who could be expected to perform the best in a physical, stressful job, empirical evidence (i.e., criterion-related validity) that the examination would actually accomplish that goal was required. In addition, the Court declared that greater evidence of validity was required because of the dissimilarity between the work situation and the multiple-choice exam. As noted in *Guardians*, such demonstration must be very substantial when a test procedure is used that does not closely approximate the job in order to reflect the fine gradations required for rank ordering.

Similarly, in *Louisville Black Police Officers v. Louisville*, the multijurisdictional test was found valid, based on a "commendable job analysis," and was found to "have greater relevance to the functions of a police officer than does the test in *Washington v. Davis*." Nevertheless, the Court found that "use of the ranking device violates the mandate of *Griggs*" and could not be used as before because of its substantial disparate impact. More precisely, the Court ruled that there was no evidence that those who scored highest on the exam would necessarily be the best qualified police officers, even though the test itself was found valid. The use of the cutoff score was also declared impermissible where a disproportionate impact on minority candidates resulted. Accordingly, an appellate court (*Sarabia* v. *Toledo Police Patrolman's Association*) approved a decision to require the certification of all black candidates passing the most recent test, citing expert witness testimony that "all those passing the tests were relatively equally qualified." Rank ordering may be justified on the basis of a job analysis, but if not, random selection from within a group validly determined to have passed an exam is an available option (*Association Against Discrimination in Employment v. City of Bridgeport*).

The "Inferential Leap"

Job analysis information should provide evidence that the measures of future work performance and behaviors are as relevant to the job as possible. This is particularly critical when using written examinations to test for stressful, physically demanding, or supervisory or management positions where cognitive measures may not be as important as noncognitive measures. Several decisions have upheld the need to stay as close as possible to work behaviors to minimize the "leap" between test and job duties; most notably, the case referenced earlier in this chapter as precedential for job analysis, *U.S. v. State of New York*. One of the primary issues in the case was whether the job analysis approach met the federal enforcement agency regulations' expressed desire for "minimizing the inferential leap between tests and performance" and the regulatory emphasis on observable work behaviors. The decision found that use of the Job Element approach was unacceptable and susceptible to bias because it failed to establish sufficient linkage between observable work behaviors (job tasks) and other characteristics identified as important for job success. The state's primary reliance on the judgment of incumbent personnel contributed to the possibility of exclusionary selection procedures. As this case illustrates, job analysis procedures which emphasize observable work behaviors and allow for outside input will best survive a court challenge.

Relevance of Criteria

The relevance of criterion measures has also been scrutinized more rigorously by judges during the past few years (Shaycroft, 1980). Criteria must be relevant and represent important or critical work behaviors. For example, tests that measure training success, consisting of paper and pencil tests, have been closely reviewed for evidence of job relevance, and in most instances have been found wanting. Job analysis information was successfully employed in *Washington v. Davis* to make it an exception in this regard.

More commonly, criteria used in validation strategies have been inadequately supported by job analysis information and thus have not been shown to be job relevant, as with the exams in *Ensley Branch, NAACP v. Seibels*. In this case, three criteria were used in the validation studies for the police and firefighter exams: (a) training academy grades, (b) official supervisory ratings, and (c) experimental ratings conducted by supervisors, but used only for exam development. The appellate court in *Ensley* ruled that the training academy grades were not proper, as these grades had not been shown to be related to job performance. Official supervisory ratings were untrustworthy assessments, the court said. The third criterion was suspect in part because the experimental ratings were positively correlated with the academy grades of employees with less than three years of service and negatively correlated with grades of those with more than three years of service. Similarly, in *Association Against Discrimination v. City of Bridgeport*, a job analysis which did not result in a detailed list of critical work behaviors and their relative importance was held to be perfunctory and inadequate to support the validity study. Thus, criteria with which test results are compared must be good, relevant measures of job performance (*James v. Stockham Valves & Fittings Co.*).

Alternative Methods of Assessment

The Guidelines' requirement that employers whose validated selection or promotion procedure has an adverse impact must investigate alternatives with less adverse impact has drawn severe criticism from employers and many psychologists. A supplementary question to the Questions and Answers on the Uniform Guidelines attempts to provide more guidance and to mitigate the concern over the "cosmic search" (as the alternatives section has been termed by those who believe it to be an endless search).

Starting with *Albemarle*, judicial endorsement of this federal requirement emphasizes that an employer consider alternative procedures and methods of selection and use the method having lesser adverse impact so long as it serves the "user's legitimate interest in efficient and trustworthy workmanship" and is "substantially equally valid." Employers have all too frequently construed this requirement to mean an endorsement of alternatives to written tests or an encouragement to focus on the bottom line. For example, some employers believed it was easier to stop giving written tests and hire the appropriate numbers of minorities and women rather than to investigate alternatives with lesser adverse impact and equal validity.

The U.S. Supreme Court decisions in *Kaiser Aluminum v. Weber* and *Fullilove v. Klutznick* alleviated many employers' fear of reverse discrimination suits; consequently, alternatives such as dual certification lists and other voluntary race-conscious hiring procedures are becoming increasingly common and judicially approved (Lorber and Horstman, 1980). For example, the U.S. Supreme Court recently declined to review a case where the California Supreme Court endorsed the voluntary adoption of a race-conscious program requiring one minority attorney to be hired for every two nonminority attorneys (*Price v. Sacramento County CSC*). As noted previously, information collected during job analysis can help to demonstrate that alternative methods of assessment with equivalent validity have been considered. There is at present some uncertainty over whose burden it is to find these alternatives, so employers and personnel analysts would be wise to utilize job analysis documentation procedures which include information showing the consideration of alternatives in order to assure legal compliance.

Professional Standards

Federal regulations and judicial decisions refer directly or implicitly to the prevailing professional standards; generally these are the existing standards of the psychological profession as set forth in the *Standards for Educational and Psychological Tests* of the American Psychological Association, the American Educational Research Association, and the National Council on Measurement in Education and in the *Principles of Division 14*, the Industrial-Organizational Division of the American Psychological Association. Textbooks, articles, research studies, and surveys of personnel practices have also been considered in determining of what is professionally acceptable. Legal standards have typically incorporated professional standards without conflict; however, this has not always been the case. Indeed, initially there was general uncertainty as to judicial acceptance of the Guidelines when they might conflict with professional standards (Cahoon, 1978; Lerner, 1979); however, the judiciary has increasingly accorded deference to the Guidelines principles (Rose, 1980). The appellate courts have uniformly endorsed the federal regulations with the possible exception of the *Guardians* case, where the court noted the difficulty of strict compliance with the Guidelines.

The 1980 revision of the *Principles of Division 14* proclaims disagreement with the federal enforcement regulations, the Uniform Guidelines. While this pronouncement is believed by some experts to be more philosophical than substantive, there have been no legal cases to test or resolve this seeming disparity.

The proposed revision of the *Standards* is expected to have more import, especially as it is the premier standard-setter. In addition, the revision of the *Standards* comes at a time of considerable debate about the Guidelines themselves. Hence, many individuals had looked to the new *Standards* for guidance in any revision of the Guidelines. A preliminary draft of the proposed 1984 Joint Technical Standards for Educational and Psychological Testing was released for comment in 1983. Portions of this draft met with substantial adverse reaction from many psychologists and employers, who felt the proposed standards were too idealistic and could be inappropriately interpreted and applied by attorneys and judges. The original schedule for revisions and approvals was considerably extended, with new standards now anticipated in 1985.

The changing, ambiguous nature of the professional and legal standards may be a primary reason why none of the current methods completely satisfies the need for job analysis information which meets management, legal, and psychometric concerns (Levine, Bennett, and Ash, 1979). The better known job analysis methods are considered in more depth in Chapter 2.

Putting It All Together—The Four-Factor Framework

Faced with ambiguous standards, changing laws, conflicting decisions, and expensive remedies, some personnel managers or employers have decided to give up sound personnel practices and wait until they are sued.

In 1975 over 115 books and articles on legal aspects of selection were cited in a bibliography published by the Equal Employment Opportunity Commission; the number has quadrupled since that time (Ashe, 1976; BNA, 1983; Brady, 1980; Sharf, 1975). This plethora of books and talks on compliance has aggravated the situation for most employers, and will probably continue to do so in the next decade. The following scheme has been developed by the authors to alleviate the pressure on employers by providing a framework for understanding the complexities of the laws and decisions with which to evaluate one's own priorities for job analysis. The Four-Factor Framework is a way for managers to "put it all together."

The underlying theory is that judicial decisions are based on *administrative, psychological, social,* and *legal* considerations which may be categorized to assess employer vulnerability and assign priorities to resources for compliance (Horstman, 1979). These factors or areas are catalysts for stimulating thinking, rather than rigorous categories. The four areas may be generally defined as follows:

Administrative. The administrative factor includes the extent of management's awareness and commitment to equal employment, the organization's information systems for collecting and analyzing data and for conducting periodic organizational audits, and the monies and efforts it expends on human resource management. For example, the use of legal and psychological experts to review and analyze objectively an organization's practices has been viewed positively by judges.

Psychological. The psychological or psychometric factor refers to the degree of compliance with the existing standards of the psychological profession as set forth primarily in the *Standards for Educational and Psychological Tests* and the Division 14 *Principles* of the American Psychological Association. Textbooks, articles, research studies, and surveys of personnel practices may also contribute to professional standards as previously explained.

Social. The social factor includes such matters as the prior industry practices, work atmosphere and conditions, attitude of employees, the visibility of the company or industry, and societal attitude toward the company. For example, a utility company is considered to be more vulnerable to discrimination suits than the Secret Service. While both organizations are known to the public, the Secret Service is more favorably perceived by the general public and is accorded more latitude on a variety of matters due to its protection mission.

Legal. The legal factor refers to the degree of compliance with the actual laws and regulations and previous judicial findings on the issue at question. For example, use of a test would be harder to justify by job analysis if the test had been found to be unlawfully discriminatory in several instances.

A judicial decision is rarely made on the basis of one factor alone; most decisions are made on the basis of all four factors. Each factor may be categorized as high (+), medium ($\sqrt{}$), or low (−) in relation to applicable standards. Generally, if more than two factors are high, the decision will be in the employer's favor; alternately, if more than two factors are low, the decision will be for the plaintiff.

In a situation where two factors are clearly high or low, and another factor which would "tilt the scales" is not clearly high or low, that factor will become the focus of the case. Exhibit 33 exemplifies how this four-factor framework could be used to analyze several major cases concerned

Exhibit 33. Four-Factor Framework

	Legal	Administrative	Psychological	Social	Decision in Favor of
Griggs*	−	−	−	−	P
Albemarle	−	−	−	√	P
Davis	−	+	−	+	E
Weber	+	+	n/a	−	E
Ensley	−	+	+	−	P
New York State Police	−	+	−	−	P
PPG Industries	−	+	+	√	E
Pegues	√	+	+	√	E

*Refer back to the beginning of the chapter for case descriptions. Other case examples may be obtained on request.

with job relatedness and where job analysis would be therefore significant.

For example, the factors in the *New York State Police* decision discussed earlier would be rated as follows: legal (−), administrative (+), social (−). The adequacy of the psychological technique was questionable. The legal factor would be rated low principally because of the extreme adverse impact, noncompliance with federal regulations, and prior case law involving police departments. The monies expended and initiation of a major validation study qualified for a (+) for the administrative factor, but the obvious bias of many of the troopers and administrators rated a low social (−). The psychological factor and the adequacy of the Job Element approach to job analysis was the focal point and thus became the crucial issue in the case. The judge determined the Job Element procedure did not meet professional standards for content validity. The psychological factor therefore was deemed a (−), and with three factors low, the decision was in favor of the plaintiff (P), not the employer (E). Note that the way a factor is rated may be determined on a comparative basis; thus, relevant technical issues were raised as to the psychological factor in *Ensley*, but the (+) rating reflects the better-than-average techniques employed.

These four factors establish a framework or set of standards derivable from judicial rulings which allows one to determine the degree of effort that must be put into the job analysis. It enables a manager or personnel analyst to have a complete picture of his or her organization's situation, which otherwise could be deduced only in fragments.

The Four-Factor Framework may be used *proactively* and not ʂ in reaction to events. For example, if a large, traditional comp social factor) with limited managerial concern for and action in sonnel area (the administrative factor) uses interviews (the psychological factor) resulting in adverse impact (the legal factor), it would have all four factors rated low and would need a much better job analysis to show job relatedness and nondiscrimination than if only two or three factors were low. The framework also may be used to determine the likelihood of success in court and where future efforts should be concentrated.

6. Future Issues in Job Analysis

Job analysis concepts are in a state of rapid change, as are the various techniques used to generate and analyze data. While it is difficult at this stage of development to arrive at many generally accepted principles of "proper job analysis" (Division of Industrial-Organizational Psychology, 1980), it is even more difficult to predict the nature and direction of future changes and to postulate future issues in the area of job analysis. Yet we must, for job analysis clearly will continue to be a topic of considerable interest.

This interest results in large part from the role which job analysis has been accorded by Federal courts and, as a consequence, by federal enforcement agencies in determining whether employment practices are discriminatory to members of any race, sex, and ethnic group. Several legal decisions have recognized that an adequate job analysis is essential to demonstrating that a test or other selection procedure is job related. In addition, as part of their responsibility to determine whether there has been a violation of equal employment opportunity laws, the courts must decide whether a particular job analysis method is legally and professionally adequate. By focusing on the strenghs and weaknesses of the various job analysis methods, these legal decisions have had a significant effect on the direction of job analysis research and design. Whether the courts will continue to have such a major role will depend in large part on the willingness of the developers and users of job analysis systems to address the problems which concern the courts before such problems become the subject of a lawsuit.

This chapter was contributed by Donald J. Schwartz, Ph.D., Chief Psychologist at the Equal Employment Opportunity Commission in his private capacity. No official support or endorsement by the United States Equal Employment Opportunity Commission or any other agency of the United States Government is intended or should be inferred.

Standards and the Law

The appropriateness of various job analysis methods for use in specific situations is a matter of current and future concern, because information gathered from job analysis is used to make decisions about the job, about people hired, or about procedures used to hire. The decision as to which method best meets the needs of a given situation is a professional choice. While a professional conducting a job analysis in the absence of a showing of adverse impact is relatively free to choose which job analysis method is to be used, the application of data resulting from that method in a way that adversely affects any race, sex, or ethnic group may require a close look at the underlying rationale, and at the legal and professional bases for its use. An excellent example of such a "close look" can be found in recent court decisions involving a large city fire department.

The city had a history of excluding women from applying for the position of firefighter. Then, in 1973, organizations representing black and Hispanic firefighters sued the city and won a court order requiring the city to prepare a new examination in accordance with professionally accepted methods of test preparation and to assure that it did not discriminate against black and Hispanic firefighter candidates. The consulting firm hired to develop the examination used two job analysis methods for constructing the physical portion of the examination but submitted data from five different methods of job analysis.

The results of the examination, while not adversely affecting black and Hispanic applicants, continued the exclusionary effect on the selection of women. Therefore, the issue of the validity of the new examination came before the court. The judge examined in detail the methods used to analyze the jobs, including the three methods that were not used to develop the examination. In fact, the results of one method were used to question the reliability of another method, and the consultant was criticized for not reconciling the results of the various methods. The judge also determined that not all of the methods provided sufficient information to support the validity of the examination under all strategies. The court ruled that the test was discriminatory in part because the validation strategy used was not supported by the data obtained from the job analysis (*Berkman v. City of New York*).

There is currently no authoritative set of principles for job analysis comparable to the *Standards* or *Principles* in the area of selection procedures. (Division of Industrial-Organizational Psychology, 1980). This does not preclude the possibility that standards will arise from deliberations of professional groups or from court decisions, based on critical scrutiny of the methods used to support questioned personnel decisions.

No specific job analysis technique has received a full stamp of approval from the profession and the courts. The courts have criticized some uses of certain methods (e.g., Job Element and PAQ), but this should not be considered an indictment of them in all contexts. A different application of one of these methods, or its use in a different context, might be fully acceptable. One of the methods described in Chapter 2 (GOJA) was fashioned toward meeting legal decisions with apparently less attention to professional concerns. Most of the others were developed around professional needs with little attention to legal constraints. Neither approach guarantees acceptability by either the profession or the courts.

While no particular job analysis method is prescribed, government regulations and court decisions clearly indicate a belief that job analysis will lead to fair job-related personnel practices. Very little research has been done on this belief or on other general job analysis questions. A preliminary study on this question conducted by researchers at the Center for Government and Public Affairs at Auburn University in Montgomery indicates that blacks and whites may respond differently to judgmental job analysis questions (Boyles et al., 1980).

What is an employer to do? There are five steps employers are urged to take to improve the chances that, if an employment decision is challenged as discriminatory, a judge will determine that the information obtained from the job analysis was sufficient to support the employment decision.

1. Articulate the purposes of the job analysis, with the assistance of a psychologist or other professional in the area of job analysis.

2. Select or develop a technique that produces information relevant to the purposes. This means that the job analyst must:
   a. Ensure that sources are reliable.
   b. Obtain information from several sources (levels, locations, ethnic groups) to ensure a broad data base.
   c. Resolve inconsistent or questionable information.
   d. Use quantitative checks on the accuracy of the information where possible.

3. Apply the techniques consistently to ensure that the information is valid and reliable.

4. Document all steps, results, and data analysis procedures.

5. Use the job analysis results properly in employment decision making.

Job Comparability

Job analysis data is important in determining the comparability of jobs. Such job information is frequently considered in determining how to classify a job. If two jobs are classified the same, then the same selection procedures and pay scales may be used. There are other reasons for determining the comparability of jobs, such as the determination of comparable worth and the establishment of layoff procedures.

Comparable Worth

Employers have traditionally considered the problem of classifying and evaluating positions to determine rates of pay as a different problem from deciding how to select people for these positions, even though both problems use job analysis data. The job analysis techniques used to classify jobs have had little relationship to the job analysis techniques used to develop or to justify selection procedures.

Recent developments provide a challenge for this type of categorical thinking. One of these is the belated realization that in the past not all jobs have been considered appropriate for members of different races, sexes, and ethnic groups. This nation has a long history of classifying jobs, for example, as "male" or "female," as "white" or "negro". The passage of the Civil Rights Act in 1964, while generally eliminating any legal basis for these classifications (except for bona fide occupational qualifications) has not eliminated the fact that men and women, whites and blacks, and other groups are concentrated in certain jobs. Moreover, there are disparities in rates of pay among these groups of jobs, as jobs historically held by women pay less than jobs historically held by men, and jobs considered "negro" pay less than those considered "white." There is, therefore, growing pressure to require employers having such disparities to show the relevance and accuracy of the job analysis systems used to classify jobs and determine pay rates, as well as the appropriateness of job analysis techniques used for selection. That is, an employer who has classified jobs in such a way that jobs with a high female concentration have lower pay than those with a high male concentration may have to show that jobs that pay less are in fact worth less.

Both the Civil Rights Act and the Equal Pay Act require that jobs with essentially the same duties and responsibilities be paid the same except for differences based on such factors as productivity or length of service. Accurate and relevant information about jobs is needed to determine which jobs are the same. The issue for the future is how to determine whether jobs with different duties and responsibilities have comparable worth.

The issue of comparable worth of jobs is highly complex and emotionally charged. How does one compare, for example, the "physical danger" component of firefighting with the mental and emotional demands of nursing? Yet, that is precisely the kind of comparison which must be made. Comparable worth is a problem that concerns civil rights groups and EEO regulatory agencies, and courts are not reticent about considering the issue.

Any system for evaluating jobs has three overlapping components. Each component may be subject to challenge, although it may be hard to distinguish them separately in any job evaluation system. These components are:

1. The procedure used to document the content, context, and requirements of the job. This is, of course, the job analysis component of the system.

2. The factors considered in comparing jobs. This is the job evaluation component of the system.

3. The value placed on the factors considered. This component of the system should reflect informed judgment on the importance of each factor to the health and growth of the organization.

A major problem in job comparability is the use of separate job evaluation systems (and sometimes different job analysis methods) for shop, clerical, and executive jobs. The use of different systems makes it difficult, if not impossible, to compare a job in one system with a job in another. A job with a high level of responsibility, for example, may be paid less than a similar job in another category because one is classified using the "clerical" system and the other using the "executive" system. The final report of the National Academy of Sciences (NAS) (Treiman and Hartman, 1981) indicates that the committee was divided on the question of whether jobs within a firm can be adequately evaluated using only one job evaluation method. However, the proposed guidelines for Job Evaluation Plans, released unofficially by the NAS Committee on Occupational Classification and Analysis, advocate the replacement of multiple job evaluation systems with one single top-to-bottom system where every job is evaluated according to the same factors. It is clear that the development of such a system is critically dependent on an accurate identification of the relevant dimensions of worth by which jobs can be compared. The burden of providing relevant and accurate information about jobs, then, is thrown back on the job analysis system. A paragraph in the NAS final report is encouraging:

> In our judgment job evaluation plans provide measures of job worth that, under certain circumstances, may be used to discover and reduce wage discrimination for persons covered by a given plan. Job evaluation plans provide a way of systematically rewarding jobs for their content—for the skill, effort, and responsibility they entail and the conditions under which they are performed. By making the criteria of compensation explicit and by applying the criteria consistently, it is probable that pay differentials resulting from traditional stereotypes regarding the value of "women's work" or work customarily done by minorities will be reduced (p. 95)

Layoffs

In a tight economy, many employers will cut back on the number of workers carried on the payroll, either permanently, to "trim the fat," or temporarily, to reduce costs until additional contracts are received. In unionized, blue collar positions, the layoffs will usually be based on seniority—last hired, first fired. For other positions, the health of the organization and EEO liabilities dictate that job performance be considered when determining who will go, and when. If the most recently hired are let go, the layoff will probably affect minorities and women most severely. If higher-paid employees are let go, the layoff will probably affect those over 40 most severely.

Attorneys are recommending objective appraisal systems to make sure that the employer who lays off low producers can prove that they are in fact poorer job performers. Walter P. Connolly, Jr., a labor law-attorney with Pepper, Hamilton and Scheetz, was quoted by the *Washington Post* (Connolly, 1981) as saying,

> You have to set up an assessment system that is candid, brutally candid, because the day may come when you're not going to want to promote someone or you're going to intend to lay off someone and you're going to have to live with the results of your assessment system (p. 1).

Job analysis is a critical component in determining which factors should be rated, and in determining which jobs are comparable. The comparability issue is very important during layoffs—it is the way that employers determine which employees to compare when some are targeted for layoff. In some organizations, the number of job titles may almost equal the number of people, so without job analysis there is no comparison group—that is, every job is different. In other situations, a manager may try to protect a favored employee from layoff consideration by giving him or her a unique job title. Job analysis data is needed to identify this employee and to make sure he or she is evaluated on the basis of merit, not "buddyism."

Employers should have a job analysis based employee evaluation system. Employers who do not have such a system—and who face a layoff situation—may want to install a system that allows for an equitable comparison of employees before proceeding with the layoff.

Job Analysis and the Changing Work Force

The work force is changing in many significant ways. As more women enter the work force, the two-wage-earner family is becoming the norm. As birthrates fluctuate, as mandatory retirement ages go up or disappear, and as retirement incomes look inadequate, a greater number of older workers remain in the work force. As transportation costs go up and as the quality of life becomes more important to many, some workers look for jobs they can do at home or close to home. As we automate more and more, skilled workers become increasingly important, and our need for unskilled and semiskilled workers decreases. Modern managers recognize these trends and look for the best ways to operate in the changing environment. Job analysis can be a very useful tool for adapting the job to the needs and abilities of the available work force.

Where a job traditionally has been filled exclusively or predominantly by members of one sex, or of one race, certain biasing factors may have become built into the job or the equipment related to it. In these cases, "valid" selection procedures reflect the biasing factors, and groups favored in the past continue to be favored by the "validated" selection procedures. The Sheridan study at American Telephone and Telegraph (Sheridan, 1975), for example, found that field positions which had been exclusively occupied by men before the passage of the Civil Rights Act, but which were required by a consent decree to be open to women, required the use of equipment designed for the physical strength and characteristics of men. Other examples are found in minimum height requirements.

To compensate for such built-in biases, federal contractors, state and local governments, federal agencies, and some other employers who are subject to consent decrees or conciliation agreements must take affirmative action to eliminate irrelevant barriers and to ensure that true equal employment opportunity is provided for women and disadvantaged groups. London and Bray (1980) pointed out that professional ethical standards of psychologists recognize this obligation for all employers using professionally developed selection procedures. (The most recent edition of these standards were published after the London and Bray article (American Psychological Association, 1981).) The information provided by job analysis can be a useful basis for affirmative action through job restructuring or redesign. The same procedures used to identify the critical or important tasks of a job can be used to identify tasks that are more difficult for women or minority group members, that present unnecessary burdens to handicapped workers, or that perpetuate past patterns of discrimination. With these data, it may be possible to remove barriers by modifying these tasks or the equipment used in performing them.

Women in Nontraditional Jobs

One application of job analysis is to find ways to restructure jobs and design equipment to make it easier for women to move into nontraditional occupations. Sheridan's analysis of telephone company field jobs, cited above, resulted in several suggestions for relatively inexpensive equipment modifications that reduced the impact of physical requirements on women. For example, a simple metal extension rod, costing about a dollar, enabled women to position ladders against buildings and telephone poles—a task which had caused them great physical difficulty. The change made the task easier for men as well as women. Other employers faced with the need or desire to hire women into traditionally male jobs such as firefighting have also reduced physical strength requirements by simple equipment modifications. In other cases, redesign of job tasks and working conditions to accommodate the social needs of a sexually mixed work force (such as provision of privacy for inmates and staff in correctional institutions) have proven useful in providing employment opportunities for women. Finally, job analysis studies focusing on nonphysical characteristics, such as assertiveness or competitiveness, which are sometimes thought necessary for higher level jobs, and which affect the opportunities of women, may prove to be worthwhile in finding ways to reduce or eliminate barriers.

Employment of the Handicapped

Federal contractors, federal agencies, and other recipients of federal funds are required to take affirmative action to remove discriminatory barriers affecting the employment opportunities of the handicapped. At a minimum, federal agencies and contractors are expected to review all physical and mental job standards to ensure that they are job related and consistent with business necessity whenever these standards tend to screen out otherwise qualified handicapped individuals. In these cases, the burden is on the employer to demonstrate business necessity or job relatedness— a burden which can be partially met through careful job analysis. Ideally, this job analysis should also be designed to identify which job-related barriers unnecessarily impede the employment opportunities of handicapped individuals and to suggest remedies to remove these barriers. Often, simple changes in the job or in the job setting can accommodate the needs of many handicapped individuals.

Even where these changes are not required by law or by executive order, they make good business sense—both in meeting the spirit of equal employment opportunity and in providing a larger pool of qualified applicants from which to make selections. In times of economic stress, employers must be creative in using the full potential of their human resources as well as in holding down the cost of disability retirement and workers' compensation. It makes little sense to pay large sums of money to a disabled employee to sit at home when a simple job change would enable that employee to be productive. Similarly, it makes little sense to allow a job to go unfilled when an equipment modification would enable an otherwise qualified handicapped individual to perform the job. The problem, of course, is to ensure that these handicapped individuals can do the job. Providing employment opportunities for the handicapped and ensuring that those hired can perform the job safely and adequately requires a job analysis system which takes barriers and remedies, as well as performance and safety factors, into account. Such a job analysis approach is the Medical Standards Project undertaken by the County of San Bernardino (1978), using Fleishman's Physical Abilities Analysis to assess the physical requirement of the tasks of a job in terms of 19 abilities.

Factors working against persons with obvious handicaps, such as blindness or deafness, may be revealed by even cursory job analysis. It is more difficult to detect and to correct the impact of so-called "hidden handicaps," such as heart disease, high blood pressure, cancer, seizure disorders, and some forms of back injury. Often, applicants with these handicaps are automatically eliminated from consideration without evidence from the job analysis that the job requires tasks or duties that they cannot perform. In some of these cases, individuals have filed suit claiming illegal discrimination and have won. For example, an applicant with a history of epilepsy as a child who had been eliminated from consideration for a police position in Tampa, Florida, sued and obtained a court order admitting him to the police academy. It is clear that these "hidden handicaps" have equal status under the law with the more obvious handicaps.

The Aging Work Force

By the year 2030, more than one-fifth of our population will be over 65. The entry level labor force will expand less rapidly, and the work force will have to depend on the willingness or necessity of workers to remain productive past age 65 in order to meet the economy's needs. This information, and the fact that most people want to continue working if they can, was reported by Iseli Krauss at a meeting of the Personnel Testing Council of Southern California (Krauss, 1981). She cited a study finding that 51 percent of employed people want to work past age 65, and an additional 26 percent wish to remain employed at least until they reach the "normal" retirement age.

Federal law prohibits discrimination on the basis of age against most employees between 40 and 70 and federal employees 40 or over. Under the pressure of law and regulations, mandatory retirement ages of less than 70 are being eliminated. Thus, most of those who wish to remain employed may work as long as they can do the job. An adequate job analysis system, therefore, must also provide criteria against which the continued ability of workers to perform their jobs as they grow older can be evaluated. Such a system would provide (1) a means to redesign jobs to accommodate the progressively disabling effects of age, (2) a means to identify other jobs to which the worker might transfer, and (3) a means to justify the involuntary retirement of those totally unable to perform available jobs. This provides another fruitful area for research and application in job analysis.

Changing Attitudes Toward Work

Many potential employees will be seeking opportunities to work less than full time or to work in their homes or neighborhoods. Employers will need to adapt to their workers' preferences to obtain needed skills. Further, there are usually financial advantages to employers who can structure their jobs to adapt to these workers. Job redesign, or restructuring, based on job analysis data can be part of the answer. A few examples will illustrate the kinds of changes employers will be making in the future to accommodate these workers.

- Several potential professional employees wish to work only part time. By dividing a job into two logical components, the employer can hire two half-time employees to share the job. Rather than seeking employees who are strong in several areas, the employer can hire one who is strong in one cluster of areas and one who is strong in the remaining areas. Scheduling could provide for one of the workers to be on the job at any given time, or could allow for overlap so that their combined strength could be brought to bear simultaneously on a difficult problem. For instance, *The Sunday Record* (Werlheimer, 1980) reports that Information Science, Inc. has one woman working three days a week and one working two days a week who "together are the full-time benefits administrator . . . ."
- An efficient word processor operator wants to work at home to minimize transportation or child care costs. Sophisticated transcription and data transmission gadgetry may make it cost effective to place word processing equipment in the employee's home and have the home-stationed employee do production transcription, with final copy run by an office-stationed word processor. A variation on this theme would be to station word processing equipment at several dispersed locations, to allow operators to come to nearby locations in their communities to do transcription on either a part-time or full-time basis.
- A programmer works best in the late evening hours, which is also when computer access time is less expensive. With a terminal in

his or her home, the employee can work almost exclusively at home according to the schedule that best suits him or her. (This is probably the most rapidly growing job accommodation.)

- A severely handicapped employee who is not mobile enough to commute regularly to the office could do telephone solicitation from home, on a company-installed telephone. Appointments or orders could be relayed to a central office or to a salesperson through a data transmission device, or by telephone.

- Some employers may find that certain functions can be subcontracted to the resurgent cottage industry. Typing, subpart assembly, development of training programs, for example, may be more efficiently done by subcontractors in their homes, thus saving considerable overhead for the employer who can use job analysis data to subdivide functions within jobs.

Role of the Computer

Computer technology provides us with an almost infinite number of ways to do things faster or better. While it is safe to say that the future will bring advances with direct applications to job analysis, the nature of these is hard to predict. There are two areas where the basic technology exists, and the future application to job analysis appears to be both desirable and profitable. These involve making data more accessible for decision making, and skills matching.

Ready Availability of Data

Once job analysis data have been documented, the challenge is to find a way to make sure that the data are used in decision making. To be useful, the data must be easily available to those who need it, when they need it, and the data must be updated as changes occur. A computerized data base can help assure continued usefulness of job analysis data if managers and personnel experts have ready access to use and to update the data file through terminals. In many organizations, enough job activities are performed through terminals to make terminal access to an established job analysis data base feasible.

A computerized data base could be used and updated daily in several ways, for example:

- Managers could key in any changes in positions or equipment as they occur.
- Classifiers could request a current listing of all tasks, responsibilities, and skill requirements.

- Recruiters could request a current listing of the three most important duties, and any unusual context factors.
- Staffers could request a listing of basic and special competencies not learned on the job.
- Trainers could request a listing of all positions where operation of a specific type of equipment is required.
- Validation experts could request a listing of all positions where certain specific tasks are performed.
- Managers could cross reference to tasks in existing positions rather than write up new tasks descriptions.

Computers and Skills Matching

A major possibility in job analysis results from the increasing use of computers for personnel decisions and for more effective use of human resources. As technology in this area becomes more sophisticated, there is a growing tendency to use computers to make personnel decisions, often by matching applicants with jobs. This type of skills matching depends on the capability of job analysis systems to provide quantified information about job requirements and organizational needs that can be stored and processed by computers. In other words, a data bank of "job profiles" can be created against which the individual skills and interests can be matched.

Such a data bank would greatly benefit recruitment and selection, as well as other personnel functions. An employer could, for example, concentrate his or her recruitment efforts in locations where the computer indicates the relevant skills for the job profiles are most likely to be found. Mathematical computations could be used to reduce discrepancies between applicants and job profiles, to increase the chances for an effective and balanced work force, and to identify new sources of individuals with needed skills. Finally, some of the issues discussed earlier—comparable worth, validity generalization, and job restructuring—could be brought into clearer focus by a job profile data base covering all or a large number of the jobs in the country.

Computerized skills matching will require an integration of the job analysis system and its data requirements into the ongoing personnel operations of employers. This in turn would require resolution of the job analysis issues discussed in this chapter.

Finally, for computerized skill matching to be maximally useful, employers in the same labor areas should share data banks. Thus, shared data could be a very useful outplacement tool for finding local employment for skilled workers who are laid off when a company undergoes economic cutbacks, automation, or changes in products or services. Such joint data banks will require cooperation among employers—a step that many of them have been reluctant to take in the past. Perhaps the needs of our developing social, legal, and technical standards will bring about this cooperation.

Appendix 1

Planning and Conducting a Job Analysis Study

Introduction

Chapter 3 presented specific and detailed instructions for developing, documenting, evaluating, and updating job analysis information. This appendix supplements that chapter. It discusses more general issues which need to be considered in planning and conducting a job analysis study and provides some specific "how to" suggestions. The appendix is directed primarily at those personnel specialists, consultants, and managers who are responsible for, or involved in, a job analysis study of several organizational units or of an entire organization. Managers and personnel specialists analyzing jobs in a specific organizational unit should refer to the procedures outlined in Chapter 3.

The needs which prompt consideration of job analysis studies and the conditions under which they are conducted are different in each case. The intent of this appendix, therefore, is to help the job analyst to think through the issues involved and ask the appropriate questions. The issues include: determining goals and objectives, selecting the sample, gathering data, establishing a schedule, documenting the data, disseminating information, and managing the study.

Determining Goals and Objectives

What is the intended purpose(s) of the job analysis study? What problems are you trying to solve? How do you plan to use the data? What applications—job design, classification or job evaluation, recruitment, selection, training, or performance appraisal—do you plan to develop? The nature and number of applications planned will influence the scope

155

and design of the study. Generally, a job analysis study is planned in response to specific problems or concerns. Even if you think that you will use the data for only one specific purpose, i.e., to improve selection procedures, you are urged to consider expanding the study to collect sufficient data for additional applications. Often, the possibility for additional uses of the data is seen only after a project has begun and it is no longer possible or convenient to collect more information. Worse still, different organizational units sometimes undertake separate studies requesting much of the same information from managers and workers. It is best to coordinate your work from the beginning.

A round table discussion or brainstorming session with those who use job information is one way to begin to address the scope and focus of the study and to generate support for it. Participants might include managers, administrative staff, and personnel specialists who are concerned with recruitment, selection, staffing, classification or job evaluation, training, and performance appraisal. Union officials and representatives of employee organizations should also be included early in the planning process.

Project goals developed should be related to broader organizational and managerial goals. Successful job analysis studies are not planned and conducted in a void but in relation to the total organizational environment.

You need to be realistic about the resources available and the constraints involved including time, money, staff, and organizational climate. The last, organizational climate, is often overlooked or its impact on the success of a study underestimated. You should consider the following questions: How receptive do you expect managers, employees, and top management to be? Is there a unit or individual who is less receptive than others to the study? Constraints can be overcome or at least neutralized if you plan for them.

Finally, consider how you plan to evaluate the project. In planning for project evaluation, differentiate between expected results of the study and expected performance of the individuals involved in the study. These are related but separate issues. You should recognize that it is difficult to evaluate long term and scattered results and you will need to be creative in setting meaningful evaluative criteria. If you want to compare "post" job analysis study results with previous efforts, be sure to collect "pre" data in a form that will be compatible.

Selecting the Sample

What is the appropriate size and composition of the sample? Who will provide information about the job? There are three significant variables affecting this issue: (1) the purpose of the job analysis, (2) the nature of the jobs being studied, and (3) the number of persons performing them.

If the purpose of the job analysis is to write position descriptions and to set performance objectives and standards for individual incumbents, then obviously, the data should be obtained from all incumbents or a 100 percent sample. One hundred percent coverage is also appropriate when an organization wants to develop or revise its classification or job evaluation system and to place jobs within the new structure. On the other hand, if the job analysis is to provide data to develop selection instruments such as a tailored application form or a structured interview guide, then a smaller representative sample should be sufficient.

Respondents in a job analysis study—those providing information about a job—should be those who perform (or who supervise) substantially the same major duties and tasks if they are to be considered representative of the total population for a specific job. If there are only a few workers performing a job, it is usually worthwhile to gather information from all of them. If there is a large number of incumbents, however, you will want to select a representative sample taking into account differences such as work location, types of assignments, and shifts worked. You also want to select a sample which mirrors the total incumbent population in terms of race, sex, age, and national origin—characteristics which could be the basis of a discrimination complaint. In those cases where the number of incumbents with these characteristics is limited, the analyst should oversample on these characteristics to ensure the accuracy of the resulting data.

Gathering Data

There are a number of different methods for gathering information about job content, competencies, and contextual factors. They include background research, observation, individual interviews, group meetings, worker logs or diaries, structured and unstructured questionnaires, and participation. Refer to Chapter 1 for a brief description of each of these data gathering techniques and to Appendix 2 for additional information on conducting a job-site visit.

Several examples of actual data-gathering forms are included as Exhibits 34 through 37. Exhibit 34 is a portion of a checklist used by job analysts to record data from interviews with a large number of incumbents in secretarial/clerical positions in one organization. Exhibit 35 is a portion of a machine readable Job Requirements Questionnaire for Managerial and Professional Classes. This example of a structured questionnaire was used to gather data from incumbents in similar positions in different financial organizations for use in developing a cooperative selection in-

Exhibit 34. Portion of an Interviewer Checklist

Checklist in Interviewing for Secretarial/Clerical Positions

		h/w	%
____	1. Obtains and sorts mail...	____	____
____	2. Answers telephone...	____	____
____	3. Places telephone calls...	____	____
____	4. Greets visitors...	____	____
____	5. Makes travel arrangements...	____	____
____	6. Requisitions cash advances/reimbursements...	____	____
____	7. Makes appointments/arranges meetings...	____	____
____	8. Schedules use of conference rooms...	____	____
____	9. Types...from handwritten copy...	____	____
____	10. Types...from typed copy...	____	____
____	11. Types forms...	____	____
____	12. Types and formats statistical tables/charts...	____	____
____	13. Types...from dictation, operating transcribing equipment...	____	____

Exhibit 35. Portion of the Job Requirements Questionnaire for Managerial and Professional Classes

PART I

PART I of this questionnaire contains a list of work elements frequently found in various managerial-professional type jobs. For each element, please indicate the extent to which the element is required in the job being reviewed.

1. If the element is _not_ a part of the job being reviewed, mark the circle under the column headed "Not Part of Job" and move on to the next element.

2. If the element _is_ a part of the job, mark the appropriate circle to indicate whether it is a "Minor Job Requirement," a "Moderate Job Requirement," or a "Major Job Requirement."

WORK ELEMENT	EXTENT TO WHICH REQUIRED IN JOB (Mark one)			
	Not Part of Job	Minor Requirement	Moderate Requirement	Major Requirement
Forecasting-estimating future workloads.	ⓞ	①	②	③
Estimating numbers and skills of employees required to complete assignments.	ⓞ	①	②	③
Planning-scheduling employee work.	ⓞ	①	②	③
Adjusting work schedules to meet priorities-emergencies	ⓞ	①	②	③
Establishing work performance standards for individual employees	ⓞ	①	②	③
Establishing work performance standards for departments or functional units	ⓞ	①	②	③
Evaluating the extent to which departments, functional units, etc. meet schedules and performance standards	ⓞ	①	②	③
Evaluating-recommending changes in organizational structure	ⓞ	①	②	③
Suggesting changes or revisions in work methods or procedures.	ⓞ	①	②	③
Initiating improvements in work methods or procedures	ⓞ	①	②	③
Preparing production-service volume reports	ⓞ	①	②	③
Establishing employee selection standards and procedures.	ⓞ	①	②	③
Evaluating employee selection procedures and their effects.	ⓞ	①	②	③
Maintaining contacts with other units-departments-shifts	ⓞ	①	②	③
Conferring with technical or other resource personnel to resolve problems.	ⓞ	①	②	③
Coordinating activities involving different parts of the organization	ⓞ	①	②	③
Serving as resource person to other work units	ⓞ	①	②	③
Revolving conflicts between work units	ⓞ	①	②	③
Serving as resource person in interpreting financial or other information	ⓞ	①	②	③
Maintaining contact with other financial institutions	ⓞ	①	②	③
Serving as liaison with regulatory agencies	ⓞ	①	②	③
Serving as liaison with state and local legislatures-officials	ⓞ	①	②	③
Identifying research objectives or problems	ⓞ	①	②	③
Directing studies, investigations or surveys.	ⓞ	①	②	③
Designing forms, procedures for collecting data	ⓞ	①	②	③
Designing methods for testing service quality	ⓞ	①	②	③
Establishing quantitative data analysis plans	ⓞ	①	②	③
Developing-adapting computer programs	ⓞ	①	②	③
Using computer programs to analyze data	ⓞ	①	②	③
Interpreting, summarizing research, survey, or other data	ⓞ	①	②	③
Consolidating data-information from numerous sources	ⓞ	①	②	③
Reviewing-evaluating project or research reports	ⓞ	①	②	③
Presenting project or research results	ⓞ	①	②	③
Setting or approving purchase specifications	ⓞ	①	②	③
Evaluating supplier proposals	ⓞ	①	②	③

Source: Copyright 1980 by Richardson, Bellows, Henry and Co., Inc., 1140 Connecticut Avenue, N.W., Washington, D.C. 20036. Reprinted with permission.

strument. Exhibit 36 is a second example of a structured questionnaire. Note that the response section of the questionnaire, with the notation of column numbers, was designed to facilitate transfer of the responses to computer cards for subsequent analysis. Exhibit 37 is an example of an unstructured questionnaire which was sent to incumbents in various managerial positions in several state social service agencies. Data from the questionnaire was used to loosely group like positions and to select those for which interviews were to be conducted.

Generally, several methods are used to gather data in a job analysis study. Multiple methods are more efficient and cost effective and provide more reliable and valid data. Again, the purpose of the job analysis, the number and location of incumbents, the nature of the work, as well as the resources available will affect the mix of data-gathering techniques used. A few preliminary questions will help to pinpoint which data-gathering techniques you should employ. What is the purpose(s) of the job analysis study? Worker logs or diaries provide useful background information needed to develop training curricula; generally, however, they would not be as useful for other purposes such as classification or job evaluation. Where are the work sites located? If incumbents are physically dispersed, it is often difficult if not impossible to arrange group meetings. What are the language requirements of the job? Questionnaires and checklists may not be appropriate if they require more complex language skills to complete than are required by the job itself. Is the work primarily physically or mentally oriented? Observation is often necessary for jobs which involve physical activity while interviews or questionnaires generate more information from jobs which have less observable actions. How many analysts are involved in the project? How much time has been or can be scheduled for data collection? Individual interviews may be preferable, but impractical or impossible, given time constraints. A few individual interviews can be conducted in order to gather data to structure a group meeting or to develop a checklist which could be completed by a larger population. This combination of data-gathering techniques enables you to collect data from a large number of respondents and is particularly useful if you are concerned about the size of your sample.

Establishing a Project Schedule

There are two variables to consider in planning for a realistic schedule on a job analysis study. First, how much time will be required to produce a particular product or to complete a work phase? Second, over what span of time will the work be done? For example, only x number of days or hours may be needed to develop a data-gathering instrument; however,

Exhibit 36. Portion of a Structured Questionnaire

VII. STENOGRAPHIC	A — Not Perf. — Not Performed On My Job	B — Importance to Overall Job Performance — Of Little Importance	Of Moderate Importance	Of Critical Importance	C — Percentage of Time Spent Throughout One Year — Very Little Less Than 5%	Little 05% – 14%	Some 15% – 39%	Much 40% – 74%	Most 75% or More
67. Take routine correspondence in shorthand and transcribe. 59,60	1	2	3	4	5	6	7	8	9
68. Take telephone conversations in shorthand and transcribe. 61,62	1	2	3	4	5	6	7	8	9
69. Take minutes of conferences in shorthand and transcribe. 63,64	1	2	3	4	5	6	7	8	9
70. Take technical memos in shorthand and transcribe. 65,66	1	2	3	4	5	6	7	8	9
71. Take technical letters or reports in shorthand and transcribe. 67,68	1	2	3	4	5	6	7	8	9
72. Take dictation on stenotype and transcribe. 69,70	1	2	3	4	5	6	7	8	9
73. Transcribe material from dictating machine. 71,72	1	2	3	4	5	6	7	8	9

Source: Psychological Services, Inc., 1735 I Street, N.W., Suite 706, Washington, D.C. 20006.

Exhibit 37. Example of an Unstructured Questionnaire

Name, Title, and Pay Level: _____

State and Office: _____

_____

Briefly, in one or two sentences, describe the purpose or focus of your job.

_____
_____
_____
_____

List, by position title and level, those staff members you directly supervise.   Indicate whether individuals are supervisory or nonsupervisory.

Position Title and Level	How Many	Supervisory	Nonsupervisory

Indicate, by position title and level, your immediate supervisor.

_____
_____

On the attached forms, please describe your work -- the tasks you perform -- as a supervisor and/or manager, e.g.:

    o   Planning and organizing work;
    o   Directing (scheduling, assigning, adjusting);
    o   Reviewing and monitoring work;
    o   Appraising and evaluating performance;
    o   Training and staff development;
    o   Counseling and disciplining;
    o   Hire/terminate; and
    o   Budgeting.

In describing the tasks you perform, please consider the following:

    What do you do, what actions do you perform?
    What resources do you use, what do you consider?
    What is the result -- the decision, product, service -- of your actions?

For example, in "Directing" you may perform a task such as:

    Reviews and evaluates work requirements/demands considering needs,
    priorities and availability, and skills of staff in order to assign
    work to individual staff members.

    What actions do you perform?

        Reviews and evaluates work requirements/demands......
    What resources do you use, what do you consider?

        considering needs, priorities and availability, and skills of staff....

    What is the result of your actions?

        in order to assign work to individual staff members.

Exhibit 37. Example of an Unstructured Questionnaire—*continued*

Please indicate the approximate percentage of time you perform each task.
In order to obtain a clear description of your work, it is important to
know that you may spend approximately 10 percent on one and only 1
percent on another. Please number each task you describe.

Task Number	Description of Task	Percentage of Time

taking into account other work load demands and the time needed for review by others, the work will be performed over a y-day period.

To estimate realistically the second variable, ask the following kinds of questions. Will time be lost to holidays or vacations? The Christmas-New Year holiday and summer are always slow data-gathering periods. Also allow additional time if you plan to mail questionnaires over the holiday period. Are there times of the month or year which have particularly heavy work loads for either specific units or all of the organization? For example, the end of the month or year would not be the best time to gather data in an accounting department. Are changes expected in existing policies or procedures? Are new programs about to be introduced? Is new equipment going to be installed? These are often busy and confusing times. Perhaps more important, until workers are more familiar and experienced with the changes, the data gathered may not be typical or normal. How long is the project? The production rate of people gathering data and analyzing jobs will not always be constant. Initially they will

be slow, speeding up as they become more familiar with, and knowledgeable about, the organization and methodology, and then slowing
down again in a lengthy project as they begin to "burn out." It is
important to plan for this latter phenomenon. How many different jobs
will be analyzed? A period of background research and familiarization will
be needed for each of the various types of jobs. Where are the jobs located?
Just as job location influences the choice of data-gathering techniques, it
can also affect the length of the project. Additional time for travel should
be scheduled if workers are located at scattered sites.

Documenting the Data

What information should be documented? The purpose of a job
analysis is, of course, to document specific facts about the content, competencies and contextual factors of a job. Some data-gathering methods,
for example, written questionnaires, checklists, worker logs and diaries,
are also basic documentation methods as well. Data from individual interviews and group meetings can be documented by other methods ranging
from note taking to voice and video taping.

It may also be necessary to gather and record additional information
to provide a "paper trail" of actions and decisions affecting the job analysis
study. How were respondents selected? What sample variables were used?
Basic identifying information about those providing job facts may be
necessary to document the representativeness of the sample. On what basis
were positions or jobs grouped for analytical purposes? Who gathered and
recorded the data? What were their qualifications in terms of study methodology and knowledge of the job(s)?

How and in what form should the information be stored? There are
numerous storage and retrieval systems ranging from hand-manipulated
systems such as McBee Key Sort cards to sophisticated computers. There
are a number of relevant questions to be asked. First, what in-house
systems are currently available? If the organization has a computer, what
are its capabilities and limitations for this purpose? Does the form in
which the data are recorded and stored need to be compatible with other
data banks or information systems such as personnel files? How much
data will need to be stored? For example, in a small organization with
only a few jobs, folders filed in the managers' desks and with a personnel
or administrative officer may be sufficient. In a large organization, the
data may be stored in a computer where data on the total work force can
be reviewed and analyzed by personnel staff, with printouts of job descriptions provided to managers for daily reference.

The concern with what information needs to be documented and
how it will be stored and retrieved should be reflected in the design of

data-gathering and documentation forms. For example, if the data are to be computerized, is it easy to input the data directly from the data-gathering form? The machine readable format of Exhibit 35 and the computer card column numbers on Exhibit 36 which were described previously are two examples.

Disseminating Information

Who needs to know what and when? How should information be disseminated? Generally, the success of a job analysis study is directly proportional to the amount of information available about the study's purpose, schedule, specific procedures and results, and the number of people that the information is shared with. Inadequate sharing of information can result in confusion, low morale of study staff, lack of support, hostility, and even sabotage—any of which can doom a job analysis study. Informing and involving individuals and groups in the study gives everyone a vested interest in its success.

As noted previously, it is often useful to include managers, personnel staff, and employee representatives in the initial planning discussions. The study benefits directly from their input to the planning process and indirectly from their input to the organizational grapevine. Once the work is ready to begin, the rest of the employees can be formally briefed by their managers through group meetings or even videotape presentations. As the study progresses, information sheets, bulletins, or articles in an organizational newsletter can provide periodic updates on study activities. Further, as basic data become available, managers can be trained in how to begin to use the data. If managers are gathering and documenting data about the jobs they supervise, weekly or bi-weekly meetings to discuss problems and to share ideas can be useful. Also, consider appointing a resource person to whom questions from anyone in the organization can be addressed.

Managing the Study

In planning how a job analysis study will be managed, there are a number of questions to be considered. What is the scope of the proposed work? How many jobs will be analyzed? How many units will be involved in the data collection phase? How will the data be stored? Is there a computer unit in the organization or will an outside firm be involved? What applications of the data are planned? How many different units will be involved in the application phase? What is the overall management philosophy or style of the organization? More specifically, should study management be centralized in a personnel unit or decentralized to individual operating units?

The need for centralized management increases with the number of different units involved in any phase—data collection, storage, and application—of the study. If all of the jobs in an organization are to be analyzed or if the jobs cross organizational lines or boundaries, as with clerical jobs, centralization helps to insure technical consistency and to realize economies of scale in data collection and analysis. If personnel staff or consultants collect the data, this also provides for their more efficient employment given the varying workloads of different jobs and units.

Who will gather, document, and evaluate the data—managers, personnel specialists, or consultants? The kind and degree of supervision exercised over the data gathering, the technical assistance and coordination needed, and the appropriate management structure to conduct the study are very different for each. For example, if managers are the primary data gatherers, a management plan should provide for general work phase deadlines, technical assistance in the methodology, use of the data as they become available, exchange of information among managers, development of generic or model data as appropriate, and monitoring overall progress. On the other hand, if a special staff of job analysts is formed, then the management plan would also need to provide for their daily supervision including scheduling, assigning and reviewing work, providing training, and evaluating performance. If the job analysis is to be conducted by consultants, the role of the study manager will primarily be one of co-ordination, information exchange and dissemination, and monitoring. Organizations contracting for work such as job analysis studies often focus on the last aspect, monitoring adherence to completion dates and budget totals while underestimating the importance of the first two functions and the time required to perform them.

Appendix 2

Suggestions for Conducting a Job-Site Visit

Arranging for the Job-Site Visit

Prior arrangements for the job-site visit should be made with local management, so that work is not unduly interrupted and union contracts are not violated. If possible, also discuss the purpose of your interview with local union officials. The objective of these contacts is to obtain assurance that management and union officials understand the aims of the study and authorize it.

Obtaining Information by Observation and Interviews

This procedure involves analyzing jobs by observing incumbents performing their jobs (when possible) and interviewing incumbents, supervisors, and others who have information pertinent to the job. It is a most desirable method for job analysis purposes because it (a) involves firsthand observation by the analyst; (b) enables the analyst to evaluate the interview data and to sift essential from nonessential facts in terms of his or her other observations; and (c) permits the worker to demonstrate various functions of the job rather than describing the job orally or in writing.

The observation-interview method can be conducted in two ways depending on the nature of the job and personal preference: (a) The analyst observes the incumbent on the job before asking questions. When satisfied that as much information as possible has been accumulated from observation, the analyst talks with the incumbent. (b) The analyst observes and interviews simultaneously. While watching the job being performed,

The material in this Appendix was adapted by Stephen Bemis and the late Harry Bose from the *Handbook for Analyzing Jobs* (U.S. Department of Labor).

the analyst talks with the incumbent about what is being done, and asks questions about what is being observed, as well as conditions under which the job is being performed. The analyst should take notes so as to record all the data pertinent to the job and its environment, or the session can be tape recorded.

The interview process is subjective—a conversational interaction between individuals. Communication is a two-way process. Therefore, the analyst must be more than a recording device. The amount and objectivity of information received depends upon how much is contributed to the situation. The analyst's contribution is one of understanding and adjusting to the incumbent and the job.

A good background preparation will enable the analyst to obtain facts quickly, accurately, and comprehensively. The analyst must be able to establish friendly relations on short notice, extract all the pertinent information, and yet be sufficiently detached to be as objective and free of bias as possible.

Suggestions for Interviewing and Note Taking

- Learn the incumbent(s) name(s) in advance. At the beginning of the interview, put the incumbent at ease by introducing yourself, and discussing general and pleasant topics long enough to establish rapport. Be at ease.
- Make the purpose of the interview clear by explaining why the interview was scheduled, what is expected to be accomplished, and how the incumbent's cooperation will help (for example, to improve selection procedures). Assure the incumbent that the interview will not affect him or her in any way. If the data being obtained will not be used for classification or job evaluation, assure the incumbent that the information being provided will not affect wages in any way.
- Encourage the incumbent to talk by always being courteous and showing a sincere interest in what he or she says.

Steering the Interview

- Help the incumbent to think and talk according to the logical sequence of the tasks performed. If tasks are not performed in a regular order, ask the incumbent to describe the tasks in a functional manner, by taking the most important activity first, the second most important next, and so forth. Request the worker to describe the infrequent tasks of the job, ones that are not part of regular activities, such as the occasional or infrequent reports. Infrequently performed tasks, however, do not include periodic or emergency activities such as an annual inventory or the emergency ordering of materials.

- Allow the incumbent sufficient time to answer each question and to formulate an answer. Ask only one question at a time.
- Phrase questions carefully, so that the answers will be more than "yes" or "no".
- Avoid leading questions.
- Conduct the interview in plain, easily understood language.
- Consider the relationship of the job being analyzed to other jobs in the organization.
- Control the interview with respect to the economic use of time and adherence to subject matter. For example, when the incumbent strays from the subject, a good technique for bringing him or her back to the topic is to summarize the data collected up to that point.
- The interview should be conducted patiently and with consideration for any nervousness or lack of ease on the part of the incumbent.

Closing the Interview

- Summarize the information obtained from the worker, indicating the major activities performed and the details concerning each of the tasks.
- Ask if you may contact the worker if there are questions after the interview notes are written up more fully.
- Close the interview on a friendly note.

Miscellaneous Do's and Don'ts for Interviews

- Do not take issue with incumbent's statements.
- Do not show any partiality to grievances or conflicts concerning employer-employee relations.
- Do not show any interest in the wage classification of the job.
- Do not "talk down" to the person.
- Do not permit yourself to be influenced by your personal likes and dislikes. (For instance, your dislike of long hair on men or slacks on women should not cause you to underrate information from incumbents so attired.)
- Do not be critical or attempt to suggest any changes or improvements in organization or methods of work. Be impersonal.
- Do show politeness and courtesy throughout the interview.
- Do talk to the worker only with permission of his supervisor.
- Do review information from the interview with the supervisor. He or she may have additional information.

● Do double-check any technical or trade terminology with supervisor and/or written sources.

Taking Notes

The analyst must develop a certain skill in combining notetaking with conversational aspects of the interview. He or she must be able to write intelligible notes while engaged in conversation or to intersperse writing with fluent conversation. Often, in deference to the analyst, the worker will stop talking while notes are being made. The analyst should make it clear whether he or she wishes the conversation continued in these circumstances.

Some workers object to a record being made of what they say. The analyst must decide how much the interview may be affected by this attitude and modify his or her practices accordingly. Some job analysts have found that a small looseleaf book such as a stenographer's notebook is best suited for recording notes while observing and interviewing, because it allows them to jot down key words without interrupting the flow of conversation. A clipboard might inhibit some incumbents because of the association some people make of this tool with time and motion study.

It is important to review notes taken during an observation/interview as soon as possible while the details are fresh and easily recalled. Review key words and phrases and write more detailed descriptions or statements. Identify issues to be clarified with the worker or supervisor. Note technical terms or procedures to be researched or verified in reference materials.

Tape Recording

Instead of taking notes, it may sometimes be possible to tape record a job analysis interview when the interview is conducted away from the job site, or at a quiet job site. Tape recording will permit the analyst to concentrate on listening to what the incumbent is saying and on asking questions to gather more information. An interview should be taped only with the permission of the incumbent. Even with the incumbent's permission, it may be difficult to get him or her to talk with the recorder on. Once the interview is off and running, the presence of the recorder will probably be forgotten. (The use of a condenser microphone rather than a directional microphone should help to assure that all comments and questions are recorded without the restriction of having to speak into a microphone.)

Even if notes are taken, the tape can be used to double-check for factual material and completeness.

Appendix 3

A Job Analysis Case Study

Extensive job analyses were conducted on four primary entry level jobs in the U.S. Postal Service: City Carrier, Distribution Clerk, Distribution Clerk (Machine) and Mail Handler. These job analyses were conducted as part of a project to validate selection tests for the four jobs. Such information is needed to (1) identify or develop selection tests, (2) determine appropriate criteria of job success, and (3) determine how to implement the resulting test batteries. The project was carried out by personnel research staff at the headquarters of the U.S. Postal Service with guidance and assistance from three external consultants. (This combined group is referred to as "team members.") Although essentially the same procedures were used for the four jobs, and similar results were obtained, data will be presented for the City Carrier job only. Complete information on this project can be found in the project technical report (U.S. Postal Service, 1981).

VERJAS procedures were not used in the project and some of the terminology conflicts with that used in VERJAS. Job context information had already been obtained and thus was not an area of concern in this project. Nevertheless, the project provides a convenient case study showing the way that several of the common job analysis techniques can be applied in large-scale job analysis projects that are quite dissimilar to the usual concerns of a manager. Further, the project utilizes a most unique way of obtaining information on task (work behavior) frequencies.

At the onset of the study, all available resource material relevant to each of the four jobs was collected and reviewed. The type of material reviewed included training manuals, instruction manuals, methods handbooks, organizational directives, position descriptions, qualification standards, and task inventories developed as a result of previous management studies. After the review of resource material, task statements were written. Finally, a two-part job analysis survey was used to identify the critical or important work behaviors, and the knowledges, skills, and abilities needed to perform each of the four jobs. Part one consisted of identifying the frequency of work behaviors for each job and obtaining subject matter expert (SME) judgments on the criticality or importance of each work behavior. Part two entailed obtaining expert judgments relative to the knowledges, skills, and abilities needed to perform each of the four jobs. These components are described in the following paragraphs.

Development of Job Content Information

Development of Task Statements

In concert with the resource material review, team members generated lists of potential tasks for each job. Once this process was completed, the lists were consolidated and a composite list of task statements, each written in the form of verb/object, was developed for each of the four jobs (e.g., carry registry mail to Registry/security section; deliver accountable mail to customers).

The preliminary task statements for the jobs of Mail Handler, Distribution Clerk, and City Carrier were then reviewed by SMEs who directly supervised the relevant work force. During the months of September and November of 1980, thirty SMEs, representative of the above three positions and the five postal regions, met for one week in Washington, D.C. to review and to modify the task statements. The SMEs added tasks that had been omitted, made recommendations for task consolidations, and clarified the wording of the task statements. These changes were incorporated into the final task statements. A similar procedure was used for the job of Distribution Clerk (Machine). Between 100 and 250 final task statements for each job resulted from this work.

Development of Work Behavior Statements

In developing the work behaviors the first step involved each team member independently grouping the finalized task statements into common functional clusters. At this point, the number of functional clusters was not predetermined nor was there an attempt to define the functional clusters used. Upon completion of this process, the functional clusters identified by each team member were consolidated and defined to arrive at a single list of functional clusters for each job.

Next the team members attempted to develop four-part functionally defined work behaviors, without reference to the task clusters. Each work behavior statement was structured to answer the following four questions:

(1) performs what action, (2) to whom or what, (3) for what purpose, and (4) using what tools, work aids, processes?

Results from the task clustering and development of the preliminary work behaviors were then compared and analyzed for content. Based on the results of this analysis, revised work behaviors written in the four-part format were then prepared by concentrating on each of the jobs. Two sample statements resulting from this process are shown below:

- D1 *Cases mail* in order to arrange *for* sequence of *delivery* by reading names and addresses on letters, flats, and parcels utilizing knowledge of case layout and comparing addresses with case label.

- D2 *Pulls down mail from carrier case* in sequence of delivery by reading pink cards, removing holdouts and address changes and strapping mail in delivery order in order to prepare mail for delivery.

Review and verification of the revised work behaviors was accomplished in two stages. Initially, twelve second- or third-level managers, knowledgeable in one or more of the subject jobs, met for two days in Washington, D.C. to supply additional information. Prior to their seeing the work behaviors developed by the staff, these managers were asked to describe the main components of each job and to discuss work activities for each of the four jobs. The work behaviors developed by the staff were withheld at this point to avoid prejudicing the managers' opinions and to maximize meaningful dialogue and exchange of information. The managers were then asked to review the work behaviors developed by the staff. Recommendations were made to clarify wording and to make minor modifications. These changes were subsequently incorporated into the final work behaviors.

The final review of the work behaviors was completed during the month of March, 1981. Two-day meetings with ten to twelve managers, knowledgeable in one or more of the subject positions, were conducted in Chicago, New York, Memphis, and San Francisco. The purpose of these meetings was (1) to verify that the work behaviors represented a good and comprehensive description of each job, and (2) to obtain preliminary information relative to critical or important work behaviors.

Determination of Work Behavior Frequency

The frequency of work behaviors was determined by reference to data covering the October 1979 to October 1980 period generated by the In-Office Cost System (IOCS). Data accumulated during this period include 384,472 documented observations of individuals performing the relevant jobs. A distribution of observations by job is as follows:

Mail Handler	39,278
Distribution Clerk	117,334
City Carrier	177,199
Distribution Clerk, Machine	50,661

In-Office Cost System. The In-Office Cost System is an ongoing Postal Service Program which has been used since the early 1970s to generate data from which cost information is developed for use in conducting management studies, in preparing budgets, and in developing requests for new postal rates. The Revenue and Cost Analysis Division, Rates and Classification Department, Postal Headquarters, Washington, D.C. is the principal user of the IOCS end-product data.

The IOCS design provides for a determination of the percentage of time attributable to specific work activities. Data are gathered by direct observation and documentation of the work activities of predetermined employees at specified times. Selection of sampled employees is made by a service-wide probability sample obtained from current payroll records. The program is closely monitored and collection of data is done by specially trained individuals.

To collect IOCS Data, Form 2600 (In-Office Cost System Questionnaire) is used (see Exhibit 38). Form 2600 is designed to include those situations necessary to classify significant employee work activities. It consists of 26 divided, then subdivided questions, three of which are representative of work activity statements relative to the four jobs. The remaining 23 questions are used to obtain general information, information on the sampled employee, the reading being taken and/or the mail being handled. Since IOCS clusters all city carrier street activities into one category called "street time", these street activities were further divided using data from a comparable source, the Carrier Cost Survey (CCS).

Carrier Cost Survey. The Carrier Cost Survey was conducted for the Rates and Classification Department, Postal Headquarters, Washington, D.C., during the period of July 1979 through October 1979. Accumulated data were obtained by field survey of 877 city delivery routes. As with IOCS, the CCS design provides for a determination of the percentage of time attributable to specific work activities. CCS data were collected by specially trained individuals who observed City Carriers at work.

Prior to computing work behavior frequencies, all available resource material relevant to IOCS and CCS was collected and reviewed. The type of material reviewed included methods handbooks, training materials, and instruction manuals. The IOCS training film was viewed and a copy of the training film script was obtained for additional review.

Exhibit 38. Portion of a Worker Log for U.S. Postal Service In-Office Cost System Questionnaire

16. If employee is a CARRIER, MESSENGER, OR VEHICLE SERVICE OPERATOR, (or if 15D is Yes) answer A, B, C, D, E, and complete rest of form. If Route Type is not found in 16B, enter Route Type in Remarks. Question 16C is at the option of the region.

(A) If PSDS Office, mark

MODS WORK CENTER

```
0  0  0
1  1  1
2  2  2
3  3  3
4  4  4  ■
5  5  5
6  6  6
7  7  7
8  8  8
9  9  9
```

(B) Mark route type: (Mark only one)

- ○ Business — Foot
- ○ Business — Motorized
- ○ Residential — Foot
- ○ Residential — Curb
- ○ Residential — Park and Loop
- ○ Mixed Business and Residential — Foot
- ○ Mixed Business and Residential — Curb
- ○ Mixed Business and Residential — Park and Loop ■
- ○ Exclusive Parcel Post
- ○ Parcel Post Combination
- ○ Non-Parcel Post Combination
- ○ Collection
- ○ Relay Route
- ○ Special Delivery
- ○ Express Mail
- ○ Metro Service

- ○ OMMS (Washington, D.C. only)
- ○ Depot Service
- ○ Inter-city service
- ○ Inter-station service
- ○ Service to BMC
- ○ Yard Hustler
- ○ Service to Airports
- ○ In-Office Light Duty —
  Not Assisting Carriers ■
  (Go to Question 17)

Rural Routes:
- ○ H — Route
- ○ J — Route
- ○ K — Route
- ○ Special Route
- ○ Mileage Route
- ○ Auxiliary Route
- ○ Tri-weekly Route

(C) Route Number and Lunch Period

Route Number

Start Lunch Period

Hours   Minutes

(D) Is employee on street-time?

○ No — If No, complete E

○ Yes ⟶ IF YES, { clock-out time or mark ↘
                  ○ PSDS } ·

■   (STOP, YOU HAVE COMPLETED THIS SAMPLE)

■

Exhibit 38. Portion of a Worker Log for U.S. Postal Service In-Office Cost System Questionnaire—*continued*

(E) IN-OFFICE ACTIVITY— If employee is not on street time at time of reading, mark whichever of the following activities he/she is doing at that time. Each activity includes incidental walking to and from the carrier's case. *(Mark only one.)*

○ Preparation of mail for sequencing

○ Sequencing deliverable mail

○ Separating and/or disposing of mail to be picked up by customer

■ Disposing of undeliverable-as-addressed mail

○ Withdrawing and strapping out mail from carrier case

○ Obtaining and/or returning accountable mail

○ Engaging in activity related to retail functions *(rural carriers only)*

○ Sweeping mail from distribution cases *(other than carrier cases)*

○ Assisting on carrier test (Form 38 or 38-C only)

○ Manual Mark-up

○ Disposing of mail collected on route

■ Routine office work

○ Clocking in or clocking out

○ Break/Personal needs

○ Going to Vehicle/Vehicle Preparation and Checking

○ Other *(Specify in REMARKS)*

IF HANDLING MAIL, GO TO QUESTION 20 ON PAGE 5.

IF NOT HANDLING MAIL BUT INVOLVED IN A SPECIAL SERVICE, GO TO QUESTION 24 ON PAGE 5.

IF NOT HANDLING MAIL OR INVOLVED IN A SPECIAL SERVICE, GO TO QUESTION 25 (BASIC FUNCTION) ON PAGE 6.

Source: U.S. Postal Service Form 2600. October 1979.

Upon completion of the material review, the IOCS and CCS activity statements were carefully examined for content. The IOCS and CCS activity statements were then matched to the corresponding work behaviors used to describe each job. This procedure resulted in the work behaviors being defined for the purpose of obtaining total frequency, according to the total of the matched IOCS and CCS activity statements.

This matching process was necessary because the IOCS and CCS activity statements are more specific than the work behaviors. The activity statements are further defined by specific examples of various work situations. Twenty-five work behaviors were matched to one or more of the IOCS and/or CCS activity statements. One work behavior, D7, was not matched because one or more of the examples defining the relevant activity statement(s) were not included in the work behavior. Five work behaviors, D11, A10, A11, A12, and A13 were not matched because they are performed simultaneously with other work activities and thus, could not be independently matched to the IOCS and/or CCS activity statements.

Once the IOCS and CCS activity statements were identified and matched to the work behavior, the results were reviewed and verified for accuracy by (1) staff members involved in developing the work behaviors, (2) three external consultants, and (3) individuals familiar with IOCS recording procedures. Throughout the matching process, individuals in the field responsible for the maintenance of IOCS were contacted as necessary to clarify the examples of the work situations included in the IOCS activity statements.

The work behavior frequencies obtained from IOCS and CCS data for City Carriers are summarized in Exhibit 39.

Rating of Criticality or Importance

During the period of September 9, 1981 through September 18, 1981, 348 Subject Matter Experts were convened for the purpose of rating the criticality or importance of work behaviors. A series of nine SME regional field meetings, each lasting approximately four hours, was conducted at seven locations.

Subject Matter Experts were selected by specific job of employee supervised. Using current payroll records, incumbent supervisors were identified by a service-wide probability sampling of the four relevant jobs, and they were scheduled to attend one of the regional field meetings.

The combined experience of the 348 SMEs supervising employees in the four jobs represents 1,828 years: an average of 63 months per SME. The total of employees in the four jobs currently being supervised by the SMEs is 9,128: an average of 26 employees per SME.

Exhibit 39. Percent of Time Accounted for City Carrier Work Behaviors

WORK BEHAVIOR		PERCENT[a] IOCS	PERCENT[b] CCS	COMBINED PERCENT	TOTAL
D1.	Cases mail for delivery.	26.3		26.3	
D2.	Pulls down mail from carrier case.	2.6		2.6	
[*D3. [*D10.	Loads vehicle. Unloads vehicle.	.1	4.9	5.0	
D4.	Operates vehicle.	.8	13.7	14.5	
D5.	Delivers mail.		9.4	9.4	
D6.	Collects mail from collection boxes or pick-up points.		.7	.7	
D7.	Prepares and maintains records and reports.		c		
D8.	Walks and climbs stairs.		35.8	35.8	
D9.	Obtains signatures or money.		.6	.6	
D11.	Communicates orally and in writing.		d		94.9
A13.	Protects revenue.		d		
Other		2.1	3.0	5.1	100.00

[a]Based on 177,199 observations of individuals performing the city carrier position—In Office Activities.
[b]Based on 877 delivery routines surveyed—Street Activities.
[c]Not measured for time—one or more of the examples defining the pertinent IOCS activity statement were not included in the Work Behavior.
[d]Not measured for time—performed simultaneously with other activities.
*D3 and D10 combined.

Each meeting was conducted by two team members. Using a standardized format, each SME was instructed to complete a four-part questionnaire pertinent only to the job they were identified to review, i.e., City Carrier supervisors responded only to questions relative to the City Carrier job. The first question asked the SME to rate the criticality or importance of the work behaviors used to describe the job. Three additional questions were included to allow the SME to identify the abilities needed to perform the job. The latter three questions will be discussed later.

The first question, "How important is it that this work behavior be performed properly?", required the SME to rate the importance of each work behavior using the following scale values: (1) unimportant, (2) important, and (3) critical.

In rating each work behavior, the SMEs were instructed to "consider the impact in terms of loss of revenue, or delay, damage of loss of mail if this work behavior were performed poorly, incorrectly or not at all." However, in the event an SME was not familiar with a particular work behavior he/she was allowed to respond "unable to rate." Only eight of the 348 SMEs used the category "unable to rate." The results from the SME judgments relative to work behavior criticality or importance for City Carriers are summarized in Exhibit 40.

Based on the results of the frequencies obtained from the IOCS and CCS data and the judgments obtained from the SMEs, the critical or important work behaviors were identified for each of the four jobs. The criteria used to define the critical or important work behaviors required that the work behavior have an SME Mean Rating of 2.0 or above and account for 1 percent or more of the total time. However, the six work behaviors (D7, D11, A10, A11, A12, A13) which were not measured

Exhibit 40. SME Mean Rating Critical or Important Work Behaviors City Carrier SMEs

WORK BEHAVIOR		MEAN RATING[a]
D1.	Cases mail for delivery.	2.9
D2.	Pulls down mail from carrier case.	2.7
D3.	Loads vehicle.	2.1
D4.	Operates vehicle.	2.6
D5.	Delivers mail.	2.8
D6.	Collects mail from collection boxes or pick-up points.	2.6
D7.	Prepares and maintains records and reports.	2.2
D8.	Walks and climbs stairs.	2.2
D9.	Obtains signatures or money.	2.8
D10.	Unloads vehicle.	2.3
D11.	Communicates orally and in writing.	2.1

N = 91
[a]Scale values assigned: 1-unimportant, 2-important, 3-critical.

for time by IOCS and/or CCS were accepted as being critical or important if they had been rated critical or important by the SMEs.

The work behaviors performed by City Carriers and found to be critical or important, are shown in abbreviated form below:

- D1. Cases mail for delivery.
- D2. Pulls down mail from carrier case.
- D3. Loads vehicle.
- D4. Operates vehicle.
- D5. Delivers mail.
- D7. Prepares and maintains records and reports.
- D8. Walks and climbs stairs.
- D10. Unloads vehicle.
- D11. Communicates orally and in writing.
- A13. Protects revenue.

Development of Job Requirement Information

Identification of Relevant Abilities

The abilities necessary to perform the Mail Handler, Distribution Clerk, City Carrier and Distribution Clerk (Machine) jobs were identified and defined through a two-step process. The process utilized information from individuals with considerable knowledge in one or more of the four positions, psychological literature, and the professional judgment of psychometric experts. The steps were as follows:

1. Knowledgeable managers attending the review of job information meetings in New York and Memphis identified a number of abilities through a structured group discussion conducted by psychologists.

2. After reviewing the information provided by these knowledgeable managers, nine abilities were identified and given preliminary definitions in a multi-step process by psychologists in the Test Development Branch and the consultants. Information considered in arriving at these abilities were standard descriptions of abilities available from psychological literature. Considered were standard textbooks (e.g., Anastasi, 1976; Cronbach, 1970) and publications from occupational research programs (e.g., Department of Labor, 1970; PAQ Services, Inc., 1977).

Linkage of Work Behaviors and Abilities

The abilities necessary to perform each job and the abilities necessary to perform each work behavior were identified by the SMEs attending the regional field meetings. Using a standardized format, the SMEs were instructed to answer the last three questions of the four-part questionnaire.

The second question "Is some level of each ability necessary in performing the job?" required a yes or no response. The third question "Would an employee with a higher level of each ability be likely to perform the job better than an employee with a lower level of each ability?" required a yes or no response. The fourth question "Is some level of each ability necessary in performing each work behavior?" also required a yes or no response. However, if the SME had rated a work behavior "unable to rate" in response to the work behavior criticality or importance question (question one), this same work behavior was automatically rated "unable to rate" in response to the fourth question.

Responses to the fourth question provided the linkage for the ability to each work behavior. The criterion considering an ability linked to a work behavior was two standard deviations above 50 percent (61) responding "yes," indicating some level of the ability was necessary in performing the work behavior. Exhibit 41 contains a summary of these findings.

Considering the response to the second question, regarding the job as a whole, all nine abilities were linked to the jobs of Mail Handler, Distribution Clerk, and City Carrier. For the Distribution Clerk (Machine) job, seven of the nine abilities were linked (excluding Oral Expression and Forms Completion). To ensure that over one-half of the SMEs felt the ability was necessary, the criterion for linkage was set again at two standard deviations above 50 percent responding "yes" the ability was necessary.

Responses to the third question allowed the SMEs to identify the abilities appropriate for ranking applicants. The criterion for acceptance that the ability was appropriate for ranking was again two standard deviations above 50 percent. Results from the second and third questions for City Carriers are summarized in Exhibit 42.

After abilities were linked to the individual work behaviors, the operational definitions were then written for each ability for each job. These operationally defined abilities are found in Exhibit 43.

Exhibit 41. Summary of Responses to Question 4

ABILITIES

Work Behavior	Visual Perception	Following Oral Instructions	Physical Strength & Stamina	Dexterity & Coordination	Memory for Codes	Oral Expression	Written Comprehension	Sequencing	Forms Completion
A1	x	x	x	x	x	0	x	x	0
A2	x	x	x	x	x	0	x	x	0
A3	x	x	x	x	x	0	x	x	0
A4	x	x	x	x	x	0	x	x	0
A5	x	x	x	x	x	0	x	x	0
A6	x	x	x	x	x	0	0	x	0
A7	x	x	x	x	0	0	0	x	0
A8	x	x	x	x	x	0	x	x	0
A9	x	x	x	x	x	0	x	0	0
A10	x	x	0	x	x	0	0	0	0
A11	x	x	0	0	0	x	x	x	x
A12	x	x	0	0	x	0	0	x	0
A13	x	x	x	x	x	0	x	0	0
B1	x	x	x	x	x	0	x	x	0
B2	x	x	x	x	x	0	x	x	0

B3	x	x	x	x	x	0	x	x	0
C1	x	x	x	x	x	0	x	x	0
C2	x	x	x	x	x	0	x	x	0
C3	x	x	x	x	x	0	x	x	0
C4	x	x	x	x	x	0	x	x	0
D1	x	x	x	x	x	0	x	x	0
D2	x	x	x	x	x	0	x	x	0
D3	x	x	x	x	x	0	x	x	0
D4	x	x	x	x	x	0	x	0	0
D5	x	x	x	x	x	0	x	x	x
D6	x	x	x	x	x	0	x	0	0
D7	x	x	x	0	0	0	x	0	x
D8	x	x	x	x	x	0	x	0	0
D9	x	x	x	0	0	x	x	0	x
D10	x	x	x	x	x	0	0	0	0
D11	x	x	x	0	0	0	0	0	0

SMEs Responding Ability Is Necessary for Each Work Behavior (Question Four)

X − 61% or more responded Yes
0 − Less than 61% responded Yes

N = 87 Responding to A Work Behaviors
N = 89 Responding to B Work Behaviors
N = 81 Responding to C Work Behaviors
N = 91 Responding to D Work Behaviors

Exhibit 42. City Carrier Subject Matter Expert Ratings of Abilities

	QUESTION	
ABILITY	#2	#3
Visual Perception	100	93
Following Oral Instructions	100	67
Physical Strength & Stamina	98	73
Dexterity & Coordination	99	92
Memory for Codes	97	87
Oral Expression	95	36
Written Comprehension	99	51
Sequencing	100	89
Forms Completion	99	53

(N = 91)

Column #2 shows the percent of SMEs who responded that the ability was necessary in performing the job of City Carrier.

Column #3 shows the percent of SMEs who responded that an employee with a higher level of the ability would be likely to perform better as a City Carrier than an employee with a lower level of the ability.

Exhibit 43. Operational Definitions of City Carrier Abilities

The following operationally defined abilities are necessary for the satisfactory performance of the City Carrier position. The work behaviors defining these abilities are listed in descending order of percentage of SMEs responding that the ability was required for the work behavior.

1. *Visual Perception* . . . The speed and accuracy with which a person can observe and act on visual information such as names, addresses, numbers and shapes as used in the following work behaviors:
   D1.   Cases mail.
   D2.   Pulls down.
   D3.   Loads vehicle.
   D5.   Delivers mail.
   D4.   Operates vehicle.
   D7.   Prepares and maintains records and reports.
   D8.   Walks and climbs stairs.
   D10. Unloads vehicle.
   D11. Communicates orally and in writing.

2. *Following Oral Instructions* . . . The ability to understand and carry out oral instructions expressed in English as used in the following work behaviors:
   D11. Communicates orally and in writing.
   D5.   Delivers mail.
   D7.   Prepares and maintains records and reports.
   D4.   Operates vehicle.
   D1.   Cases mail.
   D10. Unloads vehicle.
   D2.   Pulls down.
   D3.   Loads vehicle.
   D8.   Walks and climbs stairs.

Exhibit 43. Operational Definitions of City Carrier Abilities—*continued*

3. *Physical Strength and Stamina* . . . The ability to stand, walk, sit, bend, reach, stoop, etc., for prolonged periods of time, and the ability to lift up to 70 lbs. as used in the following work behaviors:
D8.   Walks and climbs stairs.
D10. Unloads vehicle.
D3.   Loads vehicle.
D5.   Delivers mail.
D1.   Cases mail.
D2.   Pulls down.
D4.   Operates vehicle.

4. *Dexterity and Coordination*. . . The speed and accuracy with which a person can use the fingers, hands and arms in coordination with visual input in the handling and manipulation of objects as used in the following work behaviors:
D1.   Cases mail.
D5.   Delivers mail.
D2.   Pulls down.
D3.   Loads vehicle.
D10. Unloads vehicle.
D4.   Operates vehicle.
D8.   Walks and climbs stairs.

5. *Memory for Codes* . . The ability to learn and recall pairings of addresses with numbers, letters or positions as used in the following work behaviors:
D1.   Cases mail.
D5.   Delivers mail.
D2.   Pulls down.
D3.   Loads vehicle.

6. *Oral Expression* . . . The ability to use spoken English words, phrases or sentences as used in the following work behavior:
D11. Communicates orally and in writing.

7. *Written Comprehension* . . . The ability to understand written English words, phrases or sentences and take appropriate action as used in the following work behaviors:
D7.   Prepares and maintains records and reports.
D11. Communicates orally and in writing.
D1.   Cases mail.
D5.   Delivers mail.
D2.   Pulls down.
D4.   Operates vehicle.

8. *Sequencing* . . . The ability to place things in the proper numerical, alphabetical or geographical order as used in the following work behaviors:
D1.   Cases mail.
D3.   Loads vehicle.
D2.   Pulls down.
D5.   Delivers mail.

9. *Forms Completion* . . . The ability to fill out forms accurately, completely and legibly as used in the following work behaviors:
D7.   Prepares and maintains records and reports.
D11. Communicates orally and in writing.
D5.   Delivers mail.

References

Books and Journals

Agrid, D. *Fair employment litigation: Proving and defending a Title VII case*. New York: Practicing Law Institute, 1979.

Alternative selection procedures. *Federal Personnel Manual* (Bulletin 331). Washington, D.C.: U.S. Office of Personnel Management, 1980.

American Psychological Association, American Educational Research Association, and National Council on Measurement in Education. *Standards for educational and psychological tests*. Washington, D.C.: American Psychological Association, 1974.

American Psychological Association. Ethical principles of psychologists. *American Psychologist*, 1981, 36, 639–685.

Anastasi, A. *Psychological testing*, 4th ed. New York: Macmillan, 1976.

Arvey, R. D. Unfair discrimination in the employment interview: Legal and psychological aspects. *Psychological Bulletin*, 1979, 86, 736–765.

Ash, R. A. and Edgel, S. L. A note on the readability of the Position Analysis Questionnaire (PAQ). *Journal of Applied Psychology*, 1975, 60, 765–766.

Ashe, R. L. A view from the despondent respondent. Paper presented at the American Psychological Association Eighty-Fourth Annual Convention. Washington, D.C., 1976.

Baehr, M. E. *Skills and Attributes Inventory*. Chicago, Ill.: The University of Chicago, Industrial Relations Center, 1971.

Bemis, S. E. Behavioral consistency: Breakthrough in unassembled examining. Paper presented at the American Psychological Association Eighty-Sixth Annual Convention. Toronto, Canada, 1978(a).

Biddle, R. E. *GOJA Manual*, 3rd ed. Sacramento, Calif.: Biddle and Associates, 1976.

———. *Brief GOJA: A step-by-step analysis, instruction booklet*. Sacramento, Calif.: Biddle and Associates, 1978(a).

This is a complete listing of the references embodied in the text of this book. Some references, therefore, are duplicates of references in the Job Analysis Bibliography.

————. *Brief GOJA: A step-by-step analysis, work booklet.* Sacramento, Calif.: Biddle and Associates, 1978(b).

————. Forms for a simplified job analysis. Sacramento, Calif.: Biddle and Associates, 1980.

Blumrosen, A. Strangers in paradise: *Griggs v. Duke Power Co.* and the concept of employment discrimination. *Michigan Law Review,* 1972, *71,* 59–110.

Boyles, W. R., Palmer, C. I. and Veres, J. G. Bias in content valid tests. Paper presented at the International Personnel Management Assessment Council Annual Conference. Boston, 1980.

Brady, R. L. *Law for personnel managers: How to hire the people you need without discriminating.* Hartford, Conn.: Bureau of Law & Business, 1979.

Bronson, M. A. The Hay system of job evaluation. *Classifiers Column,* 1980, *11*(9), 1–6.

Buckly, R., Ruch, W. W., Boyles, W., Mahaffey, C., and Giffin, P. *Integrated Job Analysis.* Los Angeles, Calif.: Psychological Services, Inc., 1980.

Bureau of National Affairs, Inc. ASPA-BNA Survey No. 45: Employee Selection Procedures. *Bulletin to Management,* May 5, 1983.

Cahoon, S. A. Employee selection procedures: Uniform guidelines at last? *EEO Today,* 1978, *5*(2), 139–148.

Christal, R. E. *The U.S. Air Force occupational research project* (AFHRL-TR-73-75). Springfield, Va.: National Technical Information Service, 1974.

Connolly, W. P., Jr. Cited in: Age bias cases, once a rarity, now fill courts. *Washington Post,* November 9, 1981.

Cooper, G., and Sobol, R. B. Seniority and testing under fair employment laws: A general approach to objective criteria of hiring and promotion. *Harvard Law Review,* 1969, *82,* 1598–1679.

Cirilli, M., Jones, D., and Moore, K. Alternative work schedules: Job sharing in Wisconsin. *Notes/Book Reprints.* U.S. Office of Personnel Management, Office of Intergovernmental Personnel Programs, April 1980.

Copus, D. Appellate court decisions involving use of statistics in job bias cases. *Daily Labor Report* (BNA, Inc.), 1976, No. 227, D1–D4.

Cornelius, E. T., Carron, T. J., and Collins, M. N. Job analysis models and job classification. *Personnel Psychology,* 1979, *32,* 693–708.

County of San Bernardino (M. E. Nelson, Project Director). *Medical standards project: Interim final report.* San Bernardino, Calif.: Author, 1978.

Cronbach, L. J. *Essentials of psychological testing,* 3d ed. New York: Harper and Row, 1970.

Cunningham, J. W., Tuttle, T. C., Floyd, J. R., and Bates, J. A. *The development of the Occupation Analysis Inventory: An "ergometric" approach to an educational problem.* (Center Research Monograph No. 6). Raleigh, N.C.: North Carolina State University, Center for Occupational Education, 1971. JSAS *Catalog of Selected Documents in Psychology*, 1974, 4(4), 144. (MS. No. 803).

Division of Industrial and Organizational Psychology, American Psychological Association. *Principles for the validation and use of personnel selection procedures*, 2nd ed. Berkeley, Calif.: Author, 1980.

Feild, H. S., and Holly, W. H. *The relationship of performance appraisal system characteristics to verdicts in selected employment discrimination cases.* Cited in: Written instructions, notes to employees assist in defending performance appraisal in EEO suits. *Daily Labor Reports* (BNA, Inc.), 1980, No. 249.

Fiks, A. I., Bawden, H. P., Jr., and Gaspair, J. D. *Bank teller job trial: Final technical report.* Prepared for the U.S. Department of Labor, Employment and Training Administration (contract # 82-42-72-08). Philadelphia: Job Trial Research Center, a Division of the Jewish Employment and Vocational Service, 1976.

Fine, S. A., and Bernotavicz, F. D. *Task analysis: How to use the national task bank.* Kalamazoo, Mich.: W. E. Upjohn Institute for Employment Research, 1973.

Fine, S. A., Holt, A. M., and Hutchinson, M. F. *Functional job analysis: How to standardize task statements.* Kalamazoo, Mich.: W. E. Upjohn Institute for Employment Research, 1974.

Fine, S. A., Olson, H. C., Meyer, D. C., and Jeannings, M. C. An analysis of heavy equipment operator jobs. Paper presented to the Military Testing Association, Oklahoma City, Okla., 1978.

Fine, S. A., and Wiley, W. W. *An introduction to functional job analysis: A scaling of selected tasks from the social welfare field.* Kalamazoo, Mich.: W. E. Upjohn Institute for Employment Research, 1971.

Flanagan, J. C. The critical incident technique. *Psychological Bulletin*, 1954, *51*, 327–358.

Fleishman, E. A. Toward a taxonomy of human performance. *American Psychologist*, 1975, *30*(12), 1127–1149.

Gandy, J., and Maier, W. *Utah clerical linkup study: Comparison of federal and state jobs.* Washington, D.C.: U.S. Office of Personnel Management, 1979.

Gebhardt, D. L. Determination of medical standards for physically demanding jobs. Presentation to the Personnel Testing Council of Metropolitan Washington. Washington, D.C., November 1982.

Gilpatrick, E. *The Health Services Mobility Study method of task analysis and curriculum design—basic tools: Concepts, task identification, skill scales and knowledge system* (Res. Rpt. No. 11, Vol. 1). Springfield, Va.: National Technical Information Service, 1977(a).

————. *The Health Services Mobility Study method of task and curriculum design—writing task descriptions and scaling tasks for skills and knowledge: A manual* (Res. Rpt. No. 11, Vol. 2). Springfield, Va.: National Technical Information Service, 1977(b).

————. *The Health Services Mobility Study method of task analysis and curriculum design: Using the computer to develop job ladders* (Res. Rpt. No. 11, Vol. 3). Springfield, Va.: National Technical Information Service, 1977(c).

————, and Guillion, C. *The Health Services Mobility Study method of task analysis and curriculum design—developing curriculum objectives from task data: A manual* (Res. Rpt. No. 11, Vol. 4). Springfield, Va.: National Technical Information Service, 1977.

Greenman, R. L., and Schmertz, E. J. *Personnel administration and the law*, 2d ed. Washington, D.C.: BNA Books, 1979.

Health and Education Resources, Inc. Developing strategies for implementation of the Health Services Mobility Study. In *Proceedings of Health and Education Resources, Inc., conference.* Bethesda, Md.: Author, 1979.

Horstman, D. A. *Legal standards for personnel practices: Court case compendium 1975–1976.* Washington, D.C.: National Technical Information Service, 1977.

————. *Improving the legal defensibility of management decisions* (Operational paper). Washington, D.C.: Information Science, Inc., 1979.

Hunter, J. E., and Schmidt, F. L. Fitting people to jobs: The impact of personnel selection on national productivity. In E. A. Fleishman, ed. *Human capability assessment* (Human performance and productivity ser., Vol. 1). Hillsdale, N.J.: Erlbaum Associates, 1982.

Jeanneret, P. R. Equitable job evaluation and classification with the Position Analysis Questionnaire. *Compensation Review* (AMACOM), First Quarter, 1980, 32–42.

Koenig, P. They just changed the rules on how to get ahead. *Psychology Today*, June 1974, 87–103.

Krauss, I. Testing the older applicant: Longer work life for the twenty-first century employee. Presentation at a monthly meeting of the Personnel Testing Council of Southern California. Los Angeles, Calif., April, 1981.

Lerner, B. The Supreme Court and the APA, AERA, NCME test standards: Past references and future possibilities. *American Psychologist*, 1978, *33*, 915–919.

Levine, E. L., Ash, R. A., and Bennett, N. Exploratory comparative study of four job analysis methods. *Journal of Applied Psychology*, 1980, *65*, 524–535.

Levine, E. L., Bennett, N., and Ash, R. Evaluation and use of four job analysis methods for personnel selection. *Public Personnel Management*, May–June 1979, 146–151.

Levine, E. M., and Moore, A. *Exploring ways to implement the Health Services Mobility Study: A feasibility study*. Bethesda, Md.: Health and Education Resources, 1977.

Lilienthal, R. A., and Rosen, T. H. *A design for validating selection procedures for groups of jobs*. Washington, D.C.: U.S. Office of Personnel Management, 1980.

London, M., and Bray, D. W. Ethical issues in testing and evaluation for personnel decisions. *American Psychologist*, 1980, *35*, 890–901.

Lorber, L. Z., and Horstman, D. A. Weber: Its impact on public employees. *IPMAAC Assessment News*, 1980, *3*(1), 1–3.

Manese, W. R. *Employment testing, validation and the law*. Berkeley Heights, N.J.: E.G.M. Enterprises, 1979.

McCormick, E. J. *Job analysis: Methods and applications*. New York: AMACOM, 1979.

———, DeNisi, A. S., and Shaw, J. B. Use of the Position Analysis Questionnaire for establishing job component validity of tests. *Journal of Applied Psychology*, 1979, *64*, 51–56.

McCormick, E. J., Jeanneret, P. R., and Mecham, R. C. *Position Analysis Questionnaire (PAQ), Form B*. West Lafayette, Ind.: Purdue University, Occupational Research Center, 1969.

———. A study of job characteristics and job dimensions as based on the Position Analysis Questionnaire (PAQ). *Journal of Applied Psychology*, 1972, *56*, 347–368.

———. *Technical manual for the Position Analysis Questionnaire (System II)*. Logan, Utah: PAQ Services, 1977(a).

———. *User's manual for the Position Analysis Questionnaire*. Logan, Utah: PAQ Services, 1977(b).

Miner, M. G., and Miner, J. B. *Employee selection within the law*, rev. ed. Washington, D.C.: BNA Books, 1979.

Mitchell, J. L., and McCormick, E. J. *Professional and Managerial Position Questionnaire (PmPQ), Form A^2*. West Lafayette, Ind.: Purdue Research Foundation, 1980.

Modjeska, L. *Handling employment discrimination cases*. Rochester, N.Y.: Lawyers Cooperative, 1980.

Moore, A. *The Health Services Mobility Study method of task analysis and curriculum design*. Monograph submitted by Health and Education Resources, Inc., to the Office of Research and Development of the Employment and Training Administration, U.S. Department of Labor, 1980.

Mussio, S. J., and Smith, M. K. *Content validity: A procedural manual.* Chicago, Ill.: International Personnel Management Association, 1973.

New York Stock Exchange. *Reaching a higher standard of living.* New York: Author, 1977.

PAQ Services, Inc. *Job analysis manual for the Position Analysis Questionnaire.* Logan, Utah: Author, 1977.

PAQ Newsletter, R. Mecham, ed. (PAQ Services, Inc.), 1981, No. 2-81.

Player, M. A. *Federal law of employment discrimination in a nutshell.* St. Paul, Minn.: West, 1976.

Powers, T. Defending a Title VII case. Paper presented at the American Law Association and National Civil Service League Second Annual Conference on EEO Law. Washington, D.C., 1976.

Primoff, E. S. *The job element procedure in relation to employment procedures for the disadvantaged.* Washington, D.C.: U.S. Civil Service Commission, Personnel Research and Development Center, 1972.

————. *How to prepare and conduct job-element examinations.* U.S. Civil Service Commission, Personnel Research and Development Center. Washington, D.C.: U.S. Government Printing Office, 1975.

————. Supplement to: *How to prepare and conduct job element examinations.* Unpublished draft, July 1980.

Questions and Answers on the Uniform Guidelines. *Federal Register*, 1979, 44, 11996–12009. Supplement. *Federal Register*, 1980, 45, 29530–29531.

Rose, D. L. Presentation at the University of Chicago Third Annual Conference on EEO Compliance and Human Resources Management. Cited in: Professional, legal requirements of job analysis explored at Chicago conference. *Daily Labor Report* (BNA, Inc.), 1980, No. 106, A6–A8.

Schlei, B. L., and Grossman, P. G. *Employment discrimination law.* Washington, D.C.: BNA Books, 1983.

Schmidt, F. L., Caplan, J. R., Bemis, S. E., Decuir, R., Dunn, L., and Antone, L. *The behavioral consistency method of unassembled examining.* Washington, D.C.: U.S. Office of Personnel Management, 1979.

Schuck, P. When officials are liable. *New York Times*, July 13, 1980, 21.

Schwartz, D. J. What the government is looking for in a job analysis. Cited in *Daily Labor Report* (BNA, Inc.), 1980, No. 106, A4–A6.

Seberhagen, L. W. Affirmative action in the public sector. In *Affirmative action in testing and selection: Legal and psychological perspectives.* Symposium presented at the American Psychological Association Eighty-Sixth Annual Convention. Toronto, Canada, 1978.

Sharf, J. Bibliography on fair employment practices testing. *Daily Labor Report* (BNA, Inc.), 1975, No. 66, A18–A22.

Sheridan, J. A. Designing the work environment. Paper presented at the American Psychological Association Eighty-Third Annual Convention. Chicago, 1975.

Siegel, J. *Personnel testing under EEO*. New York: American Management Association, 1980.

Singer, J. W. Equal employment agencies are beginning to shape up. *National Journal*, January 7, 1978, 19–23.

Smith, L. Equal opportunity rules are getting tougher. *Fortune*, June 19, 1978, 152–156.

Sparks, C. P. Presentation at the Second Annual Conference on EEO Compliance and Human Resources Utilitization. Cited in: Problems, progress in testing guidelines are probed at major conference in Chicago. *Daily Labor Report* (BNA, Inc.), 1979, No. 112, CC1–CC3.

————. Job analysis under the new Uniform Guidelines: Procedures, standards, requirements, and restraints. Paper presented at the University of Chicago Third Annual Conference on EEO Compliance and Human Resources Utilization. Chicago, 1980.

Stone, C. H. Evaluation of Marine Corps task analysis program (Technical Report No. 16) Los Angeles, Calif.: California State University, Los Angeles Foundation, 1976.

Taylor, L. R. The Construction of job families based upon the components and overall dimensions of the PAQ. *Personnel Psychology*, 1978, *31*(2), 325–340.

Thew, M. C., and Weissmuller, J. J. *CODAP: A current overview*. San Antonio, Tex.: U.S. Air Force Human Resources Laboratory, undated.

A time for crucial rulings on job bias. *Business Week*, October 13, 1980, 46–47.

Treiman, D. J. *Job evaluation: An analytic review* (Interim report to the Equal Employment Opportunity Commission). Washington, D.C.: National Academy of Sciences, 1979.

————, and Hartmann, H. I. *Women, work and wages: Equal pay for jobs of equal value*. Washington, D.C.: National Academy Press, 1981.

Uniform guidelines on employee selection procedures. *Federal Register*, 1978, *42*, 38290–38315.

U.S. Civil Service Commission. *BRE exam preparation manual*. Washington, D.C.: Author, 1977(a).

————. *Instructions for the factor evaluation system*. Washington, D.C.: U.S. Government Printing Office, 1977(b).

U.S. Department of Labor. *Manual for the General Aptitude Test Battery*. Section III: Development. Washington, D.C.: Author, 1970.

————. *Handbook for analyzing jobs*. Washington, D.C.: U.S. Government Printing Office, 1972.

U.S. Office of Personnel Management. *How to write position descriptions under the factor evaluation system*. Washington, D.C.: U.S. Government Printing Office, 1979(b).

————. *The behavioral consistency method of unassembled examining*. Washington, D.C.: Author, 1979.

U.S. Postal Service. *Validation report for positions of City Carrier, Mail Handler, Distribution Clerk, Distribution Clerk, Machine*. Washington, D.C.: Author, 1981.

van Rijn, P. *Job analysis for selection: An overview*. Washington, D.C.: Office of Personnel Management, Personnel Research and Development Center, 1979.

Weilheimer, R. Tailoring the job to fit the worker. *The Sunday Record* (Bergen/Passaic/Hudson Counties, N.J.), August 31, 1980.

Legal Citations

Albemarle Paper Co. v. Moody, 422 U.S. 405, 10 FEP Cases 1181 (1975).

Association Against Discrimination in Employment v. City of Bridgeport, 594 F.2d 306, 20 FEP Cases 985 (2d Cir. 1979).

Berkmam v. City of New York, 536 F. Supp. 177, 28 FEP Cases 856 (1982).

Blake v. City of Los Angeles, 595 F.2d 1367, 19 FEP Cases 1441 (9th Cir. 1979), *cert. denied*, 446 U.S. 928 (1980).

Cormier v. P.P.G. Industries, 702 F.2d 567, 31 FEP Cases 1039 (5th Cir. 1983).

Dothard v. Rawlinson, 433 U.S. 321, 15 FEP Cases 10 (1977).

Ensley Branch, NAACP v. Seibels, 616 F.2d 812, 22 FEP Cases 1207 (5th Cir. 1980).

Firefighters Institute for Racial Equality v. City of St. Louis, 616 F.2d 350, 21 FEP Cases 1140 (8th Cir. 1980), *cert. denied*, 452 U.S. 938, 25 FEP Cases 1683 (1981).

Friend V. Leidinger, 588 F.2d 61, 18 FEP Cases 1052 (4th Cir. 1978).

Fullilove v. Klutznick, 448 U.S. 448, 48 USLW 4979 (1980).

Griggs v. Duke Power Co., 401 U.S. 424, 3 FEP Cases 175 (1971).

Guardians Ass'n of New York City Police Dep't v. Civil Service Comm'n of the City of New York, 630 F.2d 79, 23 FEP Cases 909 (2d Cir. 1980), *cert. denied*, 452 U.S. 940, 25 FEP Cases 1683 (1981).

James v. Stockham Valves & Fittings Co., 559 F.2d 310, 15 FEP Cases 827 (5th Cir. 1977), *cert. denied*, 434 U.S. 1034, 16 FEP Cases 501 (1978).

Jones v. New York City Human Resources Admin., 391 F. Supp. 1064, 12 FEP Cases 264 (D.C.N.Y. 1975).

Louisville Black Police Officers v. City of Louisville, 20 FEP Cases 1195 (D.C. Ky. 1979).

McKenzie v. McCormick, 436 F. Supp 351, 15 FEP Cases (D.C.D.C. 1977).

Monell v. Department of Social Services of City of New York, 436 U.S. 658, 17 FEP Cases 873 (1978).

Pegues v. Mississippi State Employment Service, 488 F. Supp. 239, 22 FEP Cases 392 (D.C. Miss. 1980), *aff'd, rev'd, and remanded in part,* 699 F.2d 760, 31 FEP Cases 257 (5th Cir. 1983).

Price v. Sacramento County Civil Service Comm'n, 26 Cal.3d 257, 604 P.2d 1365, 161 Cal. Rptr. 475, 21 FEP Cases 1512 (Ca. S.Ct. 1980).

Sarabia v. Toledo Police Patrolman's Ass'n, 601 F.2d 914, 20 FEP Cases 153 (6th Cir. 1979).

Shack v. Southworth, 521 F.2d 51, 11 FEP Cases 273 (6th Cir. 1975).

Steelworkers v. Weber, 443 U.S. 193, 20 FEP Cases 1 (1979).

Teamsters v. United States, 431 U.S. 324, 14 FEP Cases 1514 (1977).

United States v. City of Chicago, 411 F. Supp. 218, 14 FEP Cases 417 (N.D. Ill. 1976) *aff'd in pertinent part,* 549 F.2d 415, 14 FEP Cases 462 (7th Cir.), *cert. denied,* 434 U.S. 875, 15 FEP Cases 1184 (1977).

United States v. City of Chicago, 573 F.2d 416, 16 FEP Cases 908 (7th Cir. 1978).

United States v. State of New York, 82 FRD 2 (D.C.N.Y. 1978), *dec. on merits,* 475 F. Supp. 1103 (D.C.N.Y. 1979).

Washington v. Davis, 426 U.S. 229, 12 FEP Cases 1415 (1976).

Civil Service Act, P.L. 95-454, 95 Stat. 111 (1978).

Equal Pay Act of 1963, 29 U.S.C. § 206, P.L. 88-38, 77 Stat. 56 (1963).

Title VII of the Civil Rights Act of 1964, 42 U.S.C. § 2000e et seq., P.L. 88-352, 78 Stat. 241 (1964).

Resources for Further Information on Methods

Department of Labor Job Analysis Method
    Division of Occupational Analysis
    Employment & Training Administration
    U.S. Dept. of Labor
    Patrick Henry Building
    601 D Street N.W.
    Washington, D.C. 20213

Functional Job Analysis Method
  Dr. Sidney A. Fine
  1870 Wyoming Ave. N.W.
  Washington, D.C. 20009

Critical Incident Technique
  John C. Flanagan
  American Institutes for Research
  P.O. Box 1113
  Palo Alto, California 94302

Job Element Method
  Ernest Primoff
  5504 Shawnee Drive
  Forest Heights, Maryland 20745

Position Analysis Questionnaire (PAQ)
  Dr. Ernest J. McCormick
  President, PAQ Services, Inc.
  1315 Sunset Lane
  West Lafayette, Indiana 47906

  Dr. Robert C. Mecham
  Director, PAQ Data Processing Division
  1625 North 1000 East
  Logan, Utah 84321

  Dr. P. R. Jeanneret
  Vice President
  PAQ Services, Inc.
  3223 Smith Street, Suite 212
  Houston Texas 77006

Computer Analyzed Task Inventory Approach (CODAP)
  Dr. Raymond E. Christal
  Manpower and Personnel Division
  Air Force Human Resources Laboratory
  Brooks Air Force Base, Texas 78235

Health Services Mobility Study Method
  Dr. Eleanor Gilpatrick
  Director, HSMS
  302 W. 12th Street
  New York, New York 10014

  Health and Education Resources
  4733 Bethesda Avenue
  Bethesda, Maryland 20014

Guidelines Oriented Job Analysis (GOJA)
   Richard E. Biddle
   Biddle and Associates, Inc.
   903 Enterprise Drive
   Sacramento, California 95825

Behavioral Consistency Method
   Examination Methods Development Unit
   Staffing Services Group
   U.S. Office of Personnel Management
   1900 E Street N.W.
   Washington, D.C. 20415

Factor Evaluation System
   Standards Development Center
   Staffing Services Group
   U.S. Office of Personnel Management
   1900 E Street N.W.
   Washington, D.C. 20415

Job Analysis Bibliography

Allen, J. C. Multidimensional analysis of worker-oriented and job-oriented verbs. *Journal of Applied Psychology*, 1969, *53*, 73–79.

Allen, L. Test transportability and the uniform guidelines. *Public Personnel Management*, 1979, *8*(5), 309–314.

American Psychological Association, American Educational Research Association, and National Council on Measurement in Education. *Standards for educational and psychological tests.* Washington, D.C.: American Psychological Association, 1974.

Archer, J. R., and Giorgia, M. J. Bibliography of the Occupational Research Division, Air Force Human Resources Laboratory (AFSC). JSAS *Catalog of Selected Documents in Psychology*, 1977, 5, 259. (Ms. No. 974).

Arvey, R. D., and Begalla, M. E. Analyzing the homemaker job using the Position Analysis Questionnaire. *Journal of Applied Psychology*, 1975, *60*, 513–517.

Arvey, R. D., Maxwell, S. E., and Mossholder, K. M. Even more ideas about methodologies for determining job differences and similarities. *Personnel Psychology*, 1979, *32*(3), 529–538.

Arvey, R. D., and Mossholder, K. M. A proposed methodology for determining similarities and differences among jobs. *Personnel Psychology*, 1977, *30*(3), 363–374.

Arvey, R. D., Passino, E. M., and Lounsbury, J. N. Job analysis results as influenced by sex of incumbent and sex of analyst. *Journal of Applied Psychology*, 1977, *62*, 411–416.

Ash, R. A., and Edgell, S. L. A note on the readability of the Position Analysis Questionnaire (PAQ). *Journal of Applied Psychology*, 1975, *60*, 765–766.

Augustin, J. W., Cunningham, J. W., and Heath, W. D., III. *Affective correlates of systematically derived occupational variables: A repeated study.*

This bibliography was prepared by C. Paul Sparks, while with Personnel Research, Exxon Company, U.S.A., Houston, Texas, and is reproduced here with his kind permission. This version reflects his entries through October 1, 1980. It has been partially updated by the authors.

(Center Report, Ergometric Research and Development Series No. 12). Raleigh, N.C.: North Carolina State University, Center for Occupational Education, 1975. JSAS *Catalog of Selected Documents in Psychology*, 1975, 5, 353–354. (Ms. No. 1152).

Baehr, M. E. *Skills and Attributes Inventory*. Chicago, Ill.: The University of Chicago, Industrial Relations Center, 1971.

————. *A national occupational analysis of the school principalship*. Chicago, Ill.: The University of Chicago, Industrial Relations Center, 1975.

————. *National validation of a selection test battery for male transit bus operators: Final report*. Springfield, Va.: National Technical Information Service, June 1976.

————. *A practitioner's view of EEOC requirements with special reference to job analysis*. Occasional Paper 37. Chicago, Ill.: The University of Chicago, Industrial Relations Center, September 1976.

————, Burns, F. M., McPherson, R. B., and Salley, C. *Job Functions Inventory for school principals*. Chicago, Ill.: The University of Chicago, Industrial Relations Center and Consortium for Educational Leadership, 1976.

Barrett, G. V., Alexander, R. A., O'Connor, E. O., Forbes, J. B., Balascoe, L., and Garver, T. *Public policy and personnel selection: Development of a selection program for patrol officers* (Technical Report 1). Akron, Ohio: University of Akron, Department of Psychology, April 1975.

Baxter, B. *Replacing jobs with task clusters as the work unit for test validation*. (DLMA 20-42-74-14-1). Pittsburgh, Penn.: American Institutes for Research, September 1975.

Bennett, C. A. Toward empirical, practicable, comprehensive task taxonomy. *Human Factors*, 1971, 13, 229–235.

Berwitz, C. J. *The job analysis approach to affirmative action*. New York: Wiley, 1975.

Biddle, R. E. *GOJA Manual*, 3d ed. Sacramento, Calif.: Biddle and Associates, 1976.

————. *Brief GOJA: A step-by-step analysis, instruction booklet*. Sacramento, Calif.: Biddle and Associates, 1978(a).

————. *Brief GOJA: A step-by-step analysis, work booklet*. Sacramento, Calif.: Biddle and Associates, 1978(b).

————. Forms for a simplified job analysis. Sacramento, Calif.: Biddle and Associates, 1980.

Blashfield, R. K. Mixture model tests of cluster analysis: Accuracy of four agglomerative hierarchical methods. *Psychological Bulletin*, 1976, 83, 377–388.

Boese, R. R., and Cunningham, J. W. *Systematically derived dimensions of human work*. (Center Report, Ergometric Research and Development

Series No. 14). Raleigh, N.C.: North Carolina State University, Center for Occupational Education, 1975. JSAS *Catalog of Selected Documents in Psychology*, 1976, *6*, 57–58. (Ms. No. 1270).

Borgen, F. H., and Weiss, D. J. Cluster analysis in counseling research. *Journal of Counseling Psychology*, 1971, *18*, 583–591.

Borman, W. C., Toquam, J. L., and Rosse, R. L. Dimensions of the army recruiter and guidance counselor job (U.S. Army Technical Report, 1977 (March), No. TR-77-A5). JSAS *Catalog of Selected Documents in Psychology*, 1979, *9*(4), 96. (Ms. No. 1953).

Bouchard, T. J. *A manual for job analysis*. St. Paul, Minn.: Minnesota Civil Service Department, 1972.

Bownas, D. A. *Plant operator task list*. Minneapolis, Minn.: Personnel Decisions Research Institute, 1979.

———, and Bosshardt, M. J. *Development of task inventories for three Coast Guard rates*. (Project Final Report). Minneapolis, Minn.: Personnel Decisions Research Institute, 1979.

Bownas, D. A., and Heckman, R. W. *Job analysis of the entry level fire-fighting position*. Minneapolis, Minn.: Personnel Decisions, Inc., 1976.

Brumback, G. B. Consolidating job descriptions, performance appraisals, and manpower reports. *Personnel Journal*, 1971, *50*, 604–610.

———, Edwards, D. S., Fleishman, E. A., Hahn, C. P., and Romashko, T. *Model procedures for job analysis, test development, and validation. Volume II: Final report of the second phase*. Washington, D.C.: American Institutes for Research, February, 1975.

Brumback, G. B., Romashko, T., Hahn, C. P., and Fleishman, E. A. *Model procedures for job analysis, test development, and validation. Volume I: Final report of the first phase*. Washington, D.C.: American Institutes for Research, July 1974.

Brumback, G. B., and Vincent, J. W. Jobs and appraisal of performance. *Personnel Administration*, 1970, *23*, 26–30.

———. Factor analysis of work-performed data for a sample of administrative, professional, and scientific positions. *Personnel Psychology*, 1970, *23*, 101–107.

Brush, D. H., and Owens, W. A. Implementation and evaluation of an assessment classification model for manpower utilization. *Personnel Psychology*, 1979, *32*(2), 369–383.

Buckly, R., Ruch, W. W., Boyles, W., Mahaffey, C., and Giffin, P. *Integrated Job Analysis*. Los Angeles, Calif.: Psychological Services, Inc., 1980.

Burgar, P. S. Have behavioral expectation scales fulfilled our expectations? Theoretical and empirical review. JSAS *Catalog of Selected Documents in Psychology*, 1978, *8*, 76. (Ms. No. 1745).

Campbell, J. P., Dunnette, M. D., Arvey, R. D., and Hellervik, L. V. The development and evaluation of behaviorally based rating scales. *Journal of Applied Psychology*, 1973, *57*(1), 15–22.

Campion, J. E., Greener, J., and Wernli, S. Work observation versus recall in developing examples for rating scales. *Journal of Applied Psychology*, 1973, *58*, 286–288.

Carpenter, J. B. *Sensitivity of group job descriptions to possible inaccuracies in individual job descriptions*. (AFHRL-TR-74-6) Lackland Air Force Base, Tex.: Air Force Human Resources Laboratory, 1974. JSAS *Catalog of Selected Documents in Psychology*, 1974, *4*, 149. (Ms. No. 811).

Carroll, S. J., Jr., and Taylor, W. H., Jr., Validity of estimates by clerical personnel of job time proportions. *Journal of Applied Psychology*, 1969, *53*, 164–166.

Christal, R. E. *The United States Air Force occupational research project*. (AFHRL-TR-73-75). Lackland Air Force Base, Tex.: Air Force Human Resources Laboratory, 1974. JSAS *Catalog of Selected Documents in Psychology*, 1974, *4*, 61. (Ms. No. 651). Springfield, Va.: National Technical Information Service.

———, and Weissmuller, J. J. *New Comprehensive Occupational Data Analysis Programs (CODAP) for analyzing task factor information*. (AFHRL Interim Professional Paper No. TR-76-3). Lackland Air Force Base, Tex.: Air Force Human Resources Laboratory, 1976. JSAS *Catalog of Selected Documents in Psychology*, 1977, *7*, 24–25. (Ms. No. 1444).

Colbert, G. A., and Taylor, L. R. Empirically derived job families as a foundation for the study of validity generalization. *Personnel Psychology*, 1978, *31*(2), 355–364.

Cornelius, E. T., III, Carron, T. J., and Collins, M. N. Job analysis models and job classification. *Personnel Psychology*, 1979, *32*(4), 693–708.

Cornelius, E. T., III, Hakel, M. D., and Sackett, P. R. A methodological approach to job classification for performance appraisal purposes. *Personnel Psychology*, 1979, *32*(2), 283–297.

Cronbach, L. J., and Gleser, G. C. Assessing similarity between profiles. *Psychological Bulletin*, 1953, *50*, 456–473.

Cunningham, J. W. *"Ergometrics": A systematic approach to some educational problems*. (Center Monograph No. 7). Raleigh, N.C.: North Carolina State University, Center for Occupational Education, 1971. JSAS *Catalog of Selected Documents in Psychology*, 1974 *4*(4), 144–145. (Ms. No. 804).

———, Phillips, M. R., and Spetz, S. H. *An exploratory study of a job component approach to estimating the human ability requirements of job classifications in a state competitive service system*. Raleigh, N.C.: North Carolina Office of State Personnel, 1976.

Cunningham, J. W., Slonaker, D. F., and Riegel, N. B. *The development of activity preference scales based on systematically derived work dimensions: An ergometric approach to interest measurement.* (Center Report, Ergometric Research and Development Series No. 15). Raleigh, N.C.: North Carolina State University, Center for Occupational Education, 1975. JSAS *Catalog of Selected Documents in Psychology*, 1975, 5, 355. (Ms. No. 1154).

Cunningham, J. W., Tuttle, T. C., Floyd, J. R., and Bates, J. A. *Occupation Analysis Inventory.* Raleigh, N.C.: North Carolina State University, Center for Occupational Education, 1970.

————. *The development of the Occupation Analysis Inventory: An "ergometric" approach to an educational problem.* (Center Research Monograph No. 6). Raleigh, N.C.: North Carolina State University, Center for Occupational Education, 1971. JSAS *Catalog of Selected Documents in Psychology*, 1974, 4(4), 144. (Ms. No. 803).

DeNisi, A. S. The implications of job clustering for training programs. *Journal of Occupational Psychology*, 1976, 49, 105–113.

————, and McCormick, E. J. *The cluster analysis of jobs based on data from the Position Analysis Questionnaire (PAQ).* West Lafayette, Ind.: Purdue University, Occupational Research Center, 1974.

Desmond, R. E., and Weiss, D. J. Supervisor estimation of abilities required in jobs. *Journal of Vocational Behavior*, 1973, 3, 181–194.

Dotson, C. O., Santa Maria, D. L., Davis, P. O., and Schwartz, R. A. *Development of a job-related physical performance examination for firefighters.* Washington, D.C.: U.S. Department of Commerce, National Fire Prevention and Control Administration, 1977.

Dowell, B. E., and Wexley, K. N. Development of a work behavior taxonomy for first-line supervisors. *Journal of Applied Psychology*, 1978, 63, 563–572.

Drauden, G. M. *Entry-level professionals' job analysis and selection strategy: A progress report.* St. Paul, Minn.: Minnesota Department of Personnel, Test Research and Development Section. JSAS *Catalog of Selected Documents in Psychology*, 1977, 7, 26. (Ms. No. 1447).

————, and Peterson, N. G. *A domain sampling approach to job analysis.* St. Paul, Minn.: State of Minnesota, Test Validation Center, 1974. JSAS *Catalog of Selected Documents in Psychology*, 1977, 7, 27. (Ms. No. 1449).

Dulewicz, S. V., and Keenay, G. A. A practically oriented and objective method for classifying and assigning senior jobs. *Journal of Occupational Psychology*, 1979, 52, 155–166.

Dumas, N. S., and Muthard, J. E. Job analysis methods for health-related professions: A pilot study of physical therapists. *Journal of Applied Psychology*, 1971, 55, 458–465.

Dunnette, M. D. Aptitudes, abilities, and skill. In M. D. Dunnette, Ed. *Handbook of industrial and organizational psychology*. Chicago, Ill.: Rand McNally, 1976, 473–520.

———, Hough, L. M., and Rosse, R. L. Task and job taxonomies as a basis for identifying labor supply sources and evaluating employment qualifications. *Human Resources Planning*, 1979, *2*(1), 37–51.

Equal Employment Opportunity Commission. Guidelines on employee selection procedures. *Federal Register*, 1970, *35*, 12333–12336.

———. Guidelines on employee selection procedures. *Federal Register*, 1976, *41*, 51984–51986.

———, Civil Service Commission, Department of Labor, and Department of Justice. Adoption by four agencies of uniform guidelines on employee selection procedures (1978). *Federal Register*, 1978, *43*, 38290–38315.

Equal Employment Opportunity Commission, Office of Personnel Management, Department of Justice, Department of Labor, and Department of the Treasury. Adoption of questions and answers to clarify and provide a common interpretation of the uniform guidelines on employee selection procedures. *Federal Register*, 1979, *44*, (43), 11996–12009.

Farina, A. J., Jr. *Development of a taxonomy of human performance: A review of descriptive schemes for human task behavior*. Washington, D.C.: American Institutes for Research, 1969. JSAS *Catalog of Selected Documents in Psychology*, 1973, *3*, 23. (Ms. No. 318).

———, and Wheaton, G. R. *Development of a taxonomy of human performance: The task characteristics approach to performance prediction*. Washington, D.C.: American Institutes for Research, 1971. JSAS *Catalog of Selected Documents in Psychology*, 1973, *3*, 26–27. (Ms. No. 323).

Feild, H. S., and Schoenfeldt, L. F. Ward and Hook revisited: A two-part procedure for overcoming a deficiency in the grouping of persons. *Educational and Psychological Measurement*, 1975, *35*, 171–173.

Fine, S. A. *An annotated bibliography of functional job analysis*. McLean, Va.: Human Sciences Research, Inc., 1965.

———. *Functional job analysis scales: A desk aid*. Kalamazoo, Mich.: W. E. Upjohn Institute for Employment Research, 1973.

———. Functional job analysis: An approach to a technology for manpower planning. *Personnel Journal*, 1974, *53*(11), 813–818.

———, and Bernotavicz, F. D. *Task analysis: How to use the National Task Bank*. Kalamazoo, Mich.: W. E. Upjohn Institute for Employment Research, 1973.

Fine, S. A., Holt, A. M., and Hutchinson, M. F. *Functional job analysis: How to standardize task statements*. Kalamazoo, Mich.: W. E. Upjohn Institute for Employment Research, 1974.

Fine, S. A., & Wiley, W. W. *An introduction to functional job analysis: A sealing of selected tasks from the social welfare field.* Kalamazoo, Mich.: W. E. Upjohn Institute for Employment Research, 1971.

Fivars, G. *The critical incident technique: A bibliography.* Palo Alto, Calif.: American Institutes for Research, 1973.

Flanagan, J. C. The critical incident technique. *Psychological Bulletin*, 1954, *51*, 327–358.

Fleishman, E. A. *Structure and measurement of physical fitness.* Englewood Cliffs, N.J.: Prentice Hall, 1964.

————. On the relation between abilities, learning, and human performance. *American Psychologist*, 1972, *27*, 1017–1032.

————. Toward a taxonomy of human performance. *American Psychologist*, 1975, *30*(12), 1127–1149.

————. *Physical abilities analysis manual.* Washington, D.C.: Advanced Research Resources Organization, 1977.

————. Evaluating physical abilities required by jobs. *The Personnel Administrator*, 1979, *24*(6), 82–92.

————, and Hogan, J. C. *A taxonomic method for assessing the physical requirement of jobs: The physical abilities analysis approach.* (Technical Report). Washington, D.C.: Advanced Research Resources Organization, 1978.

Fleishman, E. A., Kinkade, R. G., and Chambers, A. N. *Development of a taxonomy of human performance: A review of the first year's progress.* Washington, D.C.: American Institutes for Research, 1968. JSAS *Catalog of Selected Documents in Psychology*, 1972, *2*, 39. (Ms. No. 111).

Fleishman, E. A., and Stephenson, R. W. *Development of a taxonomy of human performance: A review of the third year's progress.* Washington, D.C.: American Institutes for Research, 1970. JSAS *Catalog of Selected Documents in Psychology*, 1972, *2*, 40–41. (Ms. No. 113).

Fleishman, E. A., Teichner, W. H., and Stephenson, R. W. *Development of a taxonomy of human performance: A review of the second year's progress.* Washington, D.C.: American Institutes for Research, 1969. JSAS *Catalog of Selected Documents in Psychology*, 1972, *2*, 39–40. (Ms. No. 112).

Foley, J. P. *Task analysis for job performance aids and related training.* Lackland Air Force Base, Tex.: Air Force Human Resources Laboratory, 1973.

Freedman, R. D., and Dubno, P. A new approach to managerial position descriptions. *Experimental Publication System*, April 1971, *11*, (Ms. No. 427-1).

Fugill, J. W. *Task difficulty and task aptitude benchmark scales for the administrative and general career field.* Lackland Air Force Base, Tex.:

Air Force Human Resources Laboratory, 1973. JSAS *Catalog of Selected Documents in Psychology*, 1974, *4*, 30. (Ms. No. 591).

Gael, S. *Development of job task inventories and their use in job analysis research.* New York: American Telephone & Telegraph Company. JSAS *Catalog of Selected Documents in Psychology*, 1977, *7*, 25. (Ms. No. 1445).

——. *Job analysis: A guide to assessing work activities.* San Francisco, Calif. Jossey Bass, 1983.

Gandy, J. A. *Validity generalization and cooperative testing: Approaches and prospects.* Washington, D.C.: U.S. Civil Service Commission, Personnel Research and Development Center, July 1976. (NTIS No. PB 261 698).

Garza, A. T., and Carpenter, J. B. *Comparative job attributes of airmen and civil service personnel having similar job types.* (AFHRL 74-75). Lackland Air Force Base, Tex.: Air Force Human Resources Laboratory, 1974. JSAS *Catalog of Selected Documents in Psychology*, 1975, *5*, 214. (Ms. No. 897).

Ghiselli, E. E. *The validity of occupational aptitude tests.* New York: Wiley, 1966.

Gilpatrick, E. *The Health Services Mobility Study method of task analysis and curriculum design-basic tools: Concepts, task identification, skill scales and knowledge system.* (Research Report No. 11, Vol. 1). Springfield, Va.: National Technical Information Service, 1977.

——. *The Health Services Mobility Study method of task analysis and curriculum design—Writing task descriptions and scaling tasks for skills and knowledge: A manual.* (Research Report No. 11, Vol. 2). Springfield, Va.: National Technical Information Service, 1977.

——. *The Health Services Mobility method of task analysis and curriculum design—Using the computer to develop job ladders.* (Research Report No. 11, Vol. 3). Springfield, Va.: National Technical Information Service, 1977.

——, and Gullion, C. *The Health Services Mobility Study method of task analysis and curriculum design—Developing curriculum objectives from task data: A manual.* (Research Report No. 11, Vol. 4). Springfield, Va.: National Technical Information Service, 1977.

Hackman, J. R., and Oldham, G. R. Development of the job diagnostic survey. *Journal of Applied Psychology*, 1975, *60*, 159–170.

Hadley, H. I., Marsh, C. N., and Korotkin, A. L. Standards for establishing grades of army assignments and for conversion of officer positions/duties to enlisted position/duties (U.S. Army Technical Report, 1977 (Dec.), No. TR-77-A19). JSAS *Catalog of Selected Documents in Psychology*, 1979, *9*(4), 96–97. (Ms. No. 1954).

Hahn, C. P., Archer, R. F., McNelis, J. R., Romashko, T., and Brumback, G. B. *Prototype job analyses of three supervisory positions within the*

New York City school system. Washington, D.C.: American Institutes for Research, June 1975.

Hanser, L. M., Mendel, R. M., and Wolins, L. Three flies in the ointment: A reply to Arvey and Mossholder. *Personnel Psychology*, 1979, *32*(3), 511–516.

Hartley, C., Brecht, M., Pageray, P., Weeks, G., Chapanis, A., and Hoecker, D. Subjective time estimates of work tasks by office workers. *Journal of Occupational Psychology*, 1977, *50*, 23–36.

Health Manpower Council of California. *Task analysis method for improved manpower utilization in the health sciences.* Orinda, Calif.: Author, 1970.

Heath, W. D., III, Cunningham, J. W., and Augustin, J. W. *Ability correlates of systematically derived occupational variables: A repeated study.* (Center Report, Ergometric Research and Development Series No. 13). Raleigh, N.C.: North Carolina State University, Center for Occupational Education, 1975. JSAS *Catalog of Selected Documents in Psychology*, 1975, *5*, 354. (Ms. No. 1153).

Hemphill, J. K. Job descriptions for executives. *Harvard Business Review*, 1959, *37* (5), 55–67.

———. *Dimensions of executive positions.* (Research Monograph No. 98). Columbus, Ohio: Ohio State University, Bureau of Business Research, 1960.

Hogan, J. C., and Fleishman, E. A. An index of the physical effort required in human task performance. *Journal of Applied Psychology*, 1979, *64* (2), 197–204.

———, and Ogden, G.D., *Assessing physical requirements for establishing medical standards in selected benchmark jobs.* (Final Report). Washington, D.C.: Advanced Research Resources Organization, 1978.

Holland, J. L., Viernstein, M. C., Kue, H., Karweit, N. L., and Blum, Z. D. A psychological classification of occupations. JSAS *Catalog of Selected Documents in Psychology*, 1972, *2*, 84. (Ms. No. 184).

Hough, L. M. *Job activities questionnaire for retail employees.* Minneapolis, Minn.: Personnel Decisions Research Institute, 1977.

———. *Professional activities description questionnaire.* Minneapolis, Minn.: Personal Decisions Research Institute, 1979.

Institute for Manpower Management. *Job task analysis.* Washington, D.C.: Author, 1977.

Jackson, V. C. *Task analysis, a systematic approach to designing new careers programs.* New York: New York University, New Careers Training Laboratory, 1971.

Jeanneret, P. R. Equitable job evaluation and classification with the Position Analysis Questionnaire (PAQ). *Compensation Review* (AMACOM), 1980, 1st Qtr.

————, and McCormick, E. J. *The job dimensions of "worker oriented" job variables and of their attribute profiles as based on data from the Position Analysis Questionnaire.* (Report No. 2) West Lafayette, Ind.: Purdue University, Occupational Research Center, January 1969.

Jenkins, G. D., Nadler, D. A., Lawler, E. E., III, and Cammann, C. Standard Observations: An approach to measuring the nature of jobs. *Journal of Applied Psychology*, 1975, *60*, 171–181.

Kleiman, L. S., and Faley, R. H. Assessing content validity: Standards set by the court. *Personnel Psychology*, 1978, *31*, 701–713.

Krzystofiak, F., Newman, J. M., and Anderson, G. A quantified approach to measurement of job content: Procedures and payoffs. *Personnel Psychology*, 1979, *32*(2), 341–357.

Lacy, D. P., Jr. EEO implications of job analyses. *Employee Relations Law Journal*, 1979, *4*(4), 525–534.

Landy, F. J. A procedure for occupational clustering. *Organizational Behavior & Human Performance*, 1972, *8*, 109–117.

————, Farr, J. L., Saal, F. E., and Freytag, W. R. Behaviorally anchored scales for rating the performance of police officers. *Journal of Applied Psychology*, 1976, *61*(6), 750–758.

Latham, G. P., Fay, C. H., and Saari, L. M. The development of behavioral observation scales for appraising the performance of foremen. *Personnel Psychology*, 1979, *32*(2), 299–311.

Latham, G. P., and Wexley, K. N. Behavioral observation scales for performance appraisal purposes. *Personnel Psychology*, 1977, *30*, 255–268.

————, and Rand, T. M. The relevance of behavioral criteria developed from the critical incident technique. *Canadian Journal of Behavioral Science*, 1975, *7*, 349–358.

Lawshe, C. H. *Individual's job questionnaire checklist of office operations.* Lafayette, Ind.: Purdue University Bookstore, 1955.

————. A quantitative approach to content validity. *Personnel Psychology*, 1975, *28*(4), 563–575.

Lecznar, W. B. *Three methods for estimating difficulty of job task.* Lackland Air Force Base, Tex.: Air Force Human Resources Laboratory, 1971.

Levine, E. L., Bennett, L. J., and Ash, R. A. *Exploratory comparative study of four job analysis methods.* Phoenix, Ariz.: Arizona State Personnel Division, February 1977.

Levine, J. M., Romashko, T., and Fleishman, E. A. Evaluation of an abilities classification system for integrating and generalizing human performance research findings: An application to vigilance tasks. *Journal of Applied Psychology*, 1973, *58*, 149–157.

Lewis, D. R., and Dahl, T. Time management in higher education administration: A case study. *Higher Education*, 1976, *5*, 49–66.

Lissitz, R. W., Mendoza, J. L., Huberty, C. J., and Markos, H. V. Some further ideas on a methodology for determining job similarities/differences. *Personnel Psychology*, 1979, *32*(3), 517–528.

Maier, M. H., and Fuchs, E. F. *Development of improved aptitude area composites for enlisted classification* (Technical Research Report 1159). Arlington, Va.: U.S. Army Behavioral Science Research Laboratory, 1969. (NTIS No. AD 701 134).

————. *Development and evaluation of a new ACB and aptitude area system* (Technical Research Note 239). Arlington, Va.: U.S. Army Behavior and Systems Research Laboratory, 1972. JSAS *Catalog of Selected Documents in Psychology*, 1975, *5*, 258 (Ms. No. 971). (NTIS No. AD 751 761).

Marquardt, L. D., and McCormick, E. J. *Attribute ratings and profiles of the job elements of the Position Analysis Questionnaire (PAQ).* (Report No. 1). West Lafayette, Ind.: Purdue University, Occupational Research Center, June 1972.

————. *Component analyses of the attribute data based on the Position Analysis Questionnaire (PAQ).* West Lafayette, Ind.: Purdue University, Occupational Research Center, 1973.

————. *The job dimensions underlying the job elements of the Position Analysis Questionnaire (PAQ). Form B.* West Lafayette, Ind.: Purdue University, Occupational Research Center, June 1974.

————. *The utility of job dimensions based on Form B of the Position Analysis Questionnaire (PAQ) in a job component validation model.* West Lafayette, Ind.: Purdue University, Occupational Research Center, July 1974.

Maslow, A. Job analysis. In G. H. Wright, Ed. *Public sector employment selection.* Chicago, Ill.: International Personnel Management Association, 1974.

Mayo, C. C., Nance, D. M., and Shigekawa, L. *Evaluation of the job inventory approach in analyzing U.S. Air Force utilization fields.* (U.S. AFHRL Final Report, 1975, June, No. TR-75-22). Houston, Tex.: Lifson, Wilson, Ferguson and Winick, Inc., 1975. JSAS *Catalog of Selected Documents in Psychology*, 1975, *5*, 347. (Ms. No. 1136).

McCall, M. W., Jr., Morrison, A. M., and Hannan, R. L. *Studies of managerial work: Results and methods.* (Technical Report No. 9). Greensboro, N.C.: Center for Creative Leadership, May 1978.

McCall, M. W., and Segrist, C. A. *In pursuit of the manager's job: Building on Mintzberg.* (Technical Report No. 14). Greensboro, N.C.: Center for Creative Leadership, March 1980.

McCormick, E. J. Job analysis: An overview. *Indiana Journal of Industrial Relations*, 1970, *6*(1), 5–14.

————. *The application of structured job analysis information based on the Position Analysis Questionnaire (PAQ).* West Lafayette, Ind.: Purdue University, Occupational Research Center, October 1974.

————. Job information: Its development and applications. In D. Yoder and H. G. Heneman, Eds. *Staffing policies and strategies*. Washington, D.C.: The Bureau of National Affairs, Inc., 1974, 35–83.

————. Job and task analysis. In M. D. Dunnette, Ed. *Handbook of industrial and organizational psychology*. Chicago, Ill.: Rand McNally, 1976, 651–696.

————. *Job analysis: Methods and applications*. New York: Amacom, 1979.

————, DeNisi, A. S., and Shaw, J. B. *Job-derived selection: Follow up report*. West Lafayette, Ind.: Purdue University, Department of Psychological Sciences, May 1977.

————. Use of the Position Analysis Questionnaire for establishing the job component validity of tests. *Journal of Applied Psychology*, 1979, 64, (1), 51–56.

McCormick, E. J., Jeanneret, P. R., & Mecham, R. C. *The development and background of the Position Analysis Questionnaire (PAQ)*. West Lafayette, Ind.: Purdue University, Occupational Research Center, 1969.

————. *Position Analysis Questionnaire (PAQ), Form B*. West Lafayette, Ind.: Purdue University, Occupational Research Center, 1969.

————. A study of job characteristics and job dimensions as based on the Position Analysis Questionnaire (PAQ). *Journal of Applied Psychology*, 1972, 56, 347–368.

————. *User's manual for the Position Analysis Questionnaire*. Logan, Utah: PAQ Services, 1977.

————, *Technical manual for the Position Analysis Questionnaire (PAQ)*. (System II). Logan, Utah: PAQ Services, 1977.

McCormick, E. J., and Mecham, R. C. Job analysis data as a basis for synthetic test validity. *Psychology Annual*, 1970, 4, 30–35.

McFarland, B. P. *Potential uses of occupational analysis data by Air Force management engineering teams*. Lackland Air Force Base, Tex.: Air Force Human Resources Laboratory, 1974.

————. *A comparison of task difficulty ratings made by nurses and medical services corpsmen*. Lackland Air Force Base, Tex.: Air Force Human Resources Laboratory, 1974. JSAS *Catalog of Selected Documents in Psychology*, 1974, 4, 98. (Ms. No. 717).

————. *Job analysis of the medical service career field*. Lackland Air Force Base, Tex.: Air Force Human Resources Laboratory, 1974. JSAS *Catalog of Selected Documents in Psychology*, 1974, 4, 98. (Ms. No. 716).

McIntyre, R. M., and Farr, J. L. Comment on Arvey and Mossholder's "A proposed methodology for determining similarities and differences among jobs." *Personnel Psychology*, 1979, 32(3), 507–510.

Mead, D. F. *Development of an equation for evaluating job difficulty*. Lackland

Air Force Base, Tex.: Air Force Human Resources Laboratory, 1970.

————. *Continuation study on development of a method for evaluating job difficulty*. Lackland Air Force Base, Tex.: Air Force Human Resources Laboratory, 1970.

Mecham, R. C., and McCormick, E. J. *The use of data based on the Position Analysis Questionnaire (PAQ) in developing synthetically-derived attribute requirements of jobs*. West Lafayette, Ind.: Purdue University, Occupational Research Center, June 1969.

————. *The rated attribute requirements of job elements in the Position Analysis Questionnaire*. West Lafayette, Ind.: Purdue University, Occupational Research Center, 1969.

Meltzer, D., and Arguello, T. *The job element approach to job analysis*. Denver, Colo. Career Service Authority, 1973.

Miller, R. B. *Development of a taxonomy of human performance: A user-oriented approach*. (AIR Technical Report 1971, Mar. No. 726/2035-2/71-TR-6). Washington, D.C.: American Institute for Research, 1971. JSAS *Catalog of Selected Documents in Psychology*, 1973, *3*, 26. (Ms. No. 322).

Mintzberg, H. Structured observation as a method to study managerial work. *The Journal of Management Studies*, 1970, *7*, 87–104.

————. Managerial work: Analysis from observation. *Management Science*, 1971, *18*, B-97-B-110.

————. *The nature of managerial work*. New York: Harper and Row, 1973.

————. The manager's job: Folklore and fact. *Harvard Business Review*, 1975, *53*, (4), 49–61.

Mobley, W. H., and Ramsay, R. S. Hierarchical clustering on the basis of inter-job similarity as a tool in validity generalization. *Personnel Psychology*, 1973, *26*, 213–225.

Moore, A. *The Health Service Mobility Study method of task analysis and curriculum design*. Monograph submitted by Health and Education Resources, Inc. to Office of Research and Development of the Employment and Training Administration, U.S. Department of Labor. 1980.

Mussio, S. J., and Smith, M. K. *Content validity: A procedural manual*. Chicago, Ill.: International Personnel Management Association, 1973.

Neeb, R. W., Cunningham, J. W., and Pass, J. J. *Human attribute requirements of work elements: Further development of the Occupation Analysis Inventory*. (Center Research Monograph, No. 7). Raleigh, N.C.: North Carolina State University, Center for Occupational Education, 1971. JSAS *Catalog of Selected Documents in Psychology*, 1974, 4(4), 145. (Ms. No. 805).

New York State Department of Civil Service. *Job Analysis for personnel selection*. March 1978.

Outtz, J. L., Valentine, H. M., and Nicholas, W. E. *Maryland Comprehensive Job Analysis System.* October 1978.

Owens, W. A., and Schoenfeldt, L. F. Toward a classification of persons. *Journal of Applied Psychology*, 1979, 65(5), 569–607. (Monograph).

Pass, J. J., and Cunningham, J. W. *A systematic procedure for estimating the human attribute requirements of occupations.* (Center Report, Ergometric Research and Development Series No. 11). Raleigh, N.C.: North Carolina State University, Center for Occupational Education, 1975. JSAS *Catalog of Selected Documents in Psychology*, 1975, 5, 353. (Ms. No. 1151).

——————. *Occupational clusters based on systematically derived work dimensions: Final report.* Raleigh, N.C.: North Carolina State University, Center for Occupational Education, 1977. JSAS *Catalog of Selected Documents in Psychology*, 1978, 8(1), 22–23. (Ms. No. 1661).

PAQ Services, Inc. *Job analysis manual for the Position Analysis Questionnaire.* Logan, Utah: Author, 1977.

Payne, S. S. *Reading ease level of D.C. Fire Department written materials required for entry-level job performance* (TM-76-12). Washington, D.C.: U.S. Civil Service Commission, Personnel Research and Development Center, August 1976. (NTIS No. PB 261 704).

——————, and van Rijn, P. *Development of a written test of cognitive abilities for entry into the D.C. Fire Department: The task-ability-test linkage procedure.* Washington, D.C.: U.S. Civil Service Commission, Personnel Research and Development Center, August 1978.

Pearlman, K. *Job families: A review and discussion of their potential utility for personnel selection.* Washington, D.C.: U.S. Civil Service Commission, March 1978. (NTIS No. PB 280 498).

——————. Job families: A review and discussion of their implications for personnel selection. *Psychological Bulletin*, 1980, 87(1), 1–28.

Pfeiffer, M. G., Kuennapau, T., and Fastiggi, C. F. Common elements approach to multidimensional similarity analysis among job tasks. *Perceptual & Motor Skills*, 1973, 36, 3–12.

Prien, E. P. Development of a supervisor position description questionnaire. *Journal of Applied Psychology*, 1963, 47, 10–14.

——————. Development of a clerical position description questionnaire. *Personnel Psychology*, 1965, 18, 91–98.

——————. The function of job analysis in content validation. *Personnel Psychology*, 1977, 30(2), 167–174.

——————, and Ronan, W. W. Job analysis: A review of research findings. *Personnel Psychology*, 1971, 24(3), 371–396.

Primoff, E. S. *Summary of job-element principles: Preparing a job-element standard.* Washington, D.C.: U.S. Civil Service Commission, Personnel Measurement and Development Center, 1971.

————. *Using a job-element study for developing tests*. Washington, D.C.: U.S. Civil Service Commission, Personnel Measurement and Development Center, 1972.

————. *The J-coefficient procedure*. Washington, D.C.: U.S. Civil Service Commission, Personnel Measurement and Development Center, 1972.

————. *The job-element procedure in relation to employment procedures for the disadvantaged*. Washington, D.C.: U.S. Civil Service Commission, Personnel Research and Development Center, 1972.

————. *How to prepare and conduct job-element examinations*. U.S. Civil Service Commission, Personnel Research and Development Center. Washington, D.C.: U.S. Government Printing Office, 1975.

Reilly, R. R., Zedeck, S., and Tenopyr, M. L. Validity and fairness of physical ability tests for predicting performance in craft jobs. *Journal of Applied Psychology*, 1979, 64(3), 262–274.

Riccobono, J. A., and Cunningham, J. W. *Work dimensions derived through systematic job analysis: A study of the Occupation Analysis Inventory*. (Center Research Monograph No. 8). Raleigh, N.C.: North Carolina State University, Center for Occupational Education, 1971. JSAS *Catalog of Selected Documents in Psychology*, 1974, 4, 145. (Ms. No. 806).

————. *Work dimensions derived through systematic job analysis: A replicated study of the Occupation Analysis Inventory*. (Center Research Monograph No. 9). Raleigh, N.C.: North Carolina State University, Center for Occupational Education, 1971. JSAS *Catalog of Selected Documents in Psychology*, 1974, 4(4), 146. (Ms. No. 807).

————, and Boese, R. R. *Clusters of occupations based on systematically derived work dimensions: An exploratory study*. (Center Report, Ergometric Research and Development Series No. 10). Raleigh, N.C.: North Carolina State University, Center for Occupational Education, 1974. JSAS *Catalog of Selected Documents in Psychology*, 1975, 5, 352. (Ms. No. 1150).

Richardson, Bellows, Henry & Co., Inc. *Job Requirements Questionnaire for Supervisory Classifications (JRQ)*. Washington, D.C.: Author, 1975.

Risher, H. W. Job analysis: A management perspective. *Employee Relations Law Journal*, 1979, 4(4), 535–551.

Robinson, D. D., Wahelstron, O. W., and Mecham, R. C. Comparison of job evaluation methods: A "policy capturing" approach using the Position Analysis Questionnaire (PAQ). *Journal of Applied Psychology*, 1974, 59, 633–637.

Romashko, T., Brumback, G. B., Fleishman, E. A., and Hahn, C. P. *The development of a procedure to validate physical tests*. (Final Report). Washington, D.C.: American Institutes for Research, 1974.

Ronan, W. W., and Latham, G. P. The reliability and validity of the critical incident technique: A closer look. *Studies in Personnel Psychology*, 1974, 6, 53–64.

Ronan, W. W., and Prien, E. P. *Perspectives on the measurement of human performance*. New York: Appleton-Century-Crofts, 1971.

————. Performance evaluation, task analysis and organization research bibliographies. JSAS *Catalog of Selected Documents in Psychology*, 1973, 3, 69.

Ronan, W. W., Talbert, T. L., and Mullet, G. W. Prediction of job performance dimensions: Police officers. *Public Personnel Management*, 1977, 6(3), 173–180.

Rosenfeld, M., and Thornton, R. F. *A case study in job analysis methodology*. Princeton, N.J.: Educational Testing Service, 1976.

————. *The development and validation of a multijurisdictional police examination*. Princeton, N.J.: Educational Testing Service, Center for Occupational and Professional Assessment, June 1976.

Rouleau, E. J., and Krain, B. F. Using job analysis to design selection procedures. *Public Personnel Management*, 1975, 4, 300–304.

Rundquist, E. A. *Job tasks and technical training criteria development*. San Diego, Calif.: Navy Training Research Institute, Naval Personnel and Training Research Laboratory. JSAS *Catalog of Selected Documents in Psychology*, 1971, 1, 29. (Ms. No. 46).

Rusmore, J. T. Position description factors and executive promotion. *Personnel Psychology*, 1973, 26, 135–138.

Salvendy, G., and Seymour, W. D. *Prediction and development of industrial work performance*. New York: Wiley, 1973.

Schmidt, F. L., Caplan, J. R., Bemis, S. E., Decuir, R., Dunn, L., and Antone, L. The behavioral consistency method of unassembled examining. Washington, D.C.: U.S. Office of Personnel Management, 1979.

Schoenfeldt, L. F. Utilization of manpower: Development and evaluation of an assessment-classification model for matching individuals with jobs. *Journal of Applied Psychology*, 1974, 59, 583–595.

Schwab, D. P., Heneman, H., and DeCotiis, T. Behaviorally anchored rating scales: A review of the literature. *Personnel Psychology*, 1975, 28, 549–562.

Selection Consulting Center. *The validation of entry-level firefighter examination in the states of California and Nevada*. Sacramento, Calif.: Author, January 1974.

Seymour, G. E., Gunderson, E. K. E., and Vallacher, R. R. Clustering 34 occupational groups by personality dimensions. *Educational and Psychological Measurement*, 1973, 33, 267–284.

Shaw, J. B., and McCormick, E. J. *The prediction of job ability requirements using attribute data based on the Position Analysis Questionnaire (PAQ)*. West Lafayette, Ind.: Purdue University, Department of Psychological Sciences, October 1976.

Smith, J. E., and Hakel, M. D. Convergence among data sources, response bias, and reliability and validity of a structured job analysis questionnaire. *Personnel Psychology*, 1979, *32*(4) 677–692.

Smith, P. C., and Kendall, L. M. Retranslation of expectations: An approach to the construction of unambiguous anchors for rating scales. *Journal of Applied Psychology*, 1963, 47, 149–155.

Sparks, C. P. Job analysis under the new uniform guidelines. In *Personnel Management: Compensation Service* (Par. 161). Englewood Cliffs, N.J.: Prentice-Hall, 1979, 379–384.

Sprecher, T. B. *Dimensions of engineers job performance*. Princeton, N.J.: Educational Testing Service, 1976.

State of Wisconsin. *Selection-oriented job analysis procedures*. Madison, Wis.: State Bureau of Personnel, 1972.

Stone, C. H. *Evaluation of the Marine Corps Task Analysis Program*. (Technical Report No. 16). Los Angeles, Calif.: California State University, Los Angeles Foundation, June 1976.

———, and Yoder, D. *Job Analysis*. Los Angeles, Calif.: California State College, 1970.

Sturm, R. Mass validation: The key to effectively analyzing an employer's job classification. *Public Personnel Management*, 1979, 8(5), 277–281.

Taylor, L. R. The construction of job families based on the component and overall dimensions of the PAQ. *Personnel Psychology*, 1978, *31*(2), 325–340.

———, and Colbert, G. A. The construction of job families based on company-specific PAQ job dimensions. *Personnel Psychology*, 1978, *31*(2), 341–354.

Technomics, Inc. *Job analysis techniques for restructuring health manpower education and training in the Navy Medical Department*. McLean, Va.: Author, 1974.

Tenopyr, M. L. Content-construct confusion. *Personnel Psychology*, 1977, *30*(1), 47–54.

Teichner, W. H., and Whitehead, J. *Development of a taxonomy of human performance: Evaluation of a task-classification system for generalizing research findings*. (AIR Technical Report, 1971, Apr. No. 726/2035-4/71-TR-8). Washington, D.C.: American Institutes for Research, 1971. JSAS *Catalog of Selected Documents in Psychology*, 1973, 3, 27–28. (Ms. No. 324).

Theologus, G. C. *Development of a taxonomy of human performance: A review of biologic taxonomy and classification*. Washington, D.C.: American Institutes for Research, 1969. JSAS *Catalog of Selected Documents in*

Psychology, 1973, *3*, 29. (Ms. No. 326).

————, and Fleishman, E. A. *Development of a taxonomy of human performance: Validation study of ability scales for classifying human tasks.* Washington, D.C.: American Institutes for Research, April 1971. JSAS *Catalog of Selected Documents in Psychology*, 1973, *3*, 29. (Ms. No. 326). (NTIS No. AD 736 194).

Theologus, G. C., Romashko, T., and Fleishman, E. A. *Development of a taxonomy of human performance: A feasibility study of ability dimensions for classifying human tasks.* Washington, D.C.: American Institutes for Research, January 1970. JSAS *Catalog of Selected Documents in Psychology*, 1973, *3*, 25–26. (Ms. No. 321).

Tordy, G. R., Eyde, L. D., Primoff, E. S., and Hardt, R. H. *Job analysis of the position of New York State Trooper: An application of the job element method.* Albany, N.Y.: New York State Police, State Campus, June 1976.

Tornow, W. W., and Pinto, P. R. The development of a managerial job taxonomy: A system for describing, classifying, and evaluating executive positions. *Journal of Applied Psychology*, 1976, *61*(4), 410–418.

Trattner, M. H. Task analysis in the design of three concurrent validity studies of the Professional and Administrative Career Examination. *Personnel Psychology*, 1979, *32*(1), 109–119.

Treiman, D. J. *Job evaluation: An analytic review*: (Interim Report to the Equal Employment Opportunity Commission). Washington, D.C.: National Academy of Sciences, February 1979.

Tryon, R. C., and Bailey, D. E. *Cluster analysis.* New York: McGraw-Hill, 1970.

Turney, J. R., and Cohen, S. L. Perceived work effort as time devoted to an activity (U.S. Army Technical Paper, 1978 (Sep), No. 337). JSAS *Catalog of Selected Documents*, 1980, *10*(1), 23–24. (Ms. No. 1982).

Tuttle, T. C., and Cunningham, J. W. *Affective correlates of systematically-derived work dimensions: Validation of the Occupation Analysis Inventory.* (Center Research Monograph No. .10). Raleigh, N.C.: North Carolina State University, Center for Occupational Education, 1972. JSAS *Catalog of Selected Documents in Psychology*, 1974, *4*(4), 147. (Ms. No. 808).

U.S Civil Service Commission. *Achieving job-related selection for entry-level police officers and firefighters.* Washington, D.C.: Author, 1973.

————. *Job analysis: Developing and documenting data—A guide for state and local governments.* Washington, D.C.: Author, 1973.

————. *Handbook of occupational groups and series of classes.* Washington, D.C.: U.S. Government Printing Office, 1973.

————. *Job analysis for improved job-related selection: A guide for state and local governments*. Washington, D.C.: Author, 1975.

————. *Job analysis for improved job-related employee development*. Washington, D.C.: Author, August 1976.

————. *BRE exam preparation manual*. Washington, D.C.: Author, 1977.

U.S. Department of Commerce, Office of Federal Statistical Policy and Standards. *Standard occupational classification manual*. Washington, D.C.: U.S. Government Printing Office, 1977.

U.S. Department of Labor. *Dictionary of occupational titles*, 3d ed. (Vol. II). Washington, D.C.: U.S. Government Printing Office, 1965.

————. *Handbook for analyzing jobs*. Washington, D.C.: U.S. Government Printing Office, 1972.

————. *Task analysis inventories: A method for collecting job information*. Washington, D.C.: U.S. Government Printing Office, 1973.

————. *Dictionary of occupational titles*, 4th ed. Washington, D.C.: U.S. Government Printing Office, 1977.

————. Employment Standards Administration, Office of Federal Contract Compliance Programs. *Federal contract compliance manual*. Washington, D.C.: U.S. Government Printing Office, 1979.

U.S. Office of Personnel Management. *The behavioral consistency method of unassembled examining*. Washington, D.C.: Author, 1979.

Vail, R. G., and Landrigan, R. F. True entrance qualifications and objective performance measures. *EEO Today*, 1978, 5(2), 129–138.

van Rijn, P. *Job analysis of entry level firefighting: A comparison of District of Columbia firefighters and a nationwide sample*. Washington, D.C.: U.S. Civil Service Commission, 1977.

————. *Job analysis of entry level firefighting in the District of Columbia Fire Department: A duty/task approach*. Washington, D.C.: U.S. Civil Service Commission, 1977.

————. *Job analysis of entry level firefighting in the District of Columbia Fire Department: Supervisory perception of the entry level job*. Washington, D.C.: U.S. Civil Service Commission, 1977.

————. *Job analysis of entry level firefighting in the District of Columbia Fire Department: Administration and results of the Position Analysis Questionnaire (PAQ)*. Washington, D.C.: U.S. Civil Service Commission, 1978.

————. *Job analysis for selection: An overview*. Washington, D.C.: Office of Personnel Management, Personnel Research and Development Center, 1979.

Ward, J. H., Jr., and Hook, M. E. Application of an hierarchical grouping procedure to a problem of grouping profiles. *Educational and Psychological Measurement*, 1963, *23*, 69–81.

Watson, W. J. *The similarity of job types reported from two independent analyses of occupational data*. Lackland Air Force Base, Tex.: Air Force Human Resources Laboratory, 1974. JSAS *Catalog of Selected Documents in Psychology*, 1974, 4, 98. (Ms. No. 715).

Wegener, E. Does competitive pay discriminate? *The Personnel Administrator*, 1980, 25(5), 38–43, 66.

Wexley, K. N., and Silverman, S. B. An examination of differences between managerial effectiveness and response patterns of a structured job analysis questionnaire. *Journal of Applied Psychology*, 1978, 63(5), 646–649.

Wheaton, G. R. *Development of a taxonomy of human performance: A review of the classificatory systems relating to tasks and performance*. Washington, D.C.: American Institutes for Research, 1968. JSAS *Catalog of Selected Documents in Psychology*, 1973, 3, 22–23. (Ms. No. 317).

White, S. K. Moderating effects of individual differences on the relationship between job characteristics and worker responses: A summary and comparison of empirical investigations. JSAS *Catalog of Selected Documents in Psychology*, 1977, 7, 56. (Ms. No. 1499).

Wiley, L. N. *Analysis of the difficulty of jobs performed by first term airmen in 11 career ladders*. Lackland Air Force Base, Tex.: Air Force Human Resources Laboratory, 1972.

Wilson, M. *Job analysis for human resource management: A review of selected research and development*. (Manpower Research Monograph No. 36, U.S. Department of Labor). Washington, D.C.: U.S. Government Printing Office, 1974.

Wright, G. H., Ed. *Public sector employment selection*. Chicago, Ill.: International Personnel Management Association, 1974.

Youngman, M. B., Oxtoby, R., Monk, J. D., and Heywood, J. *Analyzing jobs*. West Mead, England: Gower Press, Teakfield Ltd., 1978.

Zuder, P. M., Bickford, D. S., Charron, K., Jillson, E. H., and Rose, W. M. *The utility of a task checklist as a data-collection method for job analysis*. Montpelier, Vt.: State of Vermont, Department of Personnel, July 1978.

Index

219

About the Authors

Stephen E. Bemis is Vice President and the Director of the Eastern Region of Psychological Services, Inc. (PSI), a management consulting firm specializing in the development of employee assessment procedures and other human resource management activities. In his work he has used most major job analysis procedures, and trained hundreds of individuals in job analysis. He has contributed to the U.S. Department of Labor's *Handbook for Analyzing Jobs*, Biddle and Associates' *Guidelines Oriented Job Analysis*, and Psychological Services' *Integrated Job Analysis*. He is co-author of the *Behavioral Consistency Method* of job analysis and the *Versatile Job Analysis System* described in this book. Mr. Bemis resides in Oakton, Virginia and works out of the Washington, D.C. office of Psychological Services, Inc. at 1735 I St., N.W.

Ann Holt Belenky is a consultant on job analysis methodologies and their application to human resource management. She has designed and conducted training programs and provided technical assistance to a variety of organizations in both the public and private sectors. Ms. Belenky has applied a number of job analysis methodologies and was a co-author of *Functional Job Analysis: How to Standardize Task Statements*. She is one of the developers of the Versatile Job Analysis System presented in this book. Ms. Belenky lives and works in Washington D.C.

Dee Ann Soder is Vice President, Human Resources Development, with the Prudential Insurance Company of America. In her work for Prudential and other organizations, Ms. Soder has used a variety of job analysis procedures in regards to selection, human resource planning, training and development, compensation, and a broad spectrum of other personnel areas. As a psychologist for the Equal Employment Opportunity Commission and the U.S. Civil Service Commission in Washington, D.C., Ms. Soder advised officials on professional and legal standards relating to personnel measurement and management. She has spoken and written widely about personnel and the law including *Court Case Compendium: Judicial Standards for Employment*. She has a Ph.D. in Industrial/ Organizational Psychology, specializing in legal applications, from the University of Oklahoma.